CW00958774

THREE STEPS *To* STEPS
HEAVEN

by Bobby Cochran with Susan Van Hecke

THE *Eddie Cochran* STORY

HAL•LEONARD®

7777 W. BLUEMOUND RD. P.O. BOX 13819
MILWAUKEE, WISCONSIN 53213

Published by Hal Leonard Corporation
7777 West Bluemound Road
P.O. Box 13819
Milwaukee, WI 53213, USA

Trade Book Division Editorial Offices:
151 West 46th Street, 8th Floor
New York, NY 10036

Visit Hal Leonard online at **www.halleonard.com**

Library of Congress Cataloging-in-Publication Data

Cochran, Bobby.
    Three steps to heaven : the Eddie Cochran story / by Bobby Cochran
with Susan VanHecke.-- 1st ed.
        p. cm.
Includes bibliographical references (p.   ) and index.
Discography: p.
    ISBN 0-634-03252-6
    1. Cochran, Eddie, 1938-1960. 2. Rock musicians--United
States--Biography. I. VanHecke, Susan. II. Title.
    ML420.C6C63 2003
    782.42166'092--dc21

2003005276

Printed in the United States of America
First Edition

10 9 8 7 6 5 4 3 2 1

Now there are three steps to heaven
Just listen and you will plainly see
And as life travels on
And things do go wrong
Just follow steps one, two and three

TABLE OF CONTENTS

ACKNOWLEDGEMENTS

Special thanks to my family, Rita, Timmy and family, Bree, Courtney, Taylor, Aubree, Becky and family, Cindy and family, Mary and Bob Holman, Eddie and Florence, Frankie Jo and Judy and the kids, Jackie and Sheila Faust, Ronnie Ennis, Bob Denton, Ron and Vickie Wilson, Hal Carter, Sharon and Shannon Sheeley, Carole (née Ward) Commander and family, Chuck Foreman, Brian Hodgson, Howard Tibble, Gary Baldwin, Peter Baron, Albert Lee, Dave Shriver, Gene Riggio, Duane Eddy, Hank Cochran, Connie "Guybo" and Marilyn Smith, Jimmy Stivers, Jerry, JJ, Raymond, and Jeanie Capehart, Gary Lambert, Bobby Charles, Glen Glenn, Bruce Blake, Dickie Harrell, Angela and Mike Powell, John Knight, Richard McCullough, Warren Flock, Johnnie Berry Raines, Jeanne Carmen, Mamie Van Doren, Big Jim Sullivan, Brian Locking, Tony Belcher, Brian Bennett, Joe Brown, Marty and Joyce Wilde, Vince Eager, Johnny Gentle, Johnny Rook, Stan Ross, Larry Levine, Don Preston, Bud Deal, Bob Duckworth, J. I. Allison, Sonny Curtis, Joe B. Mauldin, Mike Deasy, Jim Horn, Joey Collins, Dotty Harmony, Brian Setzer, the Rockabilly Hall of Fame, Steve and Karen Hanlan, Dieter and Kathryn Ammann, Jerry Hanger, Eddie Stein, Thad Dedios, Jorge Vazquez, Pat Woertink, Todd Malm, Bill Curd, Tony Alamia, Ross Banky, Lou Savage, Jimmy Erickson, Stevie D., Tony Bowman, Joann Parker, Kirk Wall, Robyn Kirmsee, Darby Logan, Devan Meade, Jeff Hasselberger, Hartley Peavey & Ken Achard, Peavey Guitars, Amps and Effects, Jack Elliano, Bob Luly, Wayne Charvel, Buzzy Feiten, Greg Back, Skunk Baxter, Richard Cocco, Labella Strings, Shubb Capos, Tony Barrett, Bill Beard, Tim and Lillett Kelly, Carl and Betty West, Jody Reynolds, Graham Pugh, Baker Knight, Charlie Gracie, Richard Wright, Geoff Barker, Art and Mary York, Roy Elkins, Alan Clark, Glenn Mueller, Sonic Foundry, Cakewalk, Xvision Audio, Frontier Design Group, Tony and Rose D'Andrea.

STEP ONE: *Beginnings*

1
Musical Awakening

THE DAY EDDIE DIED was holy. It was Easter Sunday, the holiest day. A time of sacred transformations. New beginnings. Fresh starts.

And Eddie's death transformed me.

Though it happened more than forty years ago, Eddie's passing touched me, changing me in ways I'm only now beginning to understand. It was a day that will forever haunt my life—moments both happy and sad—and will forever alter its course.

It was April 17, 1960. Mom, my two sisters, and I were getting ready to go over to my grandmother's house for the holiday gathering. My aunts, uncles, and cousins were to be there for dinner; it was traditionally a time for fun, with the adults deriving as much joy from watching us kids hunt for hidden treasures as we did from finding them. This Easter was to be particularly special because even Uncle Eddie, Granny and Grandpa's youngest child, was expected. He'd been away in England, working, making the family proud, and was to fly in that day. He'd been gone for several weeks, and we all missed him terribly, especially Granny, the diminutive matriarch of our Cochran clan. Eddie missed us as well; since he'd been gone he had phoned Granny—whom he and my dad affectionately called "Shrimper"—just about every day.

Dad was already at Granny's, which was just a few miles away in Buena Park. Early that morning he had left our tiny, termite-ridden one-bedroom duplex in the southern California suburb of Cypress.

Our house sat across from empty fields where I ran, explored, and played hide and seek. The fields were interrupted only by a fragrant grove of towering eucalyptus. "Dad will be back to pick us up very soon," Mom had assured me, as I played army man in the converted 8x8 closets that served as my bedroom.

Though I was only ten years old, I knew that something was wrong—sickeningly wrong—the moment Dad returned through the front door. His usually placid face was taut, and his eyes were red and watery, as if he'd been crying. I'd never seen my dad cry before, and I wasn't sure I wanted to. My stomach sank. Mom rushed to him, and they spoke in hushed tones. Mom began to sob, and it was now obvious that something terrible had happened. Frightened and confused, I ran to them. We hugged and cried together, although I didn't know exactly why .

And then I understood. Eddie was dead.

A waterfall of emotion crushed me, taking my breath along with it. Eddie, my father's younger brother by ten years, the shining pride of the Cochran family—dead. Ed was a rock 'n' roll star, one of the first. A trailblazing guitarist, gifted vocalist, hit-making composer and arranger, and budding whiz-kid producer. In the late '50s he had ascended quickly from the family's lower-class obscurity to become one of nascent rock 'n'roll's leading lights, writing or recording many of the most-recognized songs in rock history— "Summertime Blues," "Nervous Breakdown," "Somethin' Else," "C'mon Everybody," "Twenty Flight Rock," and "Sittin' in the Balcony." These are songs whose distinctive sound and defiant, often wryly humorous lyrics have been eagerly digested and analyzed, and lovingly reinterpreted by generations of rockers after him, from practically every bar band across the planet to major names such as the Beatles, the Sex Pistols, the Who, Keith Richards, Led Zeppelin, Alan Jackson, and U2.

Eddie's stunning good looks—all he-man, blue-eyed and sun-blessed—had landed him in front of all kinds of cameras; he had appeared in the motion pictures *The Girl Can't Help It* (with Jayne Mansfield), *Untamed Youth* (with Mamie Van Doren and Jeanne Carmen), and *Go, Johnny, Go!* (with Alan Freed, Chuck Berry,

Ritchie Valens, and Jackie Wilson) and on countless television programs around the world. He had toured relentlessly, joining pals like Gene Vincent, the Everly Brothers, Buddy Holly, and Little Richard for endless concert junkets and gigs abroad, including England and Australia, where he had been part of that country's first-ever rock 'n' roll tour.

And now he was dead. At twenty-one.

In my ten-year-old universe, Eddie was one of the most important constellations. He was my friend, my hero, my joy. He brought light, love, and music into our troubled home, and he was especially close to my father. He was my dad's drinking, hunting, and partying buddy, as well as his musical cohort, practicing, playing, and penning songs with Dad. Though my father was a car mechanic by trade, he was a music lover at his core and in his spare moments was always singing, strumming guitar or mandolin, or crafting songs. Eddie kept the lights on in Dad's heart, kept the music going in Dad's soul. He was our struggling family's brilliant hope for a better circumstance, a life of golden plenty instead of grinding poverty. Eddie was our leader; he would conquer that promised land of status and respect, of affirmation and validation, for all of us. And, as it seemed with almost every member of the Cochran family, my father's self-worth was directly dependent on Eddie's success.

Sure, Eddie wasn't perfect. He drank. Too much, just like Dad. I can remember one early morning when he and his buddy Ronnie Ennis drove up to our house, drunk out of their minds, just as I was setting out on my bicycle.

"What you doin' there, son?" Eddie intoned in a booming impersonation of Kingfish from *Amos and Andy*, the same comical voice he'd used in "Summertime Blues" and "Weekend." He'd often use that drawling voice when he wanted to make a point without being confrontational or hurting anyone's feelings. He used to say, "Not only does I resents the allegation, I resents the alligator!" It would crack us all up.

"Paper route," I told him, surprised but positively delighted to see him at that early hour.

"Let's deliver 'em, Bobby," he had said with a brotherly clap on my back as he began tossing my freshly folded Sunday papers into the rear of his new '59 Ford Country Squire station wagon, the one that took him crisscrossing the country to perform for screaming crowds of idolatrous fans. We hadn't gone but a block or so down the street, weaving wildly from curb to curb, before we all—including the overly partied Eddie at the wheel—laughingly realized that Ed was just too smashed to drive.

"Uh, how many papers you got dere, Bobby?" Ed chuckled, Kingfish-style. I told him, and he reached into his pocket, pulled out enough cash to cover all of the undelivered papers, and handed it to me. Still giggling, we turned around for home. I didn't think of how angry my customers would be at not getting their papers that morning. Honestly, I didn't care. I was basking in the attention of the big guys, my wonderful Uncle Ed and his buddy Ron, and we were having great, mischievous fun together.

That's the way Eddie was. Generous and giving of himself, of his time, his talents, of all that he had. Whether they had known him for a few minutes or twenty years, people just adored Eddie. He was everyone's best friend. Ed had a way of making you feel close to him. You could sense the current just being near him, a magnetic connection that warmed and enveloped you. It was comforting, restorative. Safe.

One time Dad, Ed, and I were at their sister (my aunt) Pat's house for a barbecue. It was a glorious afternoon, with fat, fleecy clouds ambling slowly across the open sky. Eddie and Dad were off to one side, away from the rest of the guests, lying on the cool grass in the shade of a tree, their knees bent, hands behind their heads, silently contemplating the beautiful heavens. I went over and lay down next to them. It was perfect, an extraordinarily serene moment, just me and the two men I cared for most, wordlessly sharing a lazy summer afternoon. After a while I noticed that Eddie's change had fallen out of his pocket. I gathered the shiny coins and said, "Oh, Ed, here, you dropped your money." He put a kind hand on my shoulder—not like I was some dumb kid but as if

I was his equal, his partner. "Thanks," he said. "You keep 'em. Those are for you."

My heart swelled with joy. They were just some quarters and dimes, but we were so poor—Mom would often send us kids to beg for toilet paper from the neighbors. To me it seemed like a million bucks. It was a small gesture that might not have meant much to Ed, but to this impoverished little boy it had meant the world.

And now my world was collapsing around me.

My experiences with death had been few; certainly no one close to me had died. The mere thought of losing someone I loved was enough to send me to pieces. A year or two earlier I had burst into tears on the way to church because I had dreamt the night before that my father had died. I loved him—how could I wish that about my Dad? I had felt so ashamed and guilty, as if I'd violated my relationship with my father. I believed that my dream meant that, deep down in my heart, I wanted him dead. Because, after all, didn't the Disney song "When You Wish Upon a Star" tell us, "A dream is a wish your heart makes?" It had taken Mom the rest of the ride to church to calm me down.

And now, Eddie dead? It didn't make any sense. Radiant young souls like Eddie weren't supposed to die. How could this happen? Life was all mixed up. Radio reports throughout the day didn't help my confusion. They offered contradicting news: Eddie was alive but injured; then dead of massive injuries; then in critical condition, but there was still hope.

But there was no hope.

I was distraught and inconsolable, utterly overwhelmed with sadness. I remember feeling the loss of Eddie so acutely, so incredibly, that I was actually in physical pain. And for most of my life I never have understood why. Even many years afterward, remembering that day and the intensity of my sorrow, the intensity of that loss could reduce me to the tears of a ten-year-old child. It was a day whose full and aching significance would not become entirely clear to me until four decades later.

I was simply unable to stop crying. Blinded by grief, I shuffled, on that most sacred and holiest of days, into my closet bedroom. I climbed onto the bed, curled up with my legs tucked beneath me, and slowly, steadily, banged out with my head on the stained plaster wall the horrible finality of Eddie's death.

When I was twelve-and-a-half years old, Eddie came to me in my dreams.

Dad had just given me my very first guitar lesson. My lifelong relationship with the instrument had commenced the night before in the back of the family car, parked at a drive-in movie. Dad had taken us to see some Western flick. The sound track was simple but memorable. Dad owned a couple of cheap acoustic guitars, and one of them was lying across the floor of the backseat of the car. Fiddling with it, I noticed that the sounds of the lower strings matched the melody from the film. Intrigued, I picked out the first few notes of the tune. I was thrilled to be able to match it so closely and quickly, so effortlessly. When we got home that night, I asked Dad if he would teach me to play. Over the next couple of days, working on his Regal and Stella acoustic guitars—Eddie had also learned on that Stella—Dad showed me everything he knew. His knowledge consisted of a few open chords, maybe a dozen or so, the basics. But it was a start. He also played some mandolin, and he taught me "Green Back Dollars," "You Are My Sunshine," and some other old hillbilly tunes.

The day after our lesson, Dad left the house and didn't return for about two weeks. I assumed he was on a drinking binge, so I continued to practice on my own. I quickly found that Dad's guitars—the sunburst red Regal and the antique yellow, clear-lacquered Stella—were of rather poor quality. Both had actions like barbed wire strung across fence posts. I had to press so hard to make a note that I thought I'd cut my fingers on the high E and B strings. Added to that, the guitars didn't play in tune much, and not knowing how to tune them was even more discouraging. When Dad finally came home, I begged him to teach me how to tune a guitar. He did, and that was my second revelation: A guitar in tune is a happy thing.

From those first lessons on, I was utterly, totally obsessed. My goal was to become as fantastic a guitar player as Eddie had been. Dad had always talked about what a great guitarist Eddie was, how he could even play some of Chet Atkins's mind-bending tunes, the ones where it sounded like two guitar players going at it simultaneously. He enthused about how Eddie's playing always sounded more full, more complex than that of a lot of other "single string" players. I wanted that kind of approval. I wanted that kind of admiration. I wanted to do whatever Eddie could do. I made a solemn commitment then and there—to myself, to God, to Eddie. I prayed earnestly every night before I went to sleep, vowing to Eddie, God, and Jesus that I was going to practice every day. I was going to make Eddie proud of me. I was going to carry on for Ed.

Eddie continued to make his nocturnal visits. My dreams of Eddie were in bright, clear Technicolor. Crystal clear, unobstructed in any way. Clearer than real life. They were so vivid I could almost taste the color, feel the electric sizzle of the life force within me, within Eddie. Eddie would appear and show me how to play guitar. What was odd, though, was that when I awoke in the morning, I couldn't remember specifically what he had shown me. I could only remember that he had come to me and taught me. But guitar kept unfolding for me, like the swift undoing of some elaborately wrapped present or the way a tiny sponge swells the instant you pour water on it, growing and expanding right before your eyes.

I immediately discovered that I knew things—things that I'd never been taught, things that I simply couldn't have known. It was like when you're learning how to do multiplication and division, and all of a sudden it becomes clear to you, that correlation of things, the way that two plus two is four, and two times two is four, and six minus two is four—how it all correlates, and all of a sudden it's all clear and incontrovertible. It was exactly like that when I realized that the shape of a D chord is an F chord at the fifth fret— I can remember how clearly I heard that in my mind. And how an F chord at the fifth fret is like an A chord at the second fret. And how an F chord at the twelfth fret is the same, only higher, as an open E chord at the first fret, and the same as an A chord at the seventh fret. Within several days I knew all that, just from sitting and noodling on the guitar.

In a way, Eddie's death gave me creative life. With Eddie's spiritual encouragement—I knew that he was responsible, somehow, for this knowledge, that it was Ed feeding my hunger to become his kind of musician—I was wholly devoted to guitar and the idea of taking up for my famous uncle where he'd left off. I made a promise to myself and to Eddie, a commitment, to practice every day. I prayed that if I could just be as good as Ed, then it would be okay if I, like Eddie, had to be taken when I was twenty-one. One evening I awoke after midnight and realized I hadn't practiced that day. I got up, hauled out my guitar, lay back on the bed, and practiced until I fell asleep with the instrument in my hands. That's how committed I was.

I was always better than average at hearing and associating pitch. It wasn't something I really worked at, it was just kind of there. I'm sure this natural gift played a part in my musical ability, and I'm sure I have my parents to thank for it. Mom and Dad were both talented. Mom was a gifted vocalist who had studied opera when she was a teen. Her teachers had encouraged her to pursue singing because she was so talented. Her range, she was told, was two or three notes higher than the famous opera singer Lily Pons. But Mom was raised near Watts, in southern California, a pretty rough area. Hanging out with her friends and the area gangs had been much more important to her at the time. Mom was very intense, and way ahead of her time, a free spirit who was into all kinds of music—jazz, rock, pop, blues. Eddie recognized her musical talent and was so impressed—he thought she could be the next Julie London—that he cut a couple of songs with her; the songs were eventually released by the British independent label Rockstar on the CD titled, *One Minute to One*. Mom was so proud to be on a recording with Eddie. We all thought the world of him.

I wanted to be just like Eddie. Well, almost. I was aware that Eddie was not without faults. In addition to his drinking, I knew that Eddie probably took some things while on the road to pick himself up a bit, maybe bennies or other uppers, like a lot of musicians did. I'd learned a lot about that stuff from Mom and Dad. They were both pretty hip to what was going on out in the real world. Mom told me about her experiences around drugs and rough elements growing up in central Los Angeles. And I also had plenty of experience seeing Mom's daily reliance on prescription drugs.

I wasn't going to do either—drink or drugs—I promised myself. In fact, I wasn't going to let anything get in the way of my being good and capable—carrying on for Eddie. I wanted so much to just be *good*. I was so committed to perfection that I often practiced eight and twelve hours a day. From the fourth grade on, I missed more school than I attended. Our home life was crazy—we often didn't have clothes, we frequently went without food. So I just stayed home. Once I began playing guitar, it became my fortress, my friend, my constant companion.

Eddie had been just as hopelessly possessed by the guitar.

He was born on October 3, 1938, in Albert Lea, Minnesota, where I, too, was born little more than a decade later. His father, my grandfather, was the hard-working ex-Navy sailor Frank, who once showed me the huge scar on his shoulder, a parting gift from a .50-caliber machine gun bullet fired by a Japanese Zero. The bullet had grazed him and nearly tore his arm off. His mother was the charming Alice, my grandmother, who spoke with a drawl and carried herself with all the grace and pride of the queen of England. They had settled in Minnesota after leaving drought-demolished, economically depressed Oklahoma in the early '30s.

Albert Lea was a humble little town of neatly painted clapboard homes. Children played on the tree-lined streets and neighbors rocking on their front porches caught gentle summer breezes. The sweeping prairie land of Minnesota—vibrant with wildlife in the spring and summer, stark and silent in the brutal snowy winter—

was a vast playground for an active young boy like Edward Raymond Cochran. From an early age he enjoyed outdoor sports, fishing with cane poles with his friends, and hunting with his dad and older brothers. He loved shooting, and was given his own fancy, western-style BB rifle when he was barely as tall as a rifle. Movies, especially Tom Mix, Gene Autry, and Hopalong Cassidy Westerns, appealed to Ed, and he and his school buddies spent endless afternoons playing cowboys and Indians along the rambling yards and sidewalks of Albert Lea.

Eddie's older siblings—Gloria, born in 1924; Bill, born in 1925; Bob, my father, born in 1928; and Patricia, born in 1932—all adored their baby brother and frequently assisted Granny with his care. The family noticed Eddie's affinity for music early on; he often fell asleep sucking his thumb while brother Bill played old 78-rpm recordings of "Beer Barrel Polka" and "Hot Pretzels" on the phonograph. So when Bill left Albert Lea in the early '40s to serve in the U.S. Marine Corps, he handed his Kay acoustic guitar over to little Eddie for safe-keeping. Eddie promised to take care of it while he was gone. Bill received letters from home telling how Eddie polished that Kay every day.

Bill had shown Ed a few chords, but Eddie, who was attending Northside Elementary School, had his heart set on learning the drums. Piano lessons were a mandatory prerequisite for percussion instruments at Northside, so Eddie opted to study trombone. Told he didn't have the lip for that horn, the school's orchestra director recommended the clarinet instead; Eddie took one look at the licorice stick and flatly refused. Compelled to make music, he pulled out Bill's old Kay. Just as I would do years later, Eddie asked my Dad to teach him to play.

Eddie's technique advanced exponentially as he devoured guitar manuals—such as Nick Manaloff's guitar handbook, which I later discovered and learned from—and entertained his school buddies, strumming on the front steps of the family's humble gabled home or staging elaborate variety shows in the neighbors' back yards, charging the local kids a penny admission. An abrupt move south to Midwest City, Oklahoma, where Grandpa found work as a machinist at Tinker Air Force Base, was cut short when, mysteriously, Eddie fell seriously ill. Years later my mother told me that Eddie had almost died from a kidney infection when he was young; it's my guess that this mystery illness was that kidney ailment. (I, too, would be diagnosed with a kidney disease, although when I was an adult. I was given only nine months to live, but I survived thanks to nutritional and herbal therapies.)

Eddie, Granny, and Grandpa returned quickly to Albert Lea where Gloria, Patty, and my father, who were now all married, still lived. Dad had been in the Navy and was something of a hero, as he'd risked his life during an emergency repair to his ship's boiler, saving the crew. He had met my mother while stationed in California. Eddie recovered from his illness, and within months, in 1953, the entire family journeyed to the abundant arms of California, lured by the prospect of better jobs and a better life in the state that Ed's brother Bill now called home. As they were packing up their belongings, about to trek toward awesome possibilities, Ed stood in the backyard of the family's modest house. "You know, Mom," he said, his handsome little face brimmed by his cap, "when we go to California I'm going to make something of myself. And you're going to have everything, Mom, everything you've never had."

Eddie sought refuge from the upheaval in his beloved guitar, cradling the cherished instrument the entire trek west. After first staying with Bill, then in a trailer behind Granny's sister's house in Bell Gardens, a suburb of Los Angeles, Ed's family moved to an apartment, then finally settled into their own home at 5539 Priory Street in Bell Gardens. Finding himself the new kid in a new town, Eddie threw himself into his guitar playing, just as I later would, practicing for hours on end. He'd have picked and strummed twenty-four hours a day if Granny would have let him, and he once chided her for daring to call his guitar a mere "possession." "This guitar's my friend," he corrected her, "my best friend."

And he treated it as such, cleaning and polishing his guitar so that it gleamed like it did the day it left the factory. I shared Eddie's passion for his instrument. When I would polish the amber-red Gretsch 6120 my parents eventually purchased for me, I was so meticulous I would take the knobs off and clean all around the washers. If I didn't feel I'd gotten it spotless enough, I'd take the nuts off from around the volume and tone knobs, lift the washers up, and clean under them. It was an obsession. I honored that guitar like it had its own spirit, like it had magic in it. And I'm convinced Eddie had felt the same way. These instruments—these objects that, when stroked by a loving and persuasive hand, had the unique power to communicate in the most extraordinary ways—they were pure magic. Back then, the thought of The Who breaking their instruments was the most profane act I could think of. It was murder, plain and simple.

In the fall of 1953, Eddie was enrolled in Bell Gardens Junior High, where the handsome, intelligent, and thoroughly likable boy was appointed editor of the *Live Wire,* the school newspaper, and became chief justice of the student court, a junior tribunal where pupils were judged by their peers for school rules infractions. Eddie even found himself a girlfriend, cute and dark-haired Johnnie Berry.

Among Eddie's many new friends was Fred Conrad Smith, nicknamed "Guybo," a southern California native who played double bass for the Bell Gardens Junior High band and knew steel guitar and mandolin as well. Eddie and Guybo felt an instant musical kinship—a chemistry that would bring them together on almost all of Eddie's commercial recorded output—and began to practice together regularly at Granny and Grandpa's house. Soon they were performing together—entertaining at school functions, supermarket openings, and other area venues. As reported in the March '54 issue of *Live Wire*, "Conrad Smith play[ed] the steel guitar and Eddie Cochran [sang]" at Bell Gardens Elementary School on a junior high orchestra field trip. The "guitar duet" performed the tunes "Just Married" and "Walkin' the Dog."

My first performance experience was also at school, at the talent show. I'd been playing guitar for all of two weeks when a saxo-

phone-honking school pal of mine suggested we start a band. We'd
been watching a group audition from outside the auditorium doorway, and they really weren't all that great, the guitar player in particular. My friend turned to me and said, "You know, you play better than that guy."

With only a couple of weeks' experience under my belt, there
were whole worlds I didn't know about the guitar. But my friend
had a point, the kid was unquestionably awful. "Why don't we put
a band together?" my friend suggested. "We'll play in the talent
show, too."

I agreed, and within days we'd assembled a little combo: trum-
pet, sax, snare drum, piano, and guitar. The night of the gig the
piano player quit, but we still went on, playing a short set that
included an instrumental rendition of "Milk Cow Blues," the old
chestnut perhaps made most famous by Elvis Presley in 1955, but
which would become a particular favorite of mine through demo
tapes of Eddie's that I'd return to again and again.

I'll never forget how it felt that first time, getting up in front of
an audience to show them what you've got, scared as hell and thinking you weren't good enough. I could hear impressed murmurs rip-
ple across the audience as we started to play, and it spurred me on
to do my absolute best. I hoped my adrenaline-energized fingers
would cooperate. It was an incredible feeling—part nerves, part
excitement. Performance, I realized, was all a big risk—you could
knock their socks off, or you could get knocked on your ass. My
hands were shaking, my stomach was quivering. My knees felt weak.
I thought, "How can I play when I feel like this?" I could barely hold
on to my pick, and it felt like the strings were in the wrong place. I
was shaking inside. I later found out that Eddie was so nervous at his
first show that he dropped his pick. But the payoff was worth it.
Hundreds of pairs of approving hands—including Mom's, Dad's,
and Granny's—joined in beautiful applause, all for us.

I've always loved communicating with people. I do it in lots of
different ways. Music is the way I make my living, and, for me,
that's when making that connection is the best. Somehow, the
people in an audience, they're in my music, they're part of how it's

being made. I'm not just making it by myself. They're part of it, too. They're giving it to me, and I'm giving it to them. It's best when it just comes through me—I'm allowed to be present, but the music, the flow, is not solely of my making. Sure, my technique can help to articulate, to enunciate; it can help me do things I couldn't do otherwise. It can help that flow, to form it into credible music. But the real trick is to not let technique get in the way of the far more important aspect of communication. So many people get so lost in technique that they lose the connection to the inspiration of heart and soul. Otherwise, it's all just a one-way conversation—a player making music *at* the audience.

Standing on that school stage all those years ago, bathed in applause, it dawned on me exactly why Eddie had loved to perform, why he had chosen to make his living by entertaining people. That give and take with a crowd, that feeling of connection with a sea of souls, it was simply irresistible. And downright addictive.

Like Eddie, I wanted to do it for the rest of my life.

2

Coming into His Own

I DON'T KNOW EXACTLY when I stopped having dreams about Eddie teaching me to play guitar, but they went on for a long time, at least the first couple of years of my fledgling musical career.

I immersed myself in guitar, just as Eddie had.

By the time he was fourteen, Eddie was the owner of a blond Gibson cutaway. Originally it had been an acoustic guitar, and Ed modified it with a DeArmond pickup, hammering a metal piece out on the sidewalk, drilling a hole in it, and screwing it into the neck. With Guybo Smith and Al Garcia, another school buddy, he'd formed a band called the Melodie Boys ("Music for all occasions," shilled the trio's business card, "Western rhythms, dance, cowboy ballads") and had made the acquaintance of Chuck Foreman, a talented steel guitarist working the post-war Los Angeles western swing and country music circuit who'd grown up in the Anaheim and Buena Park areas of the city.

Though Chuck, who'd started out on piano in his sisters' all-girl band, was five years Eddie's senior, the pair became inseparable musical companions. Both had a keen interest in the technical side of music making. They spent much of the summer of 1953 experimenting with recordings made on Chuck's two-track tape machine. He had purchased the Ampro in Long Beach for less than $100. Its 5-inch reels, four tubes, and single-speed, 3 3/4 ips (inches per second) with which to record half a track allowed sounds to be captured on one half-track of a tape, which then could be played back while the tape's second half-track captured another set of sounds. The result was a sound recording far more dense, full, and complex than a one-track recording.

The pair's earliest recording efforts were fairly rudimentary—Eddie, in his assured, basso voice, singing along with his competent rhythm guitar. But within a year Ed's skills as both guitarist and vocalist had fully blossomed. His guitar playing revealed the indelible influence of intricate pickers such as Chet Atkins, Merle Travis, and Joe Maphis. Atkins was a particular favorite of Ed's, and although my uncle's hands were small—my mom referred to them as "delicate"—his mastery of Atkins's bass-melody harmony picking technique was achieved through his unusual dexterity, versatility, and precision. Vocally, the easy phrasing and ad-libbed chuckles of his future commercial recordings were already apparent. Eddie instinctively knew how to "sell" a song, and as a vocalist and a guitarist he was a storyteller of the highest caliber, able to instantly connect and communicate through his music.

Eddie had tremendous stretch to his fingers, recalled Mike Deasy, a member of Ed's road and recording group the Kelly Four. He also had a very strong wrist, which he'd place right under his guitar's neck, his thumb in the middle, offering support. When making his music Eddie never took the easy route. Most guys would play a song like "Honky Tonk" in the key of E, Deasy remembered. Not Ed. He'd play it the tough way, in the key of F. Ed just made it look easy.

Ed was one of the few players Dave Shriver, also a future band member, had ever seen who played the guitar with all of his fingers. Though Ed's hands were small, they were flexible, and almost seemed to Shriver as if they didn't have any bones. Ed would stretch his fingers all along the fingerboard. Shriver, too, was struck by how

Ed challenged himself. For example, instead of playing an open chord, Ed would strum the same notes up the neck, giving the same chord sound, and not a barre chord either. Shriver noticed that on a lot of licks, Ed would use a flat pick and two fingers, playing in a kind of rolling, Chet Atkins left-hand style. Shriver would watch in amazement as Ed would pick something like "Arkansas Traveler" and "Yankee Doodle" at the same time. Actually, I believe it was more likely "Yankee Doodle Dixie," one of Chet's arrangements, that Ed played at the same time as another tune. And he was impressed with Ed's enormous range; it seemed Ed could play any way—jazz, country, blues, rock 'n' roll—slow or fast, anything you could want. Shriver would gaze in awe as Ed would play fast licks with a thumb pick, and then right in the middle stick the thumb pick in his mouth and switch to a flat pick, all without ever missing a note.

Eddie was a quick study and an absorptive learner. Technically proficient, he benefited greatly from Chuck Foreman's great harmonic sophistication, colored brightly by jazz. When Chuck first met my uncle, Ed played strictly rhythm guitar. He was still searching for chords and movements, and often as the pair would play together Ed would suddenly stop, lean over his guitar, and say, "What was that? What chord did you go to?" or "I didn't recognize that weird change."

Both curious by nature, the two experimented with the then-advanced recording technique of overdubbing, in which several parts could be recorded onto a single track. They would lay down a basic bed of Chuck's foot tapping and singing or of Ed's strumming and humming; they would play that back and record Ed picking a bass line on the tuned-down bottom string of his guitar. Then they would play back that collection of sounds and lay in guitar or vocal leads. To conserve tape—Ed was a dirt-poor kid—they recorded at the slowest speed possible and recycled old tapes over and over again.

Chuck and Ed also researched various ways to create reverberation. They'd hang a microphone in the top of a piano near the strings and sound board; and, with the sustain pedal depressed, they'd excite the strings—causing them to ring sympathetically with sounds being sent through a speaker pointed at the strings. Or they'd place a large box over the head of whoever was singing so that the microphone would pick up the close ambience of the box. Given that one of the few musicians at the time who was releasing material using these multi-track and overdubbing techniques was Les Paul, the home recordings that teenagers Eddie and Chuck were making were remarkably advanced. Indeed, studio recording in the '50s almost unequivocally meant a well-rehearsed, unified whole: the entire band playing simultaneously behind the singing vocalist, with absolutely no room for mistakes. An out-of-tune guitar or cracking vocal meant yet another take. Eventually, multi-tracks, overdubs, and effects such as reverb would become recording-industry standards, enabling instrumental parts to be recorded long before or after vocal tracks. But in the early '50s, Eddie and Chuck, mere kids experimenting for hours on end, were tilling relatively unknown terrain.

When I met Chuck, he reminded me of so many of my close friends from my early, adolescent years as a guitarist: Jack Elliano, Bob Luly, Wayne Charvel, Jeff Hasselberger, Hartley Peavey—true innovators all. These friendships made a great impact on me as a young player and helped me design, discover, and realize my own sound and instrument preferences. Like Ed and Chuck Foreman, we helped each other perfect our ideas. I shared with these friends my musical ability, and they imparted to me their technical know-how, along with tremendous moral and practical support during much of my career.

I remember Dad saying that Eddie had once tried to get special speaker cones because he kept blowing speakers in his Fender Bassman amplifiers. Bob Luly called one time—he needed me to help him demo his new amp design for what was to become Leo Fender's new amp company, Music Man. Bob had designed a 150-watt 2-10 amp that kicked ass. He was also the hot-rod guitar guru of the "inland empire" of San Bernardino, California. He liked using me to demo and to help fine-tune his designs, because I did a lot of stuff that sounded really full, like playing bass strings and high notes simultaneously. It also helped that I was willing to drive or bum a ride fifty miles each way and spend all day. I really put the amp through its paces. The special two 10-inch speakers he had made could handle an impressive 150 watts; Ed's Bassman had four 10-inch speakers and blew out with only 40 watts. Bob had made quite an improvement.

Bob also helped me conquer pickup squeal. He assisted in customizing my amp's tone and distortion characteristics. He taught me all kinds of tricks that came in handy as I helped Fender, Ibanez, and Peavey develop the next generation of guitars, amps, and effects that I—and the world—would come to use. When Hartley Peavey decided he had to make his own speakers, Black Widows, in order to guarantee quality and delivery, I used to blow them out as fast as we could put them in my amps. Nowadays, they are some of the most reliable speakers in the world, with field-replaceable cones. These guys have changed the world with their great ideas and devotion to what they love.

My uncommon interest in exploring the world of recording, electronics, and sound was sparked and encouraged by the stories I'd heard about Eddie. I'd always been told how Eddie would try new things in the studio, and I was just the same way. It was my father who introduced me, at the age of twelve and a half, to the world of recording, when, much to the surprise of my mother and myself, he revealed that he was building a sound studio. With a couple of partners, he was transforming a space on Tweedy Boulevard in Southgate, a suburb of southeast Los Angeles, into Advance Recording Studio. The facility was close to a thousand square feet, and the adjoining apartment above it—used mostly for partying—was about half that size. The equipment was much better than most people at that time would have had at home, but it was a far cry from what was being used in Hollywood.

At first Dad had a couple of Ampex 601 quarter-track machines. I don't remember a board or mixer in the beginning, although there may have been a Shure five-channel mixer, which was very small, you could hold it in your hand—but no EQ (equalization or tone controls). There were Magnavox 15-inch monitors, replaced with JBL 15-inch D130s in the same cabinets after the original speakers blew out. Dad was never into electronics or engineering, but he must have learned some lessons hanging around with Eddie because he'd use the two Ampex machines to do bouncing and multiple overdubs: you'd record a track on one machine, then send that recorded track along with a new performance to the other machine to create a part that embodied both performances mixed together. This allowed one musician to sound like many, by layering several performances onto one final recording containing all the perform-ances. Back in those days, in a studio as modestly equipped as Dad's, it was rare to have a multi-track machine to accommodate three or four tracks. Eight, sixteen, or even twenty-four separate tracks became the industry standard within a few years.

I was playing in my first real band, Kelly and the Midnighters, at the time. The sax player, who was sixteen, had asked me to join even though I was more than three years younger than him. At first, no one in the band knew that I was Eddie Cochran's nephew; they just thought I played well. One night Dad came to our rehears-al. "Where's the bass player?" he asked. There were three of us on guitar, plus the sax player and a drummer. We hadn't even thought about a bass. "You need a bass player to make it sound right," Dad informed us, and he instructed one of the guitar players to take up the bass. Until the kid could afford one, Dad borrowed a bass and an amp whenever we rehearsed. Sometimes he borrowed Guybo Smith's Fender Bassman and Precision bass. It was incredibly cool to get to use the same bass and amp that had been heard on so many of Eddie's records.

Kelly and the Midnighters eventually started cutting tracks at Advance after we acquired a new drummer, Danny La Mont. Mom and I recommended Danny to the band after we'd heard him recording at Dad's studio with another band. Danny reminded us of Gene Krupa and Sal Mineo all in one. He was a terrific player and used his kick drum in a more syncopated way than most guys did at the time, which was very appealing to me. I later found out that years earlier Eddie, while in England, had taught Brian Bennett of the Wildcats to play with a syncopated kick-drum pattern that helped to revolutionize his playing.

I wrote a couple of songs and we did some tunes the other guys wrote. We were terribly excited to be recording, and at our inaugural session we worked all of the first night into the next afternoon—twenty-four hours straight—with disappointing results. We hadn't eaten, and we were really tired, so we decided to quit for some rest. Exhausted and exasperated, we crashed at the studio, sleeping on the couch, the floor, anywhere we could. When we got up the next morning, we went to work again. This time things were clicking. We got every song down on the first or second take.

Dad did his best to produce and guide us, but this was all very new territory for him. He tried very hard to figure out what wasn't working, to guide us and help us, but we were all so new at it. Predictably, the more he drank the less effective he became at producing and directing us, a sad cycle that I would witness again and again at Advance, where I would become a session player until I was almost fifteen, when Dad lost the studio. But his heart was always in the right place. Often Dad would try to get me to play something the way he thought Eddie would have done it. "You know, you need to listen to your Uncle Ed and do it that way," he'd say to me time and time again. He wouldn't be able to show me how to do it, but he'd become quite adamant, especially if he was drunk, that I play in exact imitation of Ed.

At one session he came out into the studio from the control room scolding me, telling me I hadn't played something correctly—which to him meant as Eddie would've played it. He said he wanted me to do the vibrato/tremolo a certain way. Enraged, he grabbed the vibrato/tremolo arm on my guitar and yanked on it. It came up high enough that the spring popped out of place. I thought he'd broken my guitar.

So there I am in this recording session: fourteen years old and all the others in their twenties. I'm this little kid playing with the big guys, and I am about to cry because I'm absolutely heartbroken that my own father broke my guitar, my pride and joy. I can still remember that choked-up feeling, trying to get it together to figure out how to fix my guitar, trying to hold the anger, frustration, and humiliation in, to not break down in front of everybody.

I had to learn early on to trust my own judgment, to become my own person, to discover the things that I liked for myself. I learned to discern the difference between my dad's good advice and the booze talking, as Dad became far less rational when drinking.

Generally he was not very affectionate; he was kind of quiet. He was loving but not especially demonstrative. After drinking a little too much, though, his affection could sometimes turn hurtful. He would grab a little too hard or wind up hurting us unintentionally. When I was little he used to give me whisker rubs on the cheeks. I loved the attention but dreaded the inevitable sudden change when things would get too rough. Sometimes he'd tickle me so hard, so long, that I'd pass out from laughing. But when Dad was sober, you just couldn't help but love him. He was smart, handsome, funny, and fun to be around.

Mom was very protective of us. She told me about the time—I was around seven years old—when she heated up the iron as hot as it would get and went into the bedroom where Dad was sleeping. She held the iron about an inch from his face until he awakened. Once he had opened his eyes, she told him, "If you ever hurt the kids, I'll kill you!" She was real feisty. I think that is part of what Dad loved about her.

I didn't always see things Dad's way, and eventually I came to resent his constant pressure on me to become Eddie's musical doppelganger. It seems there's always been someone or some force trying to mold me into Eddie's image, fashion me as an Eddie Cochran clone, starting with an article written about me in the early '60s in England's *New Musical Express* magazine. With the headline, "Cochran Genius Lives On—In His Nephew!" the article gushed,

> There never was—and probably never will be—a rock 'n' roll guitarist as good as Eddie, although over here very few people know about this aspect of his work. But the Cochran feel is not entirely extinct.

> Eddie's brother Bob runs an independent studio in Los Angeles, and a regular guitarist at sessions is Bob's son, Bobby, who has just reached thirteen.
>
> Bobby started playing the guitar two years ago. After six months he was playing so well that it was just incredible. And now Bobby is on the threshold of the Cochran brilliance.
>
> He is lucky to be able to study demonstration instrumentals that Eddie made and which are jealously guarded by Mrs. Cochran, who apparently, won't even let them out of the house to be duplicated.

I had always wanted to be like Eddie—a great and accomplished guitarist—but with my own expression and style. I wanted to communicate what was in me the way that Eddie had been able to, but I never wished to be his clone. I wanted to be me—but as perfectly me as Eddie had been Ed.

I'd been playing guitar all of half a year, and already folks wanted to prop me up and make me act like my uncle. The idea was simply appalling to me, and frightening. It was something in which I was just not interested. The concept of being compared to someone who in my family is considered a god and who musical history regards as a legend—it's pretty intimidating. I wanted to be who I was, who I could be. Sure, I worshipped Eddie, admired and took inspiration from his musical abilities, and was proud to be related to him. But there was no way in hell somebody was going to push me out into the spotlight and say, "Here, go be like Eddie." The very idea was just gross, and soon the endless comparisons to Eddie began to feel like a giant anchor around my neck.

But recording—that first time with Kelly and the Midnighters, and ever since—has always been thrilling. As a fledgling guitar player, for me the recording studio was a fascinating playground, a musical wilderness just begging for exploration. And for Dad, I'm sure, spending his days and nights in his own studio was like reliving some of those golden days with Eddie.

I'd always heard about how Eddie would experiment and try new things in the studio, and it inspired me to expand my thinking about sound and how it's made and recorded. After my Dad lost Advance, I purchased some of the recording gear from his former partners. For my live gigs, I would use the two-track stereo Ampex 601 as an echo machine. I had a one-hour tape, thirty minutes per side, that I used to create echo, flipping it over every thirty minutes so the echo would continue. I'd take a speaker line out from my dual Showman amplifier, plug it in to the input of the tape machine, run the tape machine's output to the other channel input of my amp, then adjust the levels so I could have just enough echo. It was a great sound to have during a live performance, and nobody else playing around the area had achieved it. Unlike today, back then, when playing live, musicians didn't have effects like echo, now considered fundamental. The equipment was simply not available to the average player. People would get these great sounds in the studio, but there was no easy way to duplicate those sounds in a live-performance setting.

I was always intrigued by the great guitar tones achieved on Eddie's records. Listening to my uncle's records over and over, I was compelled to understand why some guitars and amplifiers sound as they do. Ever since hearing Eddie's records, I've had an uncommon interest in exploring the world of recording, electronics, and sound, and I would dissect, assemble, and experiment with all sorts of instruments and components, seeking the perfect tone, effect, configuration. I was so obsessed with music and musical gear, I used to draw complex diagrams of my future ideal stage, with the placement and model of all the equipment scrupulously noted. All my amps were Dual Showmans with custom green pilot lights. I'd imagine every aspect of a live performance down to the tiniest detail: the venue, lighting, musicians, set list, audience reaction, and on and on.

Most of the guys in Kelly and the Midnighters were fans of Eddie's, too, so we included a few of his songs in our live show, as well as some popular vocal tunes, but most of our stuff was instrumental surf music. The band became fairly popular pretty quickly. Mom and Dad were supportive; they even promoted a series of gigs for the band. They rented the Buena Park Civic Auditorium, which

Eddie in his
sailor suit,
like Grandpa
and Dad,
approx. 1943.

Eddie back in
Albert Lea,
Minnesota,
playing cowboy,
approx. 1945.

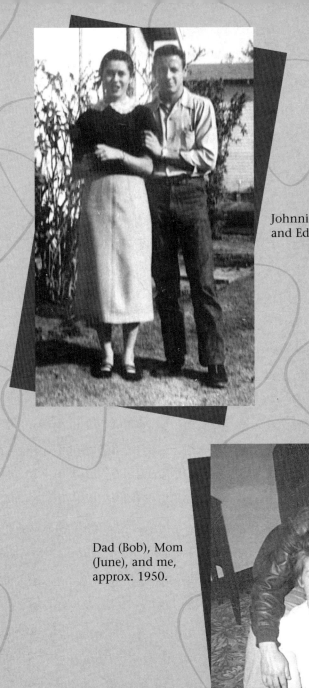

Johnnie Berry
and Eddie.

Dad (Bob), Mom
(June), and me,
approx. 1950.

Eddie kneeling in a baseball field at the high school.

Mom June, sister Becky, me, and Dad, approx. 1954.

Eddie and Hank, Cochran Brothers publicity photo. This is the Gibson guitar on which Eddie installed a modified De Armond pickup.

Eddie as Eddie Garland, American Legion Hall.

Eddie as Eddie Garland and his Country Gentleman: Ron Wilson, Richard McCullough, Guybo, and Bob Denton. It is the same band as Richard Rae and the Shamrock Valley Boys.

Eddie in hammock, publicity photo, 1957. He wore this coat in many photos throughout 1957, as well as during his tour of Australia.

My first live performance at Walker Junior High talent show.
Wayne Mills on sax. I can't remember the other fellas' names. The
piano player quit just before the show, so we did it without her.
Wayne and I went on to join Kelly and the Midnighters.

Me, 14 years old, and Larry Rendone on
sax. Benny and the Midnighters rehearsal
for Battle of the Bands.

Lil' Willie G. Garcia and me, playing with
my leg over the neck of the guitar. Benny
and the Midnighters Battle of the Bands
with the Blue Satins, about 1964. We won.
It was mom's idea for us to wear the black
masks.

Eddie lying beside that beautiful Gretsch.
Always looking for a way to make publicity
photos unique and interesting.

Dad and Eddie
in front of
Priory Street
House. Eddie's
corner bedroom
on left side of
the picture.

Jerry Capehart, Sharon, Eddie,
and Larry Levine between takes,
Goldstar recording studio.

Publicity photo. View a color version
on the Web site eddiecochran.com.

Me at dad's studio
photo shoot. I was
14 at the time.

was located downstairs at a popular mall nearby. The first weekend we had maybe ten people, the second weekend maybe a hundred. Somehow Dad persuaded Jimmy O' Neill—a big-time deejay at top LA radio station KFWB (later he was at KRLA)—to mention our shows. The third week, five hundred folks showed up, and the fourth week we had lines around the buildings and full attendance. By the fifth week we were denied permits and the hall rental; seems local clubs had complained because we were pulling away their patrons and hurting their business. We went on to do various local gigs but eventually lost our momentum. But the glamour, the excitement—the challenge—of luring and satisfying an audience was now in my blood. Like Eddie, who had recorded with countless musicians in sessions credited and uncredited, I would go on to play in more than forty bands, some famous, and to record with and produce a myriad of artists.

There was a coming together of Mom and Dad when I got my guitar at twelve and a half. For a while they set aside their looming differences and rallied around me in support. Mom had come to me not long before to tell me that she wanted to leave Dad, wanted to divorce him. I'd begged her, "Please don't, Mom, please, please, please don't. Make it work." I wanted them to be in love—I knew they were in love—and I wanted them to work it out, to be together. So I begged Mom not to leave him. She said she wanted to leave him, that it just wasn't working between them. She gave me plenty of reasons for wanting to leave: Dad was gone all the time, which I knew; he was drinking too much; he beat her up; he was mean; he was jealous. I didn't care. When you're a kid and you love your parents, none of those things matter; you still love them and want them together.

I started learning about the nature of our family relationships around that time. Dad would come home after his gallivanting; we'd be broke, with not much food. Mom would go into the bedroom with Dad and be with him sexually. Out of her doing that, suddenly we would get enough money to go to the show, get some strawberry pop, buy some tuna and bread. We'd suddenly be able to eat, plus get a treat of a movie and soda pop. Even at that age, just twelve, I understood what Mom was doing, that Mom was having sex with Dad so she could treat us. Mom and Dad were so obviously passionate about each other; you could tell at times that they were crazy about each other, but their fights were equally passionate. There were times of incredible upset, incredible dissension.

But through my music they started coming together more. We were all together as a family at the drive-in that night when I first plucked that guitar in the back seat. They were at my first gig, the talent show. They got involved in my first band. They decided to promote these gigs at the Buena Park Civic Auditorium. Dad talked to Jimmy O'Neil. It was heartwarming to see the amount of pride they both had in me, and, particularly, the overwhelming amount of love and affection my mom had for me. But something I've had conflict with all my life—and perhaps Eddie did too—was accepting that praise. I wanted to keep it at arm's length because I felt I didn't deserve it. I knew I had talent, but to me it was more of a sense of "I'm pretty good for a little kid, but compared with Duane Eddy—I can't touch him." Then when I got to the point that I could play all the Duane Eddy stuff, I still didn't have the substance of what Duane Eddy's music had. I could play the licks, but it was mere imitation.

But then there were times I could make that breakthrough and really play music with passion, even when I was little. It was hard for me because on one hand I wanted to be a success at it, and on the other hand I didn't want to be compared with Eddie, except favorably. I didn't want to have Ed's musical canvas be the one that mine was being compared with—here's Eddie's painting, now here's mine. It was more like, "Um, let's put his away, I'm just a kid."

Things were going pretty well for our family, but then we moved up to Long Beach to a wretched little neighborhood. I went to a horrible high school where the kids were just thugs. Then we moved to Cudahy. That's when the studio became the place where I hung out a lot. Mom began to invite the neighbor kids over—we lived on the second floor of an apartment building—and she had me perform for them. There'd be six to ten kids sitting on the couch or the floor watching me play "Malaguena" and other tunes.

I was around thirteen or fourteen then, and I was really getting pretty good, compared with other kids. Compared to big guys, well, I was still light years behind them. But I was actually having moments of ecstasy when I played, curious, glorious moments of swelling up inside—an outpouring from inside of me, welling out of my solar plexus and my chest. The neighbor kids would go nuts when I finished, but it was embarrassing to me. For me, those moments weren't about showing off, and that's the way it was being presented. That bothered me. My mom wanted me to show off for the neighbor kids.

My music was, and still is, a very personal thing, like communing on a very deep level. It always bothered me when my mom and sisters praised me and wanted to introduce me to all of their friends because I felt it was more like a showing off: "This is my brother. Isn't he great? Isn't he cool?" I can understand the preciousness of your kids or your brothers and sisters and your sense of pride in them, and I feel deficient that I didn't allow my family to express their pride for me in a comfortable way. I made it awkward for them. This is something I'm still trying to overcome in myself, and to make amends. After my mom died, I read a letter she had written to me in which she talked about how much she loved me. She had written something like, "If you can love me at all, then be happy. I want you to be happy."

I was spending a lot of time at Dad's studio while we lived in Cudahy, and I played there quite a bit. I was getting a lot better really fast, and my dad and the other musicians at the studio would often comment on it. My own opinion was, "God, what do they see in me?" I've always been very hard on myself. See, in the Cochran family, no one was ever good enough. And sure enough, I wasn't good enough for me. I would see these great guitar players at the studio; I remember Thumbs Carlille and Speedy West being there. Dad was having me play on sessions, as well as Guybo and some of Ed's other pals. It was really cool for me to get to play with some of Ed's friends, and, of course, I thought Guybo was God on bass. I was equal with them. They were struggling sometimes more than I was, which was surprising to me. I learned to play drums at the studio.

It was a big deal that Eddie played drums, bass, and piano. That influenced me—I thought, well, it would be good for me to learn all these things and understand how they work. And it's really come in handy; nowadays I tell the drummers what I want them to do, same as Ed used to do. I learned that partially from Dad, who hounded me to do everything like Ed had done, which made sense to me—but I also wanted to follow my own creative instincts.

As well as recording, young Eddie was performing. Throughout 1953 and into 1954, he played with an assortment of musicians in a variety of band and jam-session situations. He soaked up all the sounds he could, from the country and western of Atkins, Travis, Maphis, and Marty Robbins to the blues of greats like B. B. King and the jazz of the great Johnny Smith, whose "Moonlight in Vermont" was a particular favorite of Eddie's. Ed would intently listen to, analyze, and absorb a song, then reproduce it note for note with astounding acuity, making him a particular favorite of older, more capable players.

Soon Ed was playing in the Bell Gardens Ranch Gang with Warren Flock, a fellow Oklahoma expatriate four years Ed's senior, and bass player Dave Kohrman. The band performed locally in the Los Angeles area and was featured on area television and radio programs. They were described in advertising as "teen-age western performers." Along with fiddler Forest Lee Bibbie and vocalist/guitarist Clete Stewart, the Bell Gardens Ranch Gang combed California looking for work on radio stations from Bakersfield to San Francisco. The band didn't have much luck, though, and returned to Los Angeles, where Eddie and Chuck Foreman sat in a few times with Richard Rae and the Shamrock Valley Boys, featuring vocalist/guitarist Bob Denton. Though Denton recalls that the pair's first set during a Boys' break was so impressive that it "made us mad because they were so good," he and Eddie became close friends, especially after Eddie learned that Bob had turned down an offer of a permanent gig at the Knott's Berry Farm amusement park. Ed played there with a band on weekends and one Sunday had asked Bob to fill in for him. Because Bob sang onstage and at that time Eddie did not, the band offered Bob the gig. Loyal already to his new pal Ed, Bob refused.

The Shamrock Valley Boys occasionally used a young guest singer named Hank Cochran. Hank was a talented guitarist and vocalist with a passion for pure country music—Ernest Tubb, Lefty Frizzell, and Hank Williams, not the "flop-eared" hybrid of jazz and hillbilly that was western swing, which was immensely popular during World War II and the postwar years. He'd arrived in California in 1951 from New Mexico and by 1953 could be heard on the *Riverside Rancho* radio show on Pasadena's station KXLA. Along with the Shamrock Valley Boys, Hank also appeared on local TV programs, including *Hometown Jamboree*, which featured guitarist Jimmy Bryant and steel guitarist Speedy West, both western swing heroes.

Hank Cochran was looking for a guitar player with whom to form a country duo. He wanted to play some of the many VFW halls. He asked around and was told that there was a kid over in Bell Gardens, also by the name of Cochran, who played pretty good guitar. Since Hank also lived in Bell Gardens, he hunted Eddie up. He went to Ed's house, knocked on the door, and the two went into the bedroom, sat down and started picking.

Hank and Eddie's paths crisscrossed as each played his various gigs with various bands at various local venues, and the two became friends. Hank was aware of Eddie's growing reputation as a stellar guitarist; watching Eddie perform, and jamming with him privately, he, too, became a believer. Seventeen-year-old Hank asked fifteen-year-old Eddie to join him. Eddie agreed. The Cochran Brothers, the act with which Eddie would make his first professional recordings, was born. Eddie also fronted another combo, Eddie Garland and the Country Gentlemen. The name Garland, according to Hank, had been taken from Hank's given name, Garland Perry Cochran.

Although Eddie maintained an admirable report card, graduated from junior high, and entered Bell Gardens High School in 1954, his academic pursuits quickly took a back seat to his musical endeavors. Ed was consumed by music, almost to the detriment of his personal relationships. Music was his life, understood his junior high and high school girlfriend Johnnie Berry, who, with unusual maturity for a teenager, freely accepted Eddie's singular focus.

When I first met Johnnie Berry (in 1973 or '74), in addition to playing with Steppenwolf, I was working in a trio (two guys and a girl) called Patty, Maxine, and Laverne. I was Laverne. We took the name because we did a lot of Andrews Sisters songs. When Steppenwolf was off the road for a while, I would work clubs around Los Angeles with the trio. It was so odd running into Johnnie at the Hungry Tiger in Marina Del Rey, after all those years. She had no idea who I was, but came forward to ask me if I might possibly be the Bobby Cochran she remembered as Eddie's nephew. She hadn't seen me since I was a baby. It was just another instance of how my life has—with little or no conscious effort on my part—brought me in contact with so many people associated with Eddie.

Johnnie patiently accompanied Eddie on jaunts over to Chuck Foreman's house for reel-to-reel taping sessions, happily hung out with Hank Cochran and his wife, Shirley, and gamely went with Ed on double dates with Chuck and his girlfriends. Ed would always wear his blue suede bomber jacket, which came in very handy when they were necking in the back seat of Chuck's big, black '42 Oldsmobile sedan—they would cover up so nobody could see what they were doing. But the bomber jacket was forever falling on the floor, Chuck recalls, revealing what Eddie and Johnnie were trying to keep hidden. And ever since, whenever Johnnie would smell suede, she'd think of Eddie.

Ed was Johnnie's first serious boyfriend, and not because he was a guitar player or a star or anything, she remembers. He was just Eddie Cochran, her boyfriend. The amorous teen couple was always in the back seat of Chuck's big old four-door, Johnnie recalls, and she was always afraid of going too far. One time, she and Ed went over to the apartment of one of Chuck's girlfriends, a young lady who was pregnant, though not by him. It was the one time Ed tried to push their relationship over the edge in the backseat of Chuck's car. Of course, Ed would always bring his guitar with them into the roomy backseat. But Johnnie didn't mind; she probably carried that Gretsch guitar more than he did.

That Gretsch. The 6120 Chet Atkins hollow body guitar, available in 1955 to any young musician for $385, brand new. Endorsed by Atkins, an esteemed Nashville session guitarist who scored his first hit that year with his rendition of "Mr. Sandman," the 6120 was a powerful and fast-playing, easy-feeling, sexy-looking guitar with a full, bright sound. For a musician like Eddie who had professional aspirations, the 6120 was the stuff of which dreams were made. In Eddie's hands, that shiny, new factory-direct 6120, serial number 16942, would become part of the iconography of rock 'n' roll. With help from his parents, Eddie purchased the instrument from the Bell Gardens Music Center. The place was a popular hangout for area musicians, and Eddie had established a relationship there that allowed him to make payments on various purchases and rentals.

One of the players who frequented the Music Center was Gary Lambert, guitarist for Glen Glenn, who would eventually record classic rockabilly tunes like "Everybody's Movin'" and "One Cup of Coffee." Lambert had first seen Eddie when they were both standing in line for the amateur hour at the *Squeakin' Deacon Show* (a radio show) in 1954. When Bobby Charles, who worked on the TV show *Town Hall Party*, was getting a little band together with Connie "Guybo" Smith playing bass, Guybo officially introduced

Lambert and Eddie. Glenn and Lambert became friendly with Eddie and Hank when the Cochran Brothers dropped by the County Barn Dance in Baldwin Park, where Glenn and Lambert had a regular gig every Friday and Saturday night as the Missouri Mountain Boys.

Lambert recalls, "Every Friday night they held an amateur contest or audition contest. Eddie and Hank both came out there and played. Jerry Capehart used to come out there all the time, 'cause he was a promoter and always trying to find somebody to promote. He'd get up there and try to sing like everybody else did. One night in late 1956 or early 1957 the Everly Brothers came out and Hank and Eddie were there. I ran into Eddie again when he and Hank were playing a place I think was called the Larriet Club." They later played on the same bill with Eddie and Hank, in Salinas at a big auditorium. Gary remembers, "There were more people in the bands than in the audience."

Eddie and Lambert, who had common influences in Chet Atkins and Merle Travis, jammed together a few times at home-recording sessions, each seeking to improve his technique by gleaning all he could from the other. Gary played all sorts of pop songs, and the two worked very hard trying to perfect Chet Atkins's "Yankee Doodle Dixie," Lambert recalls.

From the Bell Gardens Music Center Gary had ordered a Gretsch Country Club model with his name inlaid in the neck, and he was given an amber-red 6120 by the local Gretsch distributor as a loaner until the custom instrument was complete. Lambert's new guitar was ready in a few months, and he exchanged the 6120 for his Country Club at the Bell Gardens store. It's long been taken for granted that the 6120 is the guitar Eddie ultimately purchased. But I don't believe that to be true. Gary's borrowed Gretsch had a natural aluminum Bigsby with a black logo area. Eddie's now infamous Gretsch, however, had a gold-anodized aluminum Bigsby. I have never found any picture or any person to confirm that Eddie's guitar had the natural aluminum tremolo; I've only found proof of the gold anodized Bigsby.

Regardless, Eddie couldn't resist when an amber-red 6120 with a gold tremolo became available at the Bell Gardens Music Center.

Eddie and his new guitar were inseparable. It was in his hands going to, during, and leaving gigs and rehearsals, on dates with Johnnie Berry, and while hanging out at home or with friends. His constant companion, never out of his sight.

I felt the same way about my Gretsch, which my parents bought for me—though I later learned that my Aunt Glo—Eddie's and my father's sister—and her husband helped pay for it when they saw how serious I was about the guitar. My first Gretsch came to me in an odd way at the most opportune time. It was just prior to the school talent show, and an insurance salesman came to our house. He noticed a picture of Eddie playing his 6120 and told us he used to play professionally, that he had a 6120 and a Magnatone amp he was trying to sell. I couldn't believe my ears. At that time I was playing a black Silvertone that Dad, who was working as a repo man, had found in the trunk of a car he'd repossessed. It was another terrible guitar, but better than the Regal or Stella.

I was about to play at that junior high talent show, my first public performance, and I could just envision myself onstage playing that gorgeous guitar that looked so much like Eddie's. My parents said they might try to get me that Gretsch, but they wanted to be sure they were making a wise investment, that I was willing to make a commitment to the instrument. So Dad made me quit Little League before he would buy it for me. He didn't want me hurting my hands. I didn't have to think twice about giving up baseball; man, I wanted that sweet guitar so badly I'd have done anything.

Those Gretschs were so beautiful: the delicate F holes; that curvaceous, seductive shape; the Bigsby tremolo; the branded "G" in the wood; and all that gleaming gold against the amber-red finish. I was in love, as I'm sure Ed must've been, too.

Eddie was no stranger to modifying his instruments. He had already been modifying them before he acquired his Gretsch. While with the Cochran Brothers, he'd converted the single cutaway Gibson from acoustic to electric by adding and altering a De Armond pickup. The pickup had a long, round metal piece that stuck out toward the neck of the guitar; Eddie pounded that metal piece with a hammer until it was flat. Then he drilled some screw holes in it so he could mount it on the neck. He ran the wires under the pick guard and mounted the control knobs. By making himself electric, Eddie thought he was ready to start changing the world. But even the best laid plans often wind up in disappointment; after all of his hard work, the sound in his mind was still superior to his reality. Something was missing.

So after purchasing his 6120, Eddie again made modifications, including changing the front pickup from a DeArmond to a Gibson P90 to achieve a mellower sound. Eddie was fascinated with the sound of some of the smooth players, particularly the silky, triad harmonies of Johnny Smith, a favorite of many guitarists of that era. The factory Gretsch had a very brittle, very bright timbre. Though the highs were astounding on the instrument, Ed wanted that mellow Gibson L5 sound. He also obscured the Chet Atkins signature on the scratchplate, first with tape and then permanently with sandpaper, and he added a homemade strap, originally crafted for him for his Gibson by Guybo's mom.

I was aware of Eddie's alterations to guitars, and they sparked my interest in hot-rodding my own guitars. When I was with a group signed to Capitol called the Knack (not the "My Sharona" band) in 1967 and '68, I had Milt Owens, a top guitar repairman in Hollywood, install a DeArmond pickup in the front position of one of my guitars, a Fender Esquire. I came to the shop early to watch how he did it and was horrified to see him hacking a hole out of my guitar with a screwdriver and a hammer. I freaked out—he should have been using a router, or a wood chisel at the very least. The guitar was all splintered, chipped, and gouged. I yelled at him to stop, whisked the scarred guitar home, and decided then and there to purchase my own router. Over the years, several guitarists had asked me if I would install pickups for them, but I never had the proper tools and never thought to make the investment. In pickup installations, that router went on to quickly pay for itself.

3
Rock Star Rising

WHEN EDDIE JOINED HANK, academia flew right out the window. In January 1955, obsessed with his instrument and intent on becoming a professional musician, my sixteen-year-old uncle dropped out of Bell Gardens High School. He never looked back.

Playing in the style of Grand Ole Opry heroes like the Wilburn Brothers and Hank Williams's protégé Ray Price, and resplendent in their showbiz finery—my Aunt Gloria, Ed's sister, had put sparkling rhinestones down the sides of their matching pant legs—the Cochran Brothers were pure country. They scoured southern California for work, which began to pay off in the form of club gigs and dance dates, and television appearances.

Warren Flock accompanied Eddie and Hank on their first audition as an opening act for some of the bigger stars. Warren remembers picking Eddie up and going into Hollywood, arriving at a little old building spartanly furnished with an office desk and a couple of chairs. There was a guy sitting there from one of the record labels, thumbing through a newspaper. Eddie and Hank had their whole show worked out. As they were giving it their all, the auditioner virtually ignored them, burying his nose behind his newspaper. Warren felt like hitting him over the head. With a club. When Ed and Hank were through, the guy gave them the standard, "Don't call us, we'll call you." Surprisingly, the Cochran Brothers did receive a call, and they got themselves placed on several shows as a warm-up act for some of the stars.

From Hank's earlier appearances on the show, the Cochran Brothers were able to guest on *Hometown Jamboree*, the hugely popular, long-running radio-turned-TV country music show whose featured performers over the years had included everyone from Tennessee Ernie Ford to Merle Travis to Johnny Cash. The show's host, Cliffie Stone, had ties to the large country-music promotion and publishing firm, American Music Corporation, and the duo's *Jamboree* work led to more gigs from the firm, plus an audition at Ekko Records.

Based in Memphis but with an office in California as well, Ekko was a small independent label that had specialized in western swing recordings in the '40s, but whose roster also boasted talents like Al Dexter, Eddie Bond, Buddy Griffin, Riley Crabtree, and Jess Willard. In May 1955, at Hollywood's Sunset Recorders, the Cochran Brothers recorded four tunes for Ekko. The pairing of "Two Blue Singin' Stars," a tribute to country legends Jimmy Rodgers and Hank Williams, and "Mr. Fiddle," featuring solo work from stalwart session fiddler Harold Hensley, became the Cochran Brothers'—and Eddie's—first commercial release. Touted as "taking the country by storm" in a July 1955 Ekko ad, which also misspelled the A-side as "Too Blue Singin' Stars," the record sales failed to make any impression. Undeterred, Ekko followed up with "Your Tomorrows Never Come" backed with "Guilty Conscience," which was penned by the pair. Both singles also missed the charts but showcased the duo's tight vocal harmonies and Eddie's evolving lead guitar style.

Two singles under their belts so early in their career also aided the Cochran Brothers in landing more performance work, particularly across the South, including an appearance on the Dallas-based TV and radio show *Big D Jamboree*, mere days after some greasy kid named Elvis Presley performed there.

Elvis Presley. A stunningly handsome, dark-haired boy with nervous legs and a strange new way with a song, Elvis was on the ascent from impoverished Memphis nowheresville to musical superstardom. His hook? A rebellious, thumping hybrid of hillbilly and rhythm and blues—heretofore unheard of—that people called rock 'n' roll. His beat-heavy songs, like "That's All Right" and a juiced-up read of Bill Monroe's "Blue Moon of Kentucky," were potent with their rhythmic locomotion and sparse instrumentation—simply guitar and snapping, slapping, upright bass. Especially daring was white boy Presley's borrowing from the rhythm and blues, or "race music," songbook, grafting the "colored" tunes, tones, and tempos onto his Anglo-hillbilly roots music. Presley's blending of the races was a colossal taboo, and a musical miscegenation that forever altered American cultural history.

Adventurous country radio stations across the nation were taking a shine to the kid, Presley, giving his unusual records, waxed on the tiny Sun label out of Memphis, loads of play. And he wasn't the only one fiddling with the new sound—tunes like Bill Haley and the Comets' "Rock Around the Clock," Chuck Berry's "Maybellene," and Little Richard's "Tutti Frutti" were also helping bring rock 'n' roll into the mainstream. Teenagers, laden with disposable income in the abundant post-war economy, snatched up the defiant new sound, helping rock 'n' roll—or rockabilly, as its earliest incarnation was known—to replace country as the record industry's latest cash cow.

Bobby Charles—a featured player on the *Town Hall Party* show who first saw Ed perform pre–Cochran Brothers on the *Squeakin' Deacon* amateur show on KXLA (Hank was there as well, playing under the name Hank Perry)—can recall a conversation he had with country music stalwart George Jones around the time of Presley's emergence. Jones was lamenting about how country acts were starting to cut rockabilly records, jumping on the rock 'n' roll bandwagon. "For cryin' out loud," he moaned to Charles, "even Porter Waggoner cut a rock 'n' roll record!" The country music establishment was in a virtual state of panic; nobody was sure how this awful rock 'n' roll racket would effect their pristine genre, and everyone was amazed at rock 'n' roll's steamrolling popularity. "Don't them people love country music?" Jones mused.

When Ed and Hank played the *Big D Jamboree*—which broadcast from the Dallas Sportatorium, an airplane-hangar-huge Quonset hut where boxing matches were held—they noticed a police officer there covered in scratches. When they asked him what had happened, he told them that police had been hired to keep the crowd away from some kid who'd played there a few days earlier. He and his fellow officers working the gig thought it was crazy, but the moment the boy "hit that damn stage, all them gals, as you can see, hell, they damn near scratched us to pieces tryin' to get to him."

"Who did you say that was?" Hank, amazed, asked the officer.

"Some kid by the name of Elvis Presley," the cop told him.

After their tour had taken them to Nashville, Ed and Hank made the trek to Memphis, where they got to know a few folks at radio station WMPS, an early Presley proponent. One evening, they were taken to a Presley gig, eager, in Hank's words, "to see what that damned kid was doin' that was eatin' them damned gals' minds up!" The two teens were knocked out—when charismatic Elvis hit the stage it was dynamic, like magic. The young women in the audience went wild. Ed and Hank knew they were witnessing a monster, the world's next musical hero. They were able to meet Presley that night and chatted with him briefly.

Eddie and Hank could hardly have known then the full extent of Presley's eventual impact on the course of pop music history. But for two kids not much younger than Elvis who were seeking their own way in the music world, the girlie-scream-inducing Elvis Presley was a downright inspiration. Ed would soon incorporate some Elvis-isms into his own stage manner. Hank recalls that prior to witnessing Elvis live, Ed didn't move about much on stage, he just shook his shoulder to the beat, a trick he'd copped from Lefty Frizzell and which Mom always told me was very sexy. But after Ed saw Elvis, Hank remembers, "He'd do damn near anything, adopting the attitude 'If Elvis can do it, why can't we?'" After their transformative Elvis experience, the two Cochrans started talking. The Presley sound hadn't yet made it as far west as California. Ed and Hank decided they'd head back to Los Angeles and give what ol' Elvis was doing a try.

Stranded by Ekko Records tour manager Red Matthews—who had simply disappeared when money got tight—and flat broke, they hocked Ed's amp and thumbed their way back home. When they weren't able to score a ride from a kindly truck driver or merciful traveling salesman, they walked. Eddie's electric Gretsch and Hank's acoustic Martin guitars were heavy; they'd trudge the highways, lugging their clothes and the hefty guitars. Big cities like Dallas took what seemed an eternity to walk through. As they traveled, Ed and Hank stopped in a few places, playing hole-in-the-wall nightclubs and roadside honky-tonks for money. Patrons in Nevada would pitch silver dollars at them, actually putting nicks and dings in Hank's guitar. But Hank would look at his partner and yell, "Keep playing, Ed!" Hank said, "You can see them nicks in my Martin, at the Country Music Hall of Fame where that guitar now resides."

One night, the two could find nowhere to sleep. When some folks offered them lodging, they were thrilled. When the accommodations turned out to be a chicken coop, Hank turned to my weary uncle and said, "I guess we hit the bottom. We got but one way to go, Eddie!"

With country music's popularity on the wane, or at least in transition, the less-than-stellar performance of the Cochran Brothers' first two records couldn't have been too surprising. Yet Ekko (perhaps trying to make up for the Red Matthews stranding incident) stood by its act, giving Ed and Hank work as session players behind some of their other artists and turning them loose on the road with label-mate Jess Willard.

One day in October 1955, while picking up some strings at the Bell Gardens Music Center, Eddie was introduced to Jerry Capehart, an ambitious air force pilot turned songwriter. Jerry had just landed a contract with the American Music Corporation, the influential publishing firm that supplied Capitol Records with many of the hits it had used to break into the once-lucrative country music market. Like Eddie and Hank, Capehart also frequented the County Barn Dance, often going onstage to sing.

Capehart, who was experimenting with the new rock 'n' roll sound, was in need of some musicians to help him make demos of his songs; the Cochran Brothers were happy to oblige. The Music Center had a tiny back studio equipped for recording directly to acetate disc, a feature that helped attract musicians like Ralph Mooney and Harlan Howard to the store. There, Eddie, Hank, and Jerry began waxing Jerry's material, including the bluesy farmer's lament "My Honest Name." Eddie and Hank would work up demos of Jerry's stuff at my parents' house as well. One of these sessions held in our living room in Bell Gardens, featuring Jerry's "Rockin' and Flyin'," was captured by Chuck Foreman in late 1955, and it is probably the earliest recorded evidence of a rock 'n' roll influence in Ed's music.

As Ed, Hank, and Jerry spent time together, Jerry took even more of an interest in the Cochran Brothers, employing them from time to time as a backing band for concert appearances and recording dates, like his session for the tiny indie label Cash, which turned out the vaguely rockabilly-esque single "Rollin'," coupled with "Walkin' Stick Boogie." "Guitar backing by the Cochran Brothers is a big help to warbler Capehart on this rhythmic tune," a music scribe wrote in early 1956 of "Rollin'," whose label read, "Jerry Capehart Sings... Walkin' Stick Boogie featuring Cochran Brothers.... Shows the Presley influence." The same critic panned the flip, stating simply, "Not much to this side." The single sank.

Undaunted, Jerry wangled another session for Cash, this time at the basement studios at Capitol Records—and he called in Eddie; one of Eddie's guitar heroes, Joe Maphis; and the Cash house band, which featured Ernie Freeman on piano. Among the tunes waxed at the session was "Rockin' and Flyin'," the song the Cochran Brothers had demoed in Mom's living room. From that stellar demo, it was clear that Eddie already had a firm grasp of some of the great licks of Chet Atkins and Merle Travis.

Ed's fingerpicking style was quite innovative; if a player simply used a pick and not his fingers, he could surely have never sounded that fluid. From listening to, learning from, and personalizing for myself Uncle Ed's and Atkins's work, I was able to incorporate that style into my playing, which ultimately proved invaluable, since hardly any West Coast guitarists played that way when I was starting my career. Ronnie Ennis showed me that rolling, pull-off technique that Ed and Atkins did so well. Eddie was one of the few who did it with two strings at once, and he would use those licks time and time again throughout his career, in the solos and intros to "Twenty Flight Rock," "Skinny Jim," "Rockin' and Flyin'," "Fast Jivin'," "Eddie's Blues #2," "Latch On," "Heart of a Fool," "Slow Down," and "Tired and Sleepy." All these songs feature those patented Cochran interpretations of Chet Atkins and Merle Travis licks, along with some of the emerging rock feel of the time.

Very few guitarists of that era were hip to some of these styles and how to do them, and Eddie was obviously swapping licks with other hip and innovative guitarists wherever and whenever he could. In my career, that has been something my buddies and I have done a lot, too. Sure, a lot of those licks were lifted from the greats like Carl Perkins, Chuck Berry, James Burton, Johnny Smith, Atkins, and Travis. But that's how most up-and-coming musicians develop their own style. Learn from the greats, then add your twists and make them your own.

A pivotal moment in my career involved such a learning experience. I was sixteen years old and with a very popular Long Beach band called the Emperors. One night we were hired to do a welcoming party in the Hollywood hills for some English group. That band, it turned out, was the Yardbirds, psychedelic rock pioneers behind the hits "For Your Love," "Heart Full of Soul," "Shapes of Things," and more. That shindig was packed to the rafters with stars and Hollywood types—a seriously well-connected crowd—and I remember thinking it was pretty cool to see Roger McGuinn of the Byrds just twenty feet away on the balcony, watching me play through binoculars. After our little set, the pros, the Yardbirds, got up and did a set of their own on our gear. Jeff Beck, just a few years older than me, was on guitar, having been recommended by Jimmy Page to replace Eric Clapton, the Yardbirds' previous guitarist.

Beck was one of the most fantastic players I'd ever heard. Although he was older and seemingly much more experienced, he was the first rock 'n' roll peer of mine that I'd ever heard doing those same rolling, pull-off licks that I'd made part of my technique, by way of Eddie and Chet, of course. He was doing a lot of what I was doing, and more—which was tremendous validation for a sixteen-year-old kid—only he was doing it with a solid-body Fender Esquire guitar. The solid-body was capable of things my 6120 just wasn't. It seemed I was blazing a stylistic trail similar to his, and it was true inspiration, a downright thrill, to hear someone that good, that close. Hearing him that night finally got me to take a solid-body guitar seriously. I went right out and bought an Esquire from a friend for sixty bucks and began hot-rodding all my guitars from then on. I was already experimenting with fuzztones and echo, and different amps and mikes. Eventually I even had a custom board built for my home studio.

Ed and Hank shoehorned the Capehart sessions into their busy performance schedule, which had the duo gigging across California, from Bakersfield to the Bay Area and beyond, including Oregon, Washington, Kansas, and Arizona. The two took up residence in northern California for a few months, where they played the same club circuit as other country music acts like Cotton Seed Clark, Black Jack Wayne, and the Maddox Brothers & Rose. Their friendship with Black Jack Wayne also landed them shows at the Garden of Allah in Niles, a popular dance hall Wayne owned with his brother Chuck. In the wine country of Napa they worked the Dream Bowl with Jess Willard for a time, and quickly became regulars on the *California Hayride*, the country music program aired by KROV TV in nearby Stockton.

The show was broadcast from venues all over the area, both indoors and out. One night Ed and Hank—who'd quickly amassed a loyal female following up north—were scheduled to perform. When it was time for them to hit the stage, Ed was nowhere to be found. Well, Hank knew where he was—somewhere behind the stage scenery. And he knew exactly what he was doing, too—and Ed wasn't doing it alone. Determined not to miss their cue, just as the announcer boomed, "Ladies and gentlemen, please welcome Hank and Eddie Cochran," Hank found Ed and pulled him off the girl. Hank wasn't sure if it was a chick from the audience or one of the girls who worked on the show, but he thought it was hilarious to watch Ed try to get himself back in his pants, zip up, and put on his guitar at the same time. Then, cool as you please, Ed and Hank walked onstage and played a flawless set on live television. Afterward, Hank didn't find the incident quite so amusing. "Christ, Eddie, you wanna get us thrown out of here into the cold?" he chided. "You gotta use more sense!"

Around the same time, while they were in the Sacramento area, a flood kept Ed and Hank stranded in a hotel room for two weeks; they were forced to find things to float on to venture out for food. They played cards and checkers, or snuck girls in, until the waters receded. But mostly they passed the time working on songs, creating new parts and harmonies. Not surprisingly, the long weeks on the road with next-to-nothing wages put a definite strain on Hank's marriage, evidenced by a pair of desperate letters to his wife from this period.

Back in southern California, in early April 1956, Jerry, Ed, and Hank—possibly with Eddie's good pal Guybo Smith on bass—were booked into LA's Goldstar Studios. Jerry's "My Honest Name," one of the songs demoed at the Bell Gardens Music Center, had been released by Crest Records, a label formed by American Music to showcase the publishing firm's newest song-writing talent. Recorded by Crest employees under the name of Jack Lewis and the Americans, "My Honest Name" was apparently impressive enough to prompt American to put Capehart into the studio to demo more of his material.

A technically sound yet relatively inexpensive recording complex, Goldstar, founded in 1950, was home to four or five hours of American Music demo sessions every Wednesday. In Goldstar's Studio B, a simple but efficient mono demo facility that went for ten bucks an hour plus tape, Eddie, Hank, and Jerry recorded four compositions that Capehart would claim as his own (although Hank recalls that Jerry didn't have a thing to do with the writing of any of the Ekko records) and one penned by two Crest employees. For the first time, Eddie took over lead vocals, handing in tentative performances on the rocking "Pink Peg Slacks" and weepers "Yesterday's Heartbreak" and "My Love to Remember." His singing showed promise, though, and a definite affinity for the burgeoning rock 'n' roll sound. Via these early demos, Jerry introduced Ed to the ears at Crest and American Music, who thought they were hearing something special.

Soon Ed, Guybo, and Jerry would become permanent fixtures at the sessions, demoing songs with a multitude of other musicians. Often they didn't know who was going to show, and frequently whomever they could round up from American at the last minute, including guys who simply worked in the office, would improvise a back beat for them by slapping a box with a brush.

Eddie would record some of his greatest records in Goldstar's Studio B, which was spartanly equipped with a pair of Ampex mono machines and a small console, a collection of Dynamic and RCA ribbon mikes, and Altec 604D monitors. Most of the echo (or slap-back) used on Ed's work was 7 1/2-ips- or 15-ips-tape echo. Sometimes masking or splicing tape would be used to increase the diameter of the capstan, a small motor-driven shaft that is pressed against by the pinch-roller. The wider you made the diameter of the capstan, the faster it pulled the tape through, thus shortening the delay (a technique that nowadays is done by the push of a button, the turn of a knob, or the click of a mouse). Only when overdubs or transfers were made in studio A would chamber echo ever be utilized, the same chamber that Phil Spector would make famous with his "wall of sound" recordings and still one of the finest sounding echo chambers ever.

Jerry, who freely admitted to Goldstar co-owner and engineer Stan Ross that he knew next to nothing about recording, listened and learned as much as he could from the Goldstar staff. Though he didn't make too much of an impression on Faith, the studio secretary, on whom he had a terrific crush (she told him he resembled a mongoose with that smile of his), he ingratiated himself to the rest of the Goldstar crew with his sense of humor. "What, can't you tell she loves me?" he'd say with a wry smile. And everyone at Goldstar loved Ed. They found him to be a beautifully mannered kid, nothing uppity about him. Though it was apparent that Eddie was coming up with the ideas in the studio, he readily took suggestions with an open mind from Jerry and others, including Stan Ross and his nephew, engineer Larry Levine, who offered critical input regarding microphone use and placement, equalization, mixing and more.

The Cochran Brothers closed out April 1956 with an appearance on *Town Hall Party*, another of the West Coast's premiere country music shows. Launched in 1953 at the town hall in the LA suburb of Compton, *Town Hall Party* started life as a Saturday night country dance, broadcast at first by the local radio station, KFI, and later by the NBC radio network. Local TV station KTTV soon added the show to its programming, expanding it to three hours broadcast live on Friday and Saturday nights.

The Cochran Brothers' undiluted country sound fit right in with other *Town Hall Party*-ers like Merle Travis; Tex Ritter; Johnny Bond, Ed's one-time session-mate; guitar hero Joe Maphis and his wife Rose; the Collins Kids; and Lefty Frizzell, with whom Hank and Ed appeared. Just a few days after their television performance, Eddie and Hank departed for Honolulu, Hawaii, joining Frizzell for a five-night stand.

One night before leaving for Hawaii, Ed and Hank got in to Hank's Nash Rambler and headed to Hollywood to visit Frizzell in the studio. On the way there, they had a flat tire. It was a frigid evening for southern California so the two quickly changed the tire and then sped to the studio. After recording some with Lefty, they climbed back into the Rambler and headed for home. On the way, the Rambler blew another tire. Without a spare, the two were stranded. They called Ed's family—Hank remembers that it was my dad—to come and get them, then left the car running to fight the cold. When help arrived, both Ed and Hank were unconscious. They had to be pulled from the car and revived. The exhaust fumes had put them completely out. Dad always said it was a wonder they were still alive.

Thanks to Elvis Presley—signed for big bucks to major label RCA—and his musical contemporaries, rock 'n' roll had captured the imagination—and piggybanks—of the vast and previously untapped American youth market. Both creatively and commercially, the genre's allure and influence could not have escaped the teenage Eddie. And working with rock 'n' roll-minded Capehart was only solidifying the direction in which Eddie's music would flow.

The transition from Eddie Cochran, country artist, to Eddie Cochran, rock 'n' roll star, was already underway by the time the Cochran Brothers returned to the studio to record again for Ekko. A drummer and pianist from the *Hometown Jamboree* program were recruited, replacing the hillbilly steel guitar and fiddle, and Eddie and Hank cut loose on a handful of rockabilly-burnished barn-burners, including "Tired and Sleepy" and "Fool's Paradise," issued as the Cochran Brothers' next single. "The Cochrans enter the triplet-backed, Presley-styled country gold with some exciting, rhythmic laments," a *Billboard* reviewer raved of "Fool's Paradise." Of "Tired and Sleepy," the critic wrote, "The lads work up a lather on this swinging blues ditty with more of the same colorful piano and down guitar." Despite the Cochran Brothers' more current sound, which featured Eddie more prominently on vocals, their third Ekko single, like their first two, tanked. Ekko soon closed up shop.

Eddie, now wholly devoted to rock 'n' roll, and Hank, still passionate for pure country, parted ways. Hank couldn't stand the often physical way rock 'n' roll fans expressed their enthusiasm; he didn't like to be touched or bothered, and he didn't care for all their screaming and hollering. It had gotten to the point where he'd just push Eddie out to the front of the stage and let him deal with it. Hank didn't care much for Jerry—he thought him to be something of an opportunist and an operator, always trying to maneuver his way into something. And it made Hank bristle the way he'd claim credit for songs he didn't write. But he seemed to have Ed hooked. Hank knew that Jerry was trying to drag Ed into the rock 'n' roll music machinery, and Hank wanted no part of it. As much as he cherished Ed, Hank had to go.

He gave Ed a big bear hug and told him, "I love you man, but I'm country to the core. I'll probably wind up in Nashville, because that's what I want to do, write. So you go out there and give 'em hell! And if that crazy son of a bitch Capehart can do you any good, go with him." Hank did eventually move to Nashville, where a string of hits waxed by others—"Make the World Go Away," "Don't Touch Me," "I Want to Go With You," "Don't You Ever Get Tired of Hurting Me?" "I Fall to Pieces," "She's Got You," "Little Bitty Tear"—would cement his status as one of country music's premier songwriters and ultimately land him in the Country Music Hall of Fame, where today you can see Hank's old guitar with all the nicks in it from those silver dollars tossed to him and Ed.

For Eddie, the uncharted possibilities and irresistible opportunities of nascent rock 'n' roll beckoned.

STEP TWO: *Riding High*

4
Rockin' the Big Screen

EDDIE'S INSATIABLE HUNGER to learn all aspects of sound-recording technique and technology, teamed with his natural ability on a variety of instruments, kept him in the recording studio throughout 1956, working his own sessions but more often playing behind others. The amazingly quick study, the rock 'n' roll-loving kid with the country-steeped roots, was garnering a stellar reputation as the versatile session player of choice for both established and fledgling artists. Country acts like Capitol Records stars Wynn Stewart and Skeets McDonald looked to Eddie as a lead guitarist to embellish their material with his capable fingerpicking or to update their sound with the intensely rhythmic style of the moment, that rock 'n' roll.

Other sessions found him strumming acoustic rhythm guitar, thumping bass, keeping time on drums, or supplying backing vocals in a whole host of genres, from jazzy to rocking. Thanks to the broad spectrum of his session work for American Music and its showcase imprint Crest, plus other labels both major and independent, Eddie was blossoming into an amazingly pliable musician, competent and comfortable in a variety of musical styles. But as a jack-of-all-trades, he had yet to establish a definitive identity as a solo artist.

Early in 1956, the wild-eyed pianist with the piled-high pompadour, Little Richard, recorded the classic "Long Tall Sally" at Master Recorders, located on LA's Fairfax Boulevard. Master was a cutting-edge sound studio with a heady resume steeped in early R&B and rock 'n' roll. Armed with this knowledge, Eddie insisted his tracks be recorded there when Jerry Capehart secured a one-off record deal with Crest. So in July 1956, seventeen-year-old Eddie and his marketeering mentor Jerry entered the studio, along with Gene Davis, another Crest hopeful, to wax a couple of solo tunes apiece.

In the 1950s, as a cost-saving measure, multiple artists often split a single session, sharing the same backing band. With Guybo Smith (who'd now also quit school to pursue his musical dreams) slapping upright bass, Ray Stanley on piano, and Jesse Sailes on drums, Eddie churned out a Cochran/Capehart composition, the frantic rock 'n' roller "Skinny Jim," as well as the flaccid ballad "Half Loved," credited to Ray Stanley and Jaye Fitzsimmons. Crest paired the two tracks, and later the next month Eddie's first solo record was released.

Owing a great debt to Richard's "Long Tall Sally," "Skinny Jim" was a righteously spirited romp, fueled by Eddie's cartwheeling guitar and Guybo's rollicking bass thumps. Falsetto Richard-esque "oos" punctuated Eddie's hoarsely hollered lyrics, and tongue-twisting "be-bop-a-lulas" nodded to fellow rocker and future friend Gene Vincent's quirky rockabilly hit of the same name, released in June 1956. "Cochran enthusiastically knocks out a driving, country-rock 'n' roller in a style similar to that of Little Richard's click 'Long Tall Sally,'" enthused one August 1956 reviewer. "Swinging side tailor-made for the teen-age hoofers." Of the flip, the reviewer opined, "On the lower end Cochran waxes a feelingful, fish-beat lover's ballad."

Eddie switched to session-player mode to accompany, along with the rest of the studio band, Gene Davis on a pair of tunes, the insistent "Drowning All My Sorrows" and "Let's Coast a While." Also released that August under the name Bo Davis, the songs, like Eddie's solo debut pairing, tanked. The studio gang, including Davis and Jerry along with Eddie and the other musicians, waxed a final song, unreleased by Crest, the swinging "Latch On," which Hank Cochran had cut as a demo back in April at Goldstar.

Looking to secure a more lucrative situation for his talented young charge, the ever-ambitious Jerry was actively seeking a label deal for Eddie that involved more than a one-off single. In the wake of Elvis Presley's phenomenal sales figures, record labels were scrambling to find their own versions of the dangerously handsome hip-shaker with the hiccup in his velvet throat. Aided by numerous television appearances, by April 1956 Elvis's "Hound Dog" had sold two million copies; "Don't Be Cruel" had sold three million; and both records, along with "Heartbreak Hotel," had straddled the Top 5 on the pop, country, and rhythm and blues charts.

In Eddie, Jerry could sense gold; he was so much more than a session player or side man. Jerry just needed to convince the label heads. So he packaged up dubs of three tunes that he, Eddie, and Guybo had knocked out at Goldstar, loose-limbed renditions of solid hits with proven sales histories and one original. Accompanied by Guybo on upright bass and Jerry on makeshift cardboard-box drum, Eddie put his own enthusiastic stamp on two rockers—Carl Perkins's "Blue Suede Shoes" (also recorded by Elvis Presley, Pee Wee King, and Boyd Bennett) and Little Richard's "Long Tall Sally" (also waxed by Marty Robbins and Pat Boone), plus "Twenty Flight Rock," written by American Music staff-writer Nelda Bingo under the pen name Ned Fairchild. Although still groping for the best way around a song with his deep, dusky vocals, Eddie's delivery was confident and crackling.

Armed with the demos, Jerry was ready to make the rounds of LA's many record labels. Fate intervened, though, in the person of Boris Petroff, a passing acquaintance of the always-networking Jerry. A movie business mainstay in the late '30s and '40s, the Russian-born writer, director, and producer—responsible for films like *Hats Off, Red Snow*, and *World Dances*—was, by 1956, grinding out B-grade horror and sci-fi titles. One day while Eddie and Jerry were working, Petroff dropped by the studio, was taken by Eddie's lens-friendly good looks, and offered him a part in a film a friend was directing.

At first, Eddie thought the out-of-the-blue invitation was a joke. But when Petroff phoned the next day, things quickly got serious.

An audition was arranged. The role of a new rock 'n' roll singing sensation in the Twentieth Century-Fox musical film *Do-Re-Mi*, later retitled *The Girl Can't Help It*, was tailor-made for Eddie, and put him in the high-profile company of a glittering host of contemporary rock 'n' roll and R&B stars, including Gene Vincent, Fats Domino, the Platters, and Little Richard, for whose song the movie was named.

The motion picture industry was eager to cash in on rock 'n' roll's gold-plated popularity among the cash-dropping youth audience and was moving swiftly to include rock 'n' roll in its celluloid fare. Music industry mavens were just as eagerly pitching their brightest young talents to Hollywood, buoyed by the resounding success of Bill Haley's "Rock Around the Clock," which was heard in February 1955 percolating under the opening credits of the film *Blackboard Jungle*. Though the single was originally released in 1954 on the Decca label, its tepid sales instantly turned torrid, carrying the tune to the top of the charts, when tied with the teen rebellion depicted in the film. Elvis Presley's three-picture, half-million-dollar movie deal with producer Hal Wallis solidified the rock 'n' roll/film connection.

The Girl Can't Help It was one of Hollywood's first big-budget rock 'n' roll extravaganzas, filmed in Cinemascope with stereophonic sound. Produced, directed, and co-written by Warner cartoons veteran Frank Tashlin, the movie featured blonde bombshell Jayne Mansfield—Fox's overly endowed answer to Marilyn Monroe—as a lovable but talentless singer being groomed by entertainment agent Tom Ewell on orders from Edmund O'Brien, her gangster-ish boyfriend. As Mansfield bounced her way through rehearsal halls and nightclubs, the film's flimsy plot afforded plenty of cameo appearances for nascent rock 'n' roll's very best and brightest.

In late July of 1955, Eddie, Guybo, and Jerry, again equipped with his trusty cardboard-box drum, entered the Goldstar studio and recorded the song that Eddie would sing in the film—and that would give the world its first, glorious glimpse of Eddie Cochran, rock 'n' roll idol—"Twenty Flight Rock." The tune—among Ed's demos that Jerry originally brought to Liberty Records and on which Ed was given co-writer credit—featured Eddie's first fully realized rock 'n' roll vocal, dripping with Goldstar echo and hopped up with a hiccuping delivery. Again, Eddie showed his considerable prowess on the guitar, handily peeling off a whirling, triplet-punched solo atop Guybo's urgent bass slaps, creating what would come to be hailed as a classic slice of rock 'n' roll.

Although Eddie's contribution to the song was indelible, if only through his performance, a contract was drawn stating he would not be entitled to any royalties on the song, that all monies would go to Nelda Bingo. It was rumored that American Music founder Sylvester Cross set this arrangement up as a favor to the song's writer "Ned," his mistress, as a way of discreetly paying her without causing undue personal complications.

Eddie's film debut was shot at Twentieth Century-Fox in August 1956. When Eddie and Jerry first arrived for rehearsals, they found sheet music left behind in their assigned practice room. It was "Love Me Tender." Elvis had been working earlier in the same rehearsal space.

Given more of a build-up in the film's final cut than most of the movie's other musical acts, Ed was introduced by a fictional TV variety show host as "Eddie Cochran, one of America's top rock 'n' rollers," as a studio audience broke into uproarious applause. Clad in a cream sport coat and tweed pegged trousers, handsome Eddie, hair coiffed into a stiff, blond pompadour, kicked off "Twenty Flight Rock" on a stage dressed with nothing but curtains and an amplifier. Outfitted with his beloved orange Gretsch, Eddie ably filled the spotlight, turning out his finest Elvis-isms—legs twitching, shoulders pumping—yet telegraphing to the world that here was an artist unlike any other, coming into his rock 'n' roll own. It was a classic performance, one that would garner him a devoted new audience.

Eddie's presence on the movie lot was noticed by Johnny Rook, an aspiring actor who had seen Ed's appearance on the *Town Hall Party* show and had immediately become a fan. Like Eddie, Rook was a young man entrenched in his first forays in front of the camera, appearing in a crowd scene in the June Allyson and David Niven comedy, *My Man Godfrey*, then shooting parts for the *Adventures of Wild Bill Hickock* television series. Rook, who was going by the screen name of Johnny Rho, had stumbled into the movie business quite accidentally. He'd been working a dead-end job at a Sears and Roebuck store in Santa Monica for a few fruitless months when he decided to play hooky and hit the beach. He was walking the oceanfront near the Palisades area when a landslide brought much of the hilly landscape lurching down onto the highway. Johnny quickly ran up from the water to find houses piled up clear across the road. He rushed to help dazed homeowners who were trying to dig their way out. He soon realized that one of the folks he was assisting was Burt Lancaster, the actor.

He and Lancaster spent the rest of the afternoon helping the actor's fellow residents climb out and clean up. Lancaster never introduced himself as a celebrity, and Rook never let on that he knew who he was. Toward the end of the day, Lancaster's blonde wife brought the two weary rescuers some lemonade. They chatted briefly before returning to their work, and Lancaster invited Rook back the next day. Johnny made his way back to Lancaster's home the following morning. Wanting to thank Johnny for his help, Lancaster made a suggestion. If Johnny had any creativity at all, he said, and wanted to become an actor or get into the movie field in any capacity, Lancaster would do all he could to help. The silver screen or Sears? Johnny's decision was easy; Lancaster introduced him to producer Maurice Kosloff, who got Johnny into the Pasadena Playhouse for acting classes (also in classes there were Sal Mineo and Natalie Wood). Because of what Kosloff called Johnny's "Grecian features and appearance" he renamed the budding young actor Johnny Rho. Then he landed his protégé the parts in *My Man Godfrey* and, because of Nebraska native Johnny's horseback-riding abilities, the Hickock show.

When Johnny saw Ed on the lot, he recalls, he sent a note to Ed at the studio message center explaining how much he appreciated Ed's *Town Hall Party* work and how he was glad to see his career progressing. The message was forwarded to Granny and Gloria, who were handling Eddie's mail, and when Granny saw Johnny's note she called Johnny. "Eddie would sure like to meet you," she told Johnny. "Do you ever get out to Bell Gardens? Can you come out about 11 a.m.? Eddie's been working late in the studio and he doesn't get up until then."

Johnny was thrilled at the invitation. But he'd never been out to Bell Gardens before and was worried about being late. Just to be sure, he left his house at 9 in the morning. He arrived in Bell Gardens about 10:15, so he parked up the street from the Cochran home and waited until 11. Then he pulled up to the house, which was painted a yellowish-green color and had a wide, uncovered porch area in front. He walked up to the door. It opened just as he was about to knock. Granny was there with her finger to her lips saying, "Shhhh. He's not up." Johnny apologized. "C'mon in," Granny said. It's time for him to be getting up. I think I heard him rustlin' in there." Johnny followed Granny inside. To the right was the kitchen, and beyond that, Eddie's bedroom. Granny showed Johnny to the living room; beyond and to the left were Granny and Grandpa's bedroom, the bathroom, and Gloria and Red's bedroom. Granny chatted with Johnny as they waited. Within minutes she'd extracted from Johnny his birthdate (October 9, six days later than Ed's), his musical tastes (which were similar to Ed's), and his favorite food, his Kentucky-bred mama's cornbread and beans (also Ed's favorite, according to Alice). Every time Ed came home from a tour, Granny told Johnny, that's what he'd want—baby white soup beans and cornbread.

Soon Gloria came into the living room from the far side of the house, sat down, and joined the conversation. Then Eddie shuffled in through the kitchen. He was wearing a bathrobe and had a cigarette in his hand. His eyes were still full of sleep and his hair was a mess. He and Johnny shook hands, Ed sat down on the couch, and the two started chatting. They continued their visit in Ed's bedroom. As Ed got cleaned up, they talked and talked, about music mostly. Ed told Johnny he loved the Coasters' hit "Young Blood." Then Ed pulled out a Marty Robbins album, the one with "Strawberry Roan" on it, and played it for Johnny. After several hours, Johnny got up to go. Maybe the two could get together in Hollywood, Ed told Johnny as he departed, because he was in town a lot these days.

Still without a record label, but with a commercially exploitable movie appearance in the can and set to hit theaters in early 1957, seventeen-year-old Eddie was a saleable commodity. Sensing opportunity, Jerry soon made his way to the office of Simon "Si" Waronker, founder of Liberty Records. It seemed a natural fit: several Liberty artists, including the label's leading light, Julie London of "Cry Me a River" fame, were featured in *The Girl Can't Help It*. Plus, Lionel Newman, whose "The Girl Upstairs"/"Conquest" had been Liberty's inaugural release in 1955, had served as the film's musical supervisor. It may have been Waronker, in fact, or perhaps Newman, who set up the movie audition for Ed at Fox, as Jerry suggested. If so, it was a confluence of synergistic events—including Petroff's discovery of Ed and Ed's collaboration with Sylvester Cross's mistress—not unusual for the entertainment business.

Waronker was no stranger to the movie industry. A child violin prodigy who fled Nazi Germany, he had played film scores for Twentieth Century-Fox from 1939 until 1955 when he launched Liberty Records at the suggestion of a cousin. When Waronker attempted to sign jazz singer Bobby Troup to his fledgling label, Troup, who was under contract elsewhere, talked Waronker into signing his girlfriend, Julie London, instead. Her "Cry Me a River" was an instant hit and she became Waronker's "Liberty Girl."

According to Waronker, he was completely unfamiliar with Ed until the two first met at Waronker's Liberty office, where Ed camped out for days until the label honcho finally granted him an audience. Armed with his Gretsch, Eddie made an instant believer of the skeptical Waronker, who was seeking an artist who could put Liberty into the rock 'n' roll game. What Waronker saw in his office went way beyond Elvis Presley and the myriad Presley wannabes who daily came knocking at Liberty's door. What Waronker discovered was an undeniably handsome vocalist who had played his own outstanding guitar style and who had a seemingly endless supply of his own good material. He was flexible—he could rock 'n' roll, but he could also sing ballads. Looker, singer, picker, writer— Eddie was a package deal too good to pass up.

Jerry Capehart's account of that first Liberty meeting is a bit different. According to Jerry, he was the one who'd waited for several hours that first day to meet the Liberty label heads. When he was finally informed that they were simply too busy to see him, the ever-persistent Jerry returned the next day. After he'd waited from sunup to nearly sundown, Jack Ames, Waronker's partner and sales manager at Liberty, emerged to see what Jerry wanted. Jack returned to his office with Ed's demos in hand and listened with Si Waronker. Jerry sat in the outer office, eagerly awaiting their reaction. He was not disappointed. The Liberty execs clearly liked what they heard; they offered a deal on the spot.

Elated, Jerry raced to Ed's house and told Eddie and Alice about the deal. The contract details were the subject of a lengthy discussion around the Cochran dinner table that evening, and the next day Ed and Jerry returned to Liberty and hammered out the final deal. I believe it was at this meeting with Ed that the record-label brass got their first real, in-person sense of Ed's irresistible charisma and profound talent on that 6120.

Although Ed and Jerry were thrilled at the opportunity to bind themselves, at long last, to a relatively large and reputable record company, the family was predictably suspicious and typically negative. Jerry said he thought the family wished for Ed to continue pursuing a country music career with Hank. But in the end, Jerry and Eddie were able to convince the family to go for the deal.

And so, on September 8, 1956, Eddie became Liberty Records' newest artist when he signed a contract giving him a royalty rate of five percent of a record's suggested retail price, with recording costs to be deducted from royalties.

For all intents and purposes, Eddie was now the "Liberty Guy."

5
Pop Star and Good Ol' Boy

EDDIE THREW HIMSELF INTO finding the perfect material for his Liberty debut, holing up at Goldstar between September and December of 1956 and hammering out demos of his songs, including "Teenage Cutie," "Never," "Sweetie Pie," "Mighty Mean," and several instrumentals. Though he was now a Liberty solo artist, he was still all too happy to play session man, evidenced by his work with Ray Stanley, Lee Denson, and the Holly Twins to record the 1956 Liberty holiday novelty single "I Want Elvis for Christmas" featuring Eddie's amusing Elvis impersonation coupled with "The Tender Age."

December 1956 found Eddie—without benefit of even his first Liberty single—making an appearance in a second movie, the low-budget quickie *Untamed Youth*, starring curvaceous platinum blonde Mamie Van Doren. Filmed in two weeks near Bakersfield, just north of Los Angeles, the teen-exploitation flick was an attempt to "fling open the door of a juvenile 'punishment' farm," screamed its sensationalized advertising, and depict "wild kids on a 'rock 'n' roll' binge—and the shocking way they get 'corrected'!"

Untamed Youth was a blatant bid by its distributor Warner Brothers to cash in on the rabid new youth audience for both rock 'n' roll and juvenile delinquency films. The corruption of America's youth, in fact, was a topic that spanned the generations; adult concern over juvenile delinquency had been mounting since the start of the decade. By 1955, national worry had reached such a fever pitch that a Senate subcommittee was established to investigate juvenile delinquency caused by—according to frenzied parents, preachers, teachers, and lawmen—the poisonous films, radio programs, comic books, and television shows consumed by American youth.

The films included 1953's *The Wild One*, the motorcycle masterpiece featuring Marlon Brando as the insolent leader of a rebellious-youth biker gang, 1955's *Blackboard Jungle*, which showcases cultural and generational dysfunction, and *Rebel Without a Cause*, depicting teenage alienation with a beautiful cast of misfits headed by the unruly James Dean. *Untamed Youth*, dubbed in one review as "an artless melodrama, compounded of sex, swing and sadism," was yet another racy log tossed on the growing juvenile delinquency fire.

In a flimsy plot revolving around the mistreatment of young offenders sentenced to labor on a cotton farm, sideburned Eddie skulks about the screen with a too-cool-to-care attitude, competently delivers a few lines, and performs a single song, the Elvis-ish "Cotton Picker," accompanying himself with his picker's bag turned air guitar.

Composer and bandleader Les Baxter helmed the film's music, which included a quartet of tunes sung by Van Doren: "Salamander, " "Go Go Calypso," "Rollin' Stone," and "Oo Ba La Baby," penned by Eddie and Jerry, with Baxter and Adelson also credited as co-writers. All four tunes were recorded by Van Doren, Baxter, and Eddie at the Capitol studios in Hollywood for release on Capitol subsidiary Prep. Indeed, a promo EP sent to deejays in advance of the film featured the Capitol tracks; the movie showcased new renditions re-recorded by Baxter.

Like *The Girl Can't Help It*, Untamed Youth further solidified Eddie's emerging image as a rock 'n' roll star of note. The sensational gossip surrounding his alleged romantic affairs with his attractive co-stars—the very-married Van Doren, lovely pin-up Jeanne Carmen, and perky Yvonne Lime, a one-time gal pal of Presley's—established him as one of Hollywood's most sought-after bachelors.

According to Carmen, his dalliance with her was for real. He sent her flowers—always bouquets of red roses with one single yellow bloom in the middle, and sang to her with his guitar. Though Ed was eight years her junior, she never thought of him as a kid. He just seemed older in spirit to her. He even walked a bit like an old man, she thought. And Jeanne couldn't deny the chemistry. They'd hold hands, sit around and kiss and hug and carry on. But they never actually had sex. Whenever they got close, something was always interfering.

One time, for a dance scene during the filming of *Untamed Youth*, Jeanne and Ed were teamed as a couple. Since neither one felt they were very good at dancing, they chose to move toward the back of the set. As all the other couples earnestly danced for the camera, Ed and Jeanne did a dance of their own, grinding pelvises for pure pleasure. They didn't care if they wound up with any screen time or not—they were horny, plain and simple, and that took precedence.

Another time on the movie set, sitting in the front seat of Carmen's Chrysler 300 convertible, the two were kissing, playing touchy-feely, getting ready to do things. Van Doren inadvertently spoiled the moment by walking by; Ed and Jeanne ducked down so she wouldn't see them. Mamie would have liked something to be happening between her and Ed, Jeanne thought. Mamie was always trying to put the make on him, but Ed always ran the other way. Mamie was just too much for him, Jeanne thought. Ed was pretty naïve. Still hot, Ed and Jeanne started in again, working themselves into a steamy heap once more. At that moment, Carmen's boyfriend—who'd secretly flown in from Texas to surprise her—strode by. And that ended that. I must add, my Mom said there was definitely a mutual attraction and some hint of hanky panky between Eddie and Mamie Van Doren. To this day both ladies have an intense sexual energy and carry themselves like women thirty years younger. I can see how Eddie would have felt the heat!

After his first movie appearances, Eddie began to wear makeup, believing it was the professional thing to do to maintain a star-like appearance, particularly onstage and in pictures. My mother was in total agreement and, in fact, had me wearing makeup for my first gigs when I was twelve and a half. She bought for me what she thought was the same shade Eddie wore, Max Factor's pancake foundation Tan #2. She actually got the whole band wearing the stuff, explaining that that's what all the stars do, and anyway, if it was good enough for Ed, it was good enough for me and the band. We all wanted to have that star look, too, so we happily put on the pancake.

Of course, an extraordinarily good-looking guy in makeup was bound to attract the attention of a few men as well. Jerry noticed that Ed had a very intense aversion to any homosexual advances, almost a phobia. Seems some fellow approached Eddie in a Hollywood restaurant, and it was all Ed could do to keep from smacking the guy. Certainly Jerry himself had a real attitude toward gay men. One time he kicked his apartment manager in the ass with his cowboy boot for flirting with him. The guy screamed and cried as he fled the apartment. Jerry was sure he had permanently altered the guy's sex life with that pointed boot.

With *The Girl Can't Help It* slated for release around the winter holidays of 1956, it was decided that "Twenty Flight Rock," his cameo in that film, would naturally be Eddie's first Liberty release, to be issued in December. The tune would be paired with the stark and evocative ballad "Dark Lonely Street," which utilized only Ed's vocal and guitar and Guybo's bass, and was recorded at the "Twenty Flight Rock" session. But a song of the South swiftly derailed those plans.

Hungry for a hit and heartened by the impressive regional sales throughout the Carolinas of a single on the independent Colonial label—"Sittin' in the Balcony," penned and performed by one John D. Loudermilk under the name Johnny Dee—Liberty head Waronker attempted to buy the rights to the record. He was beat to the punch by ABC Paramount. Not one to admit failure, Waronker ultimately decided that Liberty would release its own version of the tune, as sung by his label's new rock 'n' roll–capable pop talent, Eddie Cochran. Eddie agreed that the tune had smash hit potential, telling manager Jerry, "Well, dad, I think it's a hit!" Within days, in January 1957, Eddie—backed by Guybo and the Johnny Mann

Singers, a Liberty vocal act—had waxed the song at a long, difficult session at Liberty's newly installed studios, and his first Liberty single, "Sittin' in the Balcony," was on store shelves—before Loudermilk's original on Paramount.

On its surface a whimsical pop song of teenage romance not unlike other fare of the day from parent-friendly artists like Pat Boone, Eddie gave the tune a charmingly caddish read. His grainy near-groaning of the sugar-sweet lyrics gave the tune a subtle sexual undercurrent, while his occasional chuckles let the listener know the ditty—honeyed up with choral chants from the Mann Singers—was all in fun. Ed detuned his guitar a whole step for the song—an innovative idea that would become common practice for him—allowing him to sing in a comfortable key with a comfortable chord structure and enabling him to bend the guitar strings in a way he couldn't have otherwise. And the guitar solo was a killer, Eddie making one pass playing part of the lead line, then making another pass with a complementary lead line. From that brilliantly planned solo, it was evident that Eddie was a thinker. The entire track was draped in echo, and with the full track heads used on machines in those days, even with all of the overdubs, the sound was fantastic.

Though the results were pleasant enough, Ed was not happy with his first work for his new label. When asked by the British magazine *New Musical Express* to describe his biggest disappointment, he answered, "Hearing the playbacks after my first recording session. I cut 'Sittin' in the Balcony' and didn't like it at all." Pure perfectionism, that Cochran family trait, was making itself evident. I don't think there has ever been a mix or recording that I've done that has stood the test of time for me; I can always find a way to have made it better. I have no doubt that Ed felt the same way. "Sittin' in the Balcony" would become Eddie's second single in the U.K., released by London Records, Liberty's British distributor, after "Twenty Flight Rock" (issued in April 1957), his transatlantic debut. Neither song would crack the British charts.

With the release of his first movie—*The Girl Can't Help It* in the winter of 1956—and his debut Liberty single, by early March 1957

Eddie was poised on the precipice of pop stardom. "This one has plenty of teen-age appeal and could move out with the right exposure," predicted music industry trade magazine *Billboard* of "Sittin' in the Balcony" in its March 2, 1957 edition. "Cochran warbles with sock showmanship—à la Presley." The rag was right; with Liberty's full promotional force behind it, on March 23 "Balcony" entered *Billboard*'s Top 100 chart, where it remained for a solid thirteen weeks, cresting at a respectable Number 18. The single may have gone even further, if not for a ban on "Balcony" in a major eastern city after a fatal incident in the balcony of a local theater. I was told the song was banned out of respect for the victim's family.

The following month saw Eddie hit the road, touring behind his hot new single with Guybo Smith on bass and Jerry Capehart as manager. Among other dates across the country—including a gig at the Chicago Civic Opera House with Chuck Berry, the Everly Brothers, Charlie Gracie, and Brenda Lee—Eddie spent a week in Philadelphia for the "Rock 'n' Roll Jubilee of Stars" at the regal Mastbaum Theatre. His performance there was a pivotal moment in his early solo career, playing a posh hall in which the crowd—a mix of old and young—sat politely in their seats. All attention was focused on him, and he easily charmed the audience with his ready smile and easy mix of both rock 'n' roll and ballads. The "Jubilee Of Stars" bill of fifty artists was in itself a mixed bag, headlined by Al Hibbler, a blind, black jazz-pop crooner with an orchestra best known for "After The Lights Go Down Low" and "Unchained Melody." George Hamilton IV provided the country warm-up, and a variety of rhythm and blues, pop, and rock 'n' roll acts made up the rest.

Without benefit of charts or orchestrations—he just wasn't making the bucks yet—Ed had to flesh out his sound with just a drummer borrowed from a band and his own guitar tricks. A song like "Sittin' in the Balcony," recorded with a backing vocal septet, was difficult to recreate live; Eddie did his best to imitate the full sound of his records on stage with various guitar patterns and textures.

Also playing the Mastbaum that week was maverick rocker Gene Vincent, whose panting "Be-Bop-A-Lula" had spent fifteen weeks of 1956 in the Top 40 and whose second album for Capitol had been released that March. Although Gene and his backing band, the Blue Caps, had also appeared in *The Girl Can't Help It*, the two young rockers had never really become acquainted until Eddie rode along with Gene to the Philadelphia gig from a package tour of Ohio (which had also included Sun rockabillies Carl Perkins and Roy Orbison) onto which both artists had been booked.

On the surface, Eddie and Gene couldn't have been more different. Gene Vincent, a whip-thin, poor boy from Virginia thrust into the spotlight with the meteoric success of "Lula," had suffered a motorcycle accident that left him with a permanent leg injury. His anguished, limping fragility was in stark contrast to charismatic Eddie's all-American, milk-fed handsomeness. Still, the two shared a sweeping passion for music of all kinds, rock 'n' roll in particular, and an instinctive ability to interpret a song, each determinedly chasing the fully realized sound he heard inside his head. Ed was no doubt drawn to Gene's taste in guitar players— Cliff Gallup, the original Blue Caps guitarist, was an exceptionally virtuosic talent also of the Chet Atkins–inspired school, and his successor, Johnny Meeks, although a less articulate player, rocked intensely. In their few weeks traveling and performing together, Eddie and Gene became fast friends.

Capitalizing on the forward momentum of "Sittin' in the Balcony," Eddie pursued every promotional opportunity, glad-handing key disc jockeys across the nation, like Cleveland's Bill Randall, Chicago's Howard Miller, Pittsburgh's Barry Kaye, and Boston's Joe Smith and by personally phoning others to introduce himself and cajole airplay of his record.

In another of those synchronistic courses of events, many years later Joe Smith would become the head of Warner Brothers Records, to which my group Kindred was contracted. At that point in my career I was not mentioning my relation to Eddie unless someone pointedly asked. I didn't realize then that the Joe Smith I knew was the same Joe Smith whom Ed also knew. I would like to have talked to Joe about his experiences with my uncle.

A relatively new television program, *American Bandstand*, became another promotional venue for Ed that year. The show, an informal teen dance party originally broadcast only in Philadelphia, was now being aired coast-to-coast by ABC every weekday after school, from 3 to 5 in the afternoon. Hosted by the boyishly handsome Dick Clark—closer to thirty than thirteen in both age and mindset, and never without a proper necktie—the show featured a throng of likewise conservatively clad adolescents who, between song spins, rated records and jived to lip-synched performances by their favorite artists. *Bandstand*'s national reach and immense popularity with American youth made it an extraordinarily effective means of promotion; musicians who appeared on the show frequently sailed to the loftiest reaches of the record charts.

Though "Sittin' in the Balcony" cracked *Billboard*'s Top 20 and would go on to sell a million units (according to Eddie as well as my Dad, whose word was as good as gold to me), the single's actual sales numbers will never be known. Accounting practices in rock 'n' roll's early days were typically either woefully sloppy or artist-reaming slick, and bootlegs were prevalent. Indeed, on one of their many treks through the East not long after the release of "Balcony," Eddie and Jerry were dismayed to discover that the only copies of the record they could find in several local record shops were bootlegs.

Still, Eddie's new media presence as teen idol of radio, screen, and television impressed us all. He was receiving loads of fan mail from across the country from breathless teens requesting photos who gushed amidst a sea of exclamation points that "Your new record 'Sitting in the Balcony' is the living end," and "You are the mostest to say the leastest," and "You have a dreamy voice."

"Like all teen-agers," one Pennsylvania fan wrote in a letter to Twentieth Century-Fox, "I am a fan of Elvis Presley, but Eddie Cochran, one of the actors in *The Girl Can't Help It*, tops Elvis. He is a lot better looking than Elvis, and I like the way he sings. Would you please send me a picture of Eddie Cochran, along with any information concerning his recording career, and his acting career?"

Granny and Aunt Gloria organized a fan club for him and handled most of his mail. Eddie made sure the letter writers received replies—even coming to know regular correspondents by name—and began signing fan correspondence and autographs with the almost melancholy line "Don't forget me," an odd choice of words for a talented and ambitious teenager standing firmly on the brink of fame.

Eddie seemed almost bemused by it all. Talking to *TV and Radio Mirror* in July 1957 in a piece entitled "Hot New Singers," he said, "You go to all these places and all these people are buttering you up... the girls keep screaming and all. It's not easy to keep your feet on the ground, man. I feel kind of bad about some who have been in it longer than me, and trying hard, that don't make it."

With such public adulation, surely he was making money from his blossoming success, we assumed. So when Mom and Dad were about to lose our house to foreclosure—at that time we were living in Buena Park, another Los Angeles suburb—Dad got word to Eddie out on the road that he needed to borrow some money. All he needed was $600. To our great surprise, Eddie didn't have it. He was barely making his own ends meet on the road. The money eventually came—Eddie'd had to borrow it—but it was too late. We moved to the one-bedroom duplex in Cypress.

Some memorable moments occurred in the house in Buena Park. That's where, at age seven, I discovered the Santa Claus suit in a dresser in the garage. (Of course, I had to bring my five-year-old sister out to see for herself.) This was also the same garage where Dad butchered a cow, hanging it from the ceiling. He and Ed would often go hunting up in the high desert, and he'd brought the dead animal home after one such trip with Ed and Bob Denton, Ed's pal from the Shamrock Valley Boys. Besides their musical kinship, Ed and Bob Denton were great drinking buddies, enjoying the only beers their starving artist budgets allowed, cheap stuff like Coors, Hamm's, Brown Derby. They also shared a keen interest in guns, as did my Dad. Ed and Bob had each purchased Ruger six-shooters in .22 caliber from Weatherby's, a firearms shop in Southgate, for seventy bucks apiece. Ed also owned a Marlin 39A lever-action rifle in .22 caliber, equipped with a scope.

Bob had driven Eddie to the gun shop. Like Chuck Foreman, he often chauffered Eddie around, as Ed was not able to get a driver's license until he was at least eighteen. Bob remembers that Ed had been pulled over some time earlier while driving without a license, so as punishment the authorities denied him the precious document usually granted to sixteen-year-olds. Bob had a '54 Buick Century, so he'd frequently drive Eddie and my Dad on their hunting expeditions.

The high desert around Hesperia, northeast of Los Angeles, was witness to many a memorable time. Deep Creek was a favorite camping spot of my Dad, Ed, and his buddies. There were lots of shade trees and clean running water flowing from the snow-capped peaks around Arrowhead and Big Bear Lake. During Eddie's lifetime, I wasn't old enough to go with the guys, but it later became my favorite spot to camp and go shooting.

On my trips with Dad, when we'd get hungry we'd fire into the water in close proximity to any trout we saw, and the concussion from the blast would kill the fish and provide a quick snack while hiking. I didn't realize what we were doing was illegal. We had to always be on the watch for rattlesnakes. I nearly got it one time when I stepped over a large boulder and just missed a rattler. We were always on the lookout for rainstorms as well, because the canyon could quickly fill with water and become a rampaging river.

When Dad, Ed, and all their buddies would go on their shooting trips, they'd stock up on their beers of choice—Coors, Hamms, Brown Derby, ABC, Brew 102, the cheapest beer they could find. The guys could get kind of silly; on one excursion, after a few too many, Merle Garbisch, a close friend of Ronnie Ennis's, tried to shoot the moon down. But sometimes the combination of beers and loaded guns would get a bit dangerous. One time a rat emerged from under a rock. Bob was determined to shoot the hapless rodent, so he whipped out his gun—but it didn't quite make it out of the holster. He shot himself in the back of the leg.

On a later trip, Ed was shot in the leg as well. Most folks believed that Eddie shot himself while practicing his quick draw with live rounds in the chamber. Few knew that was an out-and-out lie, fabricated to keep Granny from killing my dad. Truth is, Dad had a Ruger semi-automatic .22-caliber pistol. One day while Dad was trying to extract a jammed round, the gun went off, hitting Eddie in the leg. Granny would have murdered Dad for shooting her pride and joy, so the two concocted the quick-draw tale.

On one trip near Hesperia, Dad, Ed, Bob, and Johnny Rook were shooting near Deep Creek. On their way home, they came upon a young cow grazing near the dirt road. There was a house just over the hill, certainly belonging to the owner of the cow. Did they dare? Ed couldn't resist. "Hold it right there, stop this son of a bitch!" he commanded. Johnny, like the rest of them, drunk as a skunk, was driving Bob's car. He slammed on the brakes, thinking Ed had to take a leak; the car screeched to a stop. Ed pulled out his Marlin 39A, silently took aim, and put a .22 right in the cow's eye. The animal went down. "Give me a hand over here, you guys!" Eddie hollered. Dad, Bob, and Johnny—giddy with drink and the sheer gall of what Ed had just done—ran out and heaved the carcass into the trunk of Bob's car, the blood making a sticky, burgundy mess of the back of the automobile. They sped to our house, where they unloaded the cow in the garage, dangling it from the ceiling to butcher it. The remains they buried in our back yard. Dad's harmless explanation to us was that they'd accidentally hit the cow on the road.

After some time Bob Denton received a call from Ed. Dogs from around the neighborhood were flocking to our yard, enticed by the seductive odor of rotting cow parts. They had to get the mess out of our yard. My ever-resourceful father, who was at that time doing demolition work for a construction company, pulled a big flat-bed truck around to the site, and he, Ed, and Bob dug up the putrid remains. They shuttled their odiferous cargo down to the beach, unloaded and buried it, and proceeded to get the truck stuck in the soft sand. The police came just as the trio were freeing the truck;

remarkably, they weren't detained, and they stopped at a couple of bars on the way home to celebrate their grand accomplishment.

That wasn't the only incident involving a cow. Dad told me about a time that he and Ed accidentally did hit a cow that was in the road. Figuring they shouldn't let it go to waste, they picked the cow up and put it in the trunk. On the way home, they suddenly heard a tremendous racket coming from the back of the car. The animal had come back to life and was kicking and mooing in the trunk. Quickly hatching a plan, Dad and Ed decided that one would open the trunk while the other would shoot the cow with Dad's Ruger semi-automatic pistol, the same gun that had left its mark in Ed's leg. They shot the flailing beast several times, and it finally stopped moving. It's a wonder the authorities didn't nab my uncle, the rock 'n' roller, for cattle rustling—would've made for some rather interesting press.

Another time, Dad, Ed, and Bob were shooting around Hemet, also in the desert, when they decided to split up. Dad took off down into the bushes near Bob's car. Ed and Bob couldn't see him, but every so often they would hear him fire off a few rounds. They headed up a densely wooded hillside, where they were able to survey the whole landscape. Soon they were startled to see a police car sidle up next to Bob's Buick. They froze in their well-camouflaged vantage point and prayed that my dad would hold his fire. No such luck. Within minutes Dad's "boom-boom-boom" had betrayed him, and Ed and Bob watched with bittersweet amusement the ensuing hot pursuit. Dad ended up having all of his guns confiscated, including one he'd borrowed from a friend. He had to go to court to get it back.

Another time, during a rabbit-hunting trip with Warren Flock and Bob Denton near Hesperia, Ed and the fellows, traveling in Bob's four-door sedan, pulled up alongside a pair of old ladies in another car stopped at a stoplight, Flock remembers. The fellows started horsing around, banging on their car doors and yelling, "Let's drag!" When the light turned green Bob popped the clutch and stomped on the accelerator. Instead of rocketing away, the car just sat there. The old ladies took off, leaving the boys in their dust.

Bob's car had dropped its drive shaft; the bolts had come loose, and the shaft was sitting in the road under the car. Ed and the guys were in hysterics for days.

Even Warren Flock's wife got in on the hunting adventures. On one rabbit-hunting trip, she was behind the wheel of the couple's '55 Ford Fairlane, with Warren in the front beside her and Eddie and Hank Cochran in the back. She was driving the car on a four-lane highway divided by a large median, heading to the Fontana turn-off toward Hesperia via the Cajon pass. "Here's the turn," Warren told her. She turned without slowing down, the car careening up onto two wheels, skidding across the median and sideways into the oncoming traffic lane. As the stunned passengers were trying to right themselves in their seats, they saw a big old Mercury barreling right for them. Inside the car was a family of Mexicans, their eyes wide open in surprise. Warren pulled himself back up in his seat just in time to make out the emblem on the Mercury's hood. He reached his foot over and punched the accelerator; the Fairlane shot out of the Mercury's path with not a hair of space to spare. The Mercury leveled several reflector road markers, but both cars—and their passengers—escaped major injury. Warren's white walls had gravel burns all over them where the sidewalls had actually been on the road; they were lucky the tires hadn't come off the rims.

Several years after Ed's death, when I was about sixteen, Dad took me to Lake Matthews, southeast of Los Angeles, with a friend of his named José—he called him "Hosee"—to do some rabbit shooting, just like he and Ed used to do. Dad and Hosee would motor up to the roads surrounding the lake late at night and use spotlights or flashlights, cruising around shooting from the car. On this trip we went by Granny's, Ed's mom's, first, and picked up Eddie's Ruger six-shooter. I liked using that gun because it was Ed's and it was real accurate. We headed up to Corona and then to the Lake Mathews area. By the time we got there, Dad, who'd been drinking a fair bit, had laid down on the back seat to sleep. Hosee was driving; I was shooting. After an hour or two, I had shot about fifty rabbits and a couple of large birds.

Soon we saw lights behind us, so we stopped firing until they passed. I could see it was a ranger on patrol. We waited until he was out of earshot, then I resumed shooting. Now, I regret all of the senseless killing of those boyhood hunting trips, and although I still enjoy shooting, inanimate objects are pretty much my limit. But hunting was simply a part of how I—and Ed and my Dad—had been raised, so when a rabbit ran across the road to my side and scurried down the embankment, I blasted away at him.

Suddenly, from a hill behind us, the ranger's lights came on. He had us cold; I was in full view. He'd lain in wait hoping to catch us, and he did. I was in a panic: They were going to get Ed's gun. Granny—the once-doting mother who was wildly possessive of her departed son's belongings—would kill me. I took the spent rounds out of Ed's six-gun and put the empties into my Ruger Bearcat. I stuffed Ed's gun into the crack between the back of the seat and the seat cushion, hoping the ranger wouldn't find it. He had us follow him to the station and, of course, they found every weapon. I figured I was one dead guitar player, once Granny got hold of me.

They were checking our police records and doing paperwork when one of the officers left the station house. A little later he came back in and whispered something in another ranger's ear. They had strange looks on their faces as they whispered some more. Finally, one of them called us to the counter. "Uh, we've had a little accident," he began. Seems the other officer had backed into our car and put a big dent in it. I didn't give a hang about Dad's car. All I cared about was getting Uncle Ed's gun back. They wanted to work out a deal, the officer told us. What luck! They returned our weapons—including that beloved Ruger of Ed's—and let us go with a warning in return for our forgetting about their little accident. And Granny never found out.

6
Show of Stars

JERRY CAPEHART WAS INTENT on making Ed a star. With the success of "Sittin' in the Balcony" and the well-received release of *The Girl Can't Help It*, they were off to a good start. But Jerry felt that Ed, with his good looks and vocal style, was garnering too many comparisons to Elvis Presley. He wanted to create a distinctive image for my uncle, his own unique identity. And he wasn't all that sure that the way to do it was with music.

For his part, Ed was delighted with the response he'd been getting from his contemporaries—kids just loved him. Girls especially, and the ability to pick up chicks with virtually no difficulty was just one of the enjoyable perks. The mania he could do without; the silliness of screaming girls tearing buttons from his shirt he preferred to keep at a minimum.

Twentieth Century-Fox was receiving abundant fan mail for Ed, and the studio's brass, not unaware of his able, if limited, performance in his first dramatic role in *Untamed Youth*, thought perhaps they might have a raw talent worthy of a little grooming. But they had to be sure. So they arranged for a screen test for Ed, who'd willingly attended drama class at the suggestion of Ben Bart, Fox's head of talent. Ed had never hidden his ambitions to make movies, and he was thrilled at Fox's interest.

Ed arrived at the lot to find this was no casual chat-to-the-camera sort of screen test. This was serious stuff: a five-minute, fully costumed scene on a dressed set with a young starlet by the name of Sandra Dee. Shooting took half a day.

Later, Ed's test was screened for producer and director Frank Tashlin and other studio executives. My uncle, a bag of nerves, and Jerry were in the screening room. Filmed in black and white, the test showed Ed and Sandra Dee in a tender love scene. Ed's performance, vulnerable and intense, wowed all those in the room. They broke into applause.

But Ed, an embarrassed flush quickly spreading across his face, felt exposed. Instead of graciously accepting the applause, he turned cocky, almost defensive. "That was motherfucking good!" he blurted out.

Jerry wanted to crawl under his chair. Studio honchos might accept that kind of sycophantic behavior from established stars, but they sure as hell didn't need it from a virtual nobody. The Fox executives quietly filed out of the room. Jerry knew they were sunk.

There was still no denying that Ed had a certain something, a genuine sensitivity, that came across on celluloid. And Ben Bart still believed in him. So Ed was given one more chance, a small role in a big picture starring Paul Newman, Joanne Woodward, and Jack Carson called *Rally 'Round the Flag, Boys*. Ed would play a rebel teenager, and would have some of the most humorous scenes in the film. Though it was hardly the part of a lifetime, Bart and Jerry knew it could break great ground for Ed in Hollywood.

Jerry arrived at Ed's house early on the film's first day of production. Ed was depressed. The family didn't want him to do the movie. The part was too small, they told him. He deserved better. Jerry should've done better, they went on, even after Jerry'd arrived. They'd never really liked nor trusted Jerry.

Ed's friend Johnny Rook recalls that Grandpa was always griping about Jerry. He'd talk about how he hated Capehart, snorting, "I got no use for that son of a bitch." Ed's brother-in-law Red—who seemed to think he knew more about everything than anybody else, Johnny noted—talked about what a scoundrel Jerry was, how he and other showbiz bigwigs "were takin' advantage of poor Ed. If it weren't for Ed, Capehart couldn't make a living." My Aunt Gloria, Red's wife, didn't have a lot to say, Johnny remembers, although she didn't seem to care for Capehart much either. She was always busy mailing out pictures and fan club correspondence. Eddie was never really around when his family members disparaged Jerry, Johnny noticed. It was always stuff they said when Johnny would drop by the house while Ed was on tour, or whenever Ed wasn't in the room. The Cochran family had no knowledge of the entertainment business, Johnny concluded. With them, it was all personal.

It seemed to be an incessant, if unspoken, mantra within our family: this sense that things—or people or situations—were never good enough. My grandfather Frank, Ed's dad, who in my eyes was a war hero, was relegated to outcast status—many of Ed's friends recalled that when Frank got home from work he would grab a beer, go to the bedroom, and simply be forgotten. My father, whom I also considered a war hero, who was brilliant with cars and anything mechanical, and who was a talented songwriter, was treated like the black sheep of the family—married to "that June," no less.

I remember a time when I was fourteen when Granny came over and I played "Little Lou"—a Capehart tune Ed had demoed in January 1958, later recorded by John Ashley—because I'd just learned it and I really liked the song. I remember I was singing and pretty soon she's crying and I'm crying and I really couldn't finish it. It was a really touching moment with Granny because I could see on one hand her sense of pride in me, and I could see on the other hand the sense of loss for her. I could see the struggle in her, wanting to say something nice but not being able to bring herself to. It would always be something that wasn't quite nice, which was hurtful to me. Granny used to accuse me of riding on Eddie's coattails, saying that everything I did was trying to capitalize on Eddie's success. As much as I loved Granny, I became truly resentful about it. Nothing was ever good enough for the Cochrans, and I puzzled for most of my life as to why. Yes, the familial history of alcoholism no doubt played a part, but there had to be more. What else was it? What was tearing at the fabric of my family? It would be decades before I'd even begin to understand.

Jerry explained to Ed's family that though the part was indeed small, this was a prestigious film, and a role that could mean big things for teenage Ed's future. But it didn't matter. Ed had already phoned Fox and told them they'd have to find somebody else. Torn between Jerry and all he represented—music and movie stardom, a way out of generational poverty and lower-class obscurity—and the family, the family won.

Even Dad, who was often at the brunt of the Cochran perfectionist mindset, got sucked into that skewed way of thinking. When I was fifteen, he made me quit the band I was playing with. Although it was a "super group" of the area's best young players—we were playing a lot around town and even played on a single by then-deejay Bob Eubanks, "Smoke that Cigarette"—to Dad no one was ever good enough for me to play with. It broke my heart. They were my buddies, especially Danny LaMont, the drummer, whom I'd known since Kelly and the Midnighters, my first band after the talent show combo. Danny was a couple years older than me, played with all these bands around town, including the Midnighters, and introduced me and got me into that band. Dad had even established a relationship with Danny; when he was sixteen, we moved him into my Dad's studio because his home life was so bad. But Dad had different dreams for me, and so I was forced to quit.

With Eddie's film career now on hold, Ed and Jerry returned their focus to music. While shooting *Untamed Youth* in 1956, Eddie had become friendly with Johnny Russell, one of the young lead actors in the film. In the spring of 1957, the two collaborated to write a few songs, including "One Kiss," which would become Ed's next Liberty single, and "Sweetie Pie," which would be shelved until 1960. Liberty's Si Waronker, hopeful for a repeat victory with Ed's follow-up to "Sittin' in the Balcony," plowed extra money into the creation of a full-color picture sleeve for "One Kiss," a luxury typically accorded only to better-established stars like Elvis Presley. That Ed was an extraordinarily good-looking boy was a key factor in the decision.

A promotional postcard for fans was also printed, with Eddie announcing his new single's April release. "I'm hoping that you will enjoy playing this one as much as you did 'Sitting [sic] in the Balcony,'" the singer wrote, adding, "I sure want to thank you for the wonderful support you are giving me." Despite Waronker's best promotional intentions, plus the release of *Untamed Youth*, "One Kiss," fundamentally a hollow facsimile of "Balcony," sank on the charts. Paired with "Mean When I'm Mad," a Cochran/Capehart collaboration featuring a snarling vocal from Ed over a doo-wop-esque backing from the Mann Singers, the record failed to crack even the Top 100.

Undaunted, Liberty set Eddie to work on his first album, titled *Singin' to My Baby*. Recorded at Goldstar's Studio B with Waronker in the producer's seat, the record, as its title intimated, was a collection of both ballads and rockers, positioning Eddie as an inoffensive hybrid of Pat Boone and Elvis Presley, the cover-all-bases marketing niche Waronker envisioned for his young star. In addition to "Sittin' in the Balcony," "One Kiss," and "Mean When I'm Mad," the long-player also included a retread of "Completely

Sweet," originally demoed at the "Twenty Flight Rock" session; ballads "I'm Alone Because I Love You," "Undying Love," "Have I Told You Lately That I Love You," and "Tell Me Why"; pop fodder "Proud of You" and "Lovin' Time," featuring ukulele; and the easy-rocking "Cradle Baby" and "Stockin's 'n' Shoes," also known as "Barefoot Rock." Recorded with Guybo on upright bass, Perry Botkin on rhythm guitar, and an unknown drummer, the album followed the Waronker mold of cushy vocal backing from the Johnny Mann singers and loads of slap-back echo.

Although most of the ballads made clear Eddie's limited vocal range, the overall high quality of both musicianship and production technique made *Singin' to My Baby* a credible, if unremarkable, full-length debut. "Cochran had the 'Sittin' in the Balcony' chart item, which should give this set by the teen rock 'n' roll artist solid sales backing," opined one reviewer in October 1957. "Besides the 'Sittin' in the Balcony' number, Cochran delivers his material both in the uptempo and ballad r&r vein with a proper, echo-chambered approach the teenagers will find right up their r&r alley. Important waxing for the teen trade."

Also recorded at the album sessions at Goldstar's Studio B were a pair of tunes destined to become Eddie's third Liberty single, "Drive-in Show" and Granny's favorite, "Am I Blue." One of very few rock 'n' roll songs to incorporate ukulele, "Drive-in Show" was another cheery cameo of the 1950s teen experience, jauntily strummed by Perry Botkin, Bing Crosby's guitarist; sung by a near-chuckling Eddie and beefed up with vocal backing from the Johnny Mann Singers. Its flip, Ed's frantically souped-up twist on the standard "Am I Blue," showcased some brilliantly manic guitar work.

"Cochran has the natural warm-weather follow-up to 'Sittin' in the Balcony,'" one critic mused of the A-side in July 1957. "Similar side to the hit, and it could score similarly. A neat slice of underplaying." Of "Am I Blue," the reviewer wrote, "Cochran belts the oldie in fast rockabilly styling. Some excitement in the tempo, but flip has the appeal." "Drive-in Show" initially did well in the charts until concern was raised about its lyrics, which could be unintentionally confused. The line "Bet my peanuts to a candy bar" sounded an awful lot like "Bet my penis to a candy bar." The concern quickly passed, though only after the song's momentum had been killed. Also battling such destined-to-be classics as Little Richard's "Keep-a-Knockin'," Sun piano-pounder Jerry Lee Lewis's "Whole Lotta Shakin' Goin' On," and "That'll Be the Day" by bespectacled Texan Buddy Holly and the Crickets, "Drive-in Show" limped to Number 82, due largely to strong sales in the Midwest.

Although his two follow-ups to "Sittin' in the Balcony," "One Kiss" and "Drive-in Show," had resoundingly stiffed, Waronker still had faith in his handsome eighteen-year-old artist. *The Girl Can't Help It* and *Untamed Youth* remained popular with the younger set, and Ed's striking looks kept him on the pages of all the teen magazines. In addition to his career as a solo artist, Eddie continued to work as a session player; in 1957 and 1958 he played behind, among others, pals Bob Denton and Don Deal, Sylvester Cross's niece Paula Morgan, and Al Casey, who'd had a couple of hit records.

According to Jody Reynolds, for Casey's "Willa Mae," recorded for Liberty at Goldstar in late 1957, Eddie used a thirty-nine dollar box tremolo by DeArmond that had a vial of mercury in it that bobbed up and down to electric impulse. Duane Eddy was known for using that sound, and Eddie also employed it when Casey had him come in to play guitar behind him. When Jody heard the record, he remarked to Al how much he admired the song's guitar lick. "Actually, I didn't play it," Casey confessed. "Eddie Cochran did. But it's okay if you tell people I played it!"

Jody would run into Eddie and Jerry every couple of weeks at Goldstar, where they would be working in one studio and Jody in the other. Jody hardly ever saw Jerry unless he was with Eddie. Jerry was always nice to Jody, always spoke to him. Jody came to Hollywood from the country—he recalls he was "dumber than dirt" when he first arrived in the big city—and when anyone was friendly to him, it was a big deal. Jody thought Jerry knew how to effectively manage an artist and how to produce a good record; he thought he would have gone a lot farther if he could have gotten Jerry to manage him. In the studio, Jody noticed Eddie was extraordinarily focused. He knew what he was doing when he went in, and he knocked out his many and various guitar parts easily. He was very serious and always watched what he was doing, studying his fingers as they moved over the strings.

Ed also played behind songwriter Ray Stanley, who'd left American Music to start Sherman Publishing. When Stanley was tapped in 1958 to help run Liberty's first subsidiary label, Freedom Records, Ed continued to work with him, adding guitar to many sides for Freedom, whose roster included Jerry Stone and the Four Dots featuring Jewel Akens, and Sherman Scott.

I would follow in my uncle's footsteps, haunting recording studios with a variety of artists before I ever hit twenty. Like Eddie, I remained wholly devoted to music as I grew up, even when I moved out of the house at age fifteen, not long after Dad had made me quit my band. My family was simply breaking up. Mom and Dad were at each other's throats, constantly fighting. Dad told Ed's pal Johnny Rook that it was "just hell at home." He'd lost the studio; his partner had stolen all the equipment. Mom had had it with Dad's drinking; he was gone all the time, and we had bill collectors coming to the door. We kids had to be quiet whenever the doorbell rang—"Don't make a sound," Mom would tell us. "It's the bill collectors outside."

Before Eddie died, Dad was gone a lot—they were hanging around together. After Eddie died, Dad was gone as well, first because he was secretly assembling the studio, then later because he was out carousing. Dad had an apartment above the studio. He and his pals would get singing starlet-wannabes over to the studio, party with them, and take them upstairs; you know, "Studio time gets a lot cheaper if you come upstairs." It was party time for Dad. I knew Dad was messing around with girls because I was at the studio all the time—I slept there a lot—and I could see what was going on. Dad was a good-looking guy, the guys that were hanging around were good looking, and musicians—well, girls just seem to like a musician more than your average Joe. I could see there were a lot of shenanigans going on, with all of the guys. I'd see Dad drinking too much, and I'd feel kind of sick about the whole thing; it made me want to go home and forget what I'd seen. I can remember once when I was around fourteen Dad took me over to the house of one of his girlfriends. We were on our way to or from the studio, and Dad pulled up to this strange house. He didn't come right out and say, "This is my girlfriend," but I could tell—they were hugging and kissing. She had a couple of young kids running around. It ate me up inside.

I knew how bad it was with Mom and Dad. After Eddie died, when we were living in Cypress, Dad woke us up late one night, around midnight or one in the morning, and took us kids over to Granny's house. I slept in Ed's bedroom. He didn't tell us why at the time, but when we went back home in the morning, Mom was all beat up. Dad did that, I knew. Dad was a very jealous man, and he was extremely possessive of Mom. I got the impression that, in this case, whatever it was he was jealous about must've been true because Mom didn't leave, and there was a certain submissiveness and regretfulness about her. It was as if she probably felt that she got what she had coming, in a way. As I got older, I was beginning to see a lot of things from more of an adult's perspective, to have the beginnings of a more realistic understanding of relationships—not how they should be, but how relationships were handled in our family. Before it was just Disneyland, Ozzie and Harriet, and Ricky Nelson. That's what it was supposed to be. Our family clearly wasn't.

When I was fifteen, I started dating Laurie. Laurie used to babysit for Ed's pal Ronnie Ennis. We had started dating, and as with most adolescent romances, things turned hot and heavy pretty quickly. Her mom took a maternal interest in me because I was so wholly and unusually, for a kid my age, dedicated to my music. My dream at that time was to get a Dual Showman, the best amplifier in the world, supposedly. That was my goal—I didn't know how I was going to do it, but I was working at it. Dave Shriver, who later joined a recording and stage band of Ed's, used to come over and visit now and then, and he had talked to me about the

Dual Showman, the amp he used. Fender had given him one because he was with Trini Lopez. I thought, "Man, that's really cool, get a company to give you a piece of equipment."

I had every picture of a Dual Showman there was. I'd tested all the other amps, and that was the one for me. I was in love with that amp. I was always talking about it and how I was going to get it. But since Dad had made me quit the band, I had no income. Even when I was playing, I was lucky if I got to keep the money I was making to buy cinnamon rolls at school for fifty cents. I had to give a lot of my money back to the family so we could eat. I used to get to keep some of it, and I guess that's when I started buying things by the case, which I still do. I loved sunflower seeds, so I hooked up with a guy who sold sunflower seeds to stores and bought them by the case wholesale. I might not have had any money, but it was so for sure, me getting that amp, that I used to talk about it as if it was already mine; it was just waiting for me to come pick it up.

After dating Laurie for a while, I still hadn't really gotten to know my girlfriend's mom very well yet, but she had met me a few times and really seemed to respect my dedication to music and all that I was trying to accomplish. One day, she said, "Bobby, I want to buy you a Dual Showman." I couldn't believe my ears. After a couple of weeks of Are you sures, we took my amp down to the music store, traded it—we got almost nothing for it—and she paid full price for a Dual Showman. It was a thousand bucks back then; you could buy a Volkswagen for two thousand.

I believe Nellie wanted to help a hard-working kid. I also think she was hoping her daughter and I would eventually get more serious, maybe even marry some day. I guess she thought I'd be good for Laurie. Back then I was very religious. We were Mormon, so I didn't drink, I didn't smoke, and I didn't do drugs. Between musicians and my mother—who took medication daily for her nerves—I'd already been around more drugs than most people would in their lives. I was weird for a teenager—naïve in many ways, mature in many others, like how I was completely committed to my music. In my mind, I knew exactly what my future would be: I was going to have a Dual Showman, I was going to be a star someday, I was going to carry on for Ed, I was going to be a great guitar player. I had it all mapped out.

I continued dating Nellie's daughter. But it was costing a fortune calling each other on pay phones because we lived too far away for it to be a local call. And my family was breaking up, just disintegrating. I don't know how the discussions went, but at some point Nellie offered to Mom and Dad to let me move in with her and Laurie. So I did. It was a hard decision, and a tearful one for Mom because I was supposed to be going with her and my sisters. We didn't know what Dad was going to do.

I had been spending a lot of time with Dad, mostly in the studio, getting to know him better than I ever knew him in my earlier life, and realizing just how severe his drinking problem was. I'd go into Hollywood with him often, whenever he was going to cut acetates on the bands he was recording. We'd go by Sharon Sheeley's, Eddie's song-writing girlfriend at the time of his death. I'd go with him sometimes when he would shop his bands to someone he knew in the music industry, like Don Blocker at Liberty.

I can remember Don sitting behind his desk and Dad coming in, it clearly being because of Ed that Dad had entré to him. I remember one time watching Don listen to Dad's demo, and I could see he wasn't digging it. Dad was trying real hard to sell it, but it was unwanted. I could see that Dad was getting the brush-off from him. I was embarrassed for Dad, that he had to have me see a scene like that, that he probably knew he was being blown off too. Dad was real smart.

Dad had lost some weight by that time; he really looked good. I loved the cologne he wore. I was proud of him. But when he lost the studio he really took a nosedive. I could see that Mom and Dad didn't want to be together anymore. Mom had stuck it out for years, and it just wasn't working. To be honest, I relished the thought of being away. Of course, to get to live with my girlfriend was a pretty heavy enticement as well. So I moved out of my family's apartment and in with Laurie and Nellie.

Nellie—whose husband died a year earlier—really thought of me as her daughter's salvation. And I think she could see what was going on with my family more than I could. I think she saw that maybe if she brought me into her daughter's life in a much bigger way, I would shift the way her daughter was, would settle her down, give her some direction. For a while that worked. But Laurie wanted to be my center of attention, and she didn't realize my devotion to my instrument would leave her feeling the way it did. She and I eventually drifted apart, and the relationship became more like a brother and sister. We both became interested in other people. At first it was very uncomfortable, but by then Nellie had a genuine desire to help me succeed in achieving my dreams. Nellie had been raised in an orphanage and had a strong sense of loyalty. And so, she became my biggest supporter, next to my mom.

I had missed more school than I attended when I was living with my parents, and that continued at Nellie's but for different reasons. I was disappointed with school and my teachers. I would take the final exams and do well, but since I had missed so much school, they would give me an incomplete, even though I knew the subjects much better than students they were passing. School seemed to be more like politics. So if I was too tired for school, it was not a big deal at Nellie's house. Nellie would do homework assignments for me—and essentially home-school me—because she knew the importance of what I was missing in school. I have her to thank for her dedication in helping to educate me. I was much more interested in music and gigging.

Nellie worked tirelessly to find people for me to work with, then helped me get everywhere I needed to be by driving me before I had a license. Once I could drive, she let me use her car whenever I needed. Both she and Laurie were incredibly supportive of my goals. They were like guardian angels, in a way. In fact, a couple of years later they used to sneak food to me while I lived with a band up in Hollywood. I had replaced a much skinnier guitar player and had to fit into his expensive wardrobe. He was about five foot ten and a hundred thirty pounds, I was about five foot seven and a hundred forty five pounds at the time. The band had me on a starvation diet. Laurie and Nellie were my buddies, sneaking food into my "band prison."

Nellie loved the arts and was a pretty fair oil painter; she played some piano and was a fantastic seamstress. I think she secretly had a desire to be a world-famous clothes designer. She didn't have music world connections; she worked for social services in LA County. But she'd get to talking to people and find people, and she ultimately got me into various bands—the Aquanauts, the Prophets 5, the Starfires, the Bogorodas. She got all her neighbors mad at her and Laurie because she would always let me practice, alone or with the band in the living room, at loud volumes. The neighbors passed a petition around to shut me up, but when Casey Van Beek, a neighbor who happened to be a professional bass player, was approached, he refused to sign. He said, "In fact, that kid is getting pretty good," and within months he hired me to substitute at the Cinnamon Cinder, a popular live-music venue. I was sixteen and subbing for guys five to seven years older. Casey once told me I was third call on his sub list. First was Don Preston, a local legend, who later played with Mad Dogs and Englishmen. Then came Barry Rillera, who played with Ray Charles and the Righteous Brothers. I was honored to be considered with guys of that caliber.

Nellie helped get me into the Emperors, too, when I was fifteen and a half. The Emperors was a pretty big band in Long Beach, with the "teen canteen" kind of age range, the sixteen to twenty-one-year-old crowd. When their guitar player got drafted, Nellie talked them into letting me come to their auditions to watch because, "He's so good and he'd really learn a lot from it so please let the kid come." They went through all the auditionees until there was no one left. All the gear was still set up, so they asked me, "Well, you got your guitar with you?" I said, "Yeah, yeah, yeah!" We set up and played six or seven songs; they stopped, went into the bedroom and had a band meeting. Then they hired me. Apparently they were impressed that I could handle what their other local legend guitar player did, even though I was several years younger. I also played a 6120. Plus, I fit his coats. The Emperors actually had a record deal. They'd all bleached their hair blond; they had long hair like the Beatles and the Stones. We became one of the very most popular bands in the area, we packed them into the teen clubs. But eventually there got to be so much tension between the "band mom" of the Emperors and Nellie (also a great seamstress, she made a lot of our stage clothes), that I quit the band.

The whole time I lived with Laurie and Nellie, I continued to see my parents and sisters. Mom used to visit, Dad used to visit, and sometimes I would go over to where Mom was living. Mom would come to lots of my gigs. Mom eventually moved to Norwalk, just a few blocks away, and Dad would come over wanting to know where Mom was. I would never tell him because I was under strict orders not to. But Mom was with these boyfriends that just weren't cutting it; they were really lacking in major ways. I remember still wanting Mom and Dad to get back together. It was clear to me that Dad loved Mom and she loved him. I wanted them together.

Dad had come over sober several times; one time when he came over and said, "Please, take me over to Mom's, I want to go talk to her about getting back together," I decided to do it. Thinking I was really sly, I took him on a roundabout way to get there. At Mom's house we knocked on the door and tried the knob. It was open, so we walked in. From the front door you could see straight into the bedroom. And there was Mom with her latest boyfriend, whom I could not stand. She was in her bra and panties, and he was naked. I wanted to kill the guy. Dad did, too.

Mom jumped up out of bed and tore out of the bedroom in a screaming rage. "What the hell are you doing here, walking in my house?" she yelled, kicking and punching at my father. In his hurry to get his hands on the boyfriend, he just kind of brushed Mom aside. He hadn't intended to hurt her. But Dad was strong as an ox, and with one sweeping right hand he flung her across the room on his way through the doorway. As if in slow motion, I watched Mom fly across the room. She crashed into the side of a chair, catching her ribs. Her ribs broke and punctured her lung; she couldn't breathe. In an instant, I went from thinking, "Yeah, get Mom out of the way and let's get this jerk!" to realizing, as I made my way to the bedroom, that Mom was really hurt.

We scooped Mom up and rushed her to the hospital. The guy, in the meantime, had jumped out of bed, ran to the bathroom, and

Eddie and the Kelly Four (Hollywood Swingers, Eddie Cochran band): Gene Riggio, Mike Deasy, Dave Shriver, Jimmy Stivers, and Mike Henderson.

Left to right: unknown, Larry Levine, Eddie, Bob Denton, Levone unknown, Mary Jo Sheeley, Sharon Sheeley, Goldstar recording studio.

Left to right: Jimmy Seals on sax ,
Levone unknown, Sharon, Mary Jo,
Jimmy Stivers, Eddie, Goldstar
recording studio.

Eddie and Gene Riggio, Goldstar recording studio.

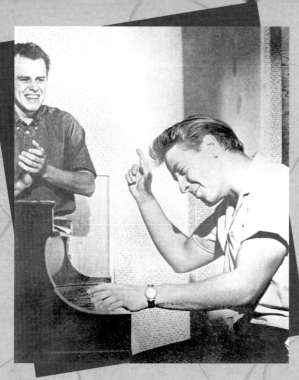

Dave Shriver clapping while Eddie hams it up on the piano. Mom said Eddie did a great Jerry Lee Lewis on the piano.

Eddie plays piano for fans at Chadron back stage after show.

Eddie, Sharon Sheeley, Mary Jo Sheeley, and Guybo at Sharon's place in Hollywood.

Eddie in a scene from the movie *Go, Johnny, Go!*

Eddie in a rare shot from the movie *The Girl Can't Help It*.

Lori Nelson and Eddie between scenes for the movie *Untamed Youth*.

Untamed Youth cast, playing around for the camera.

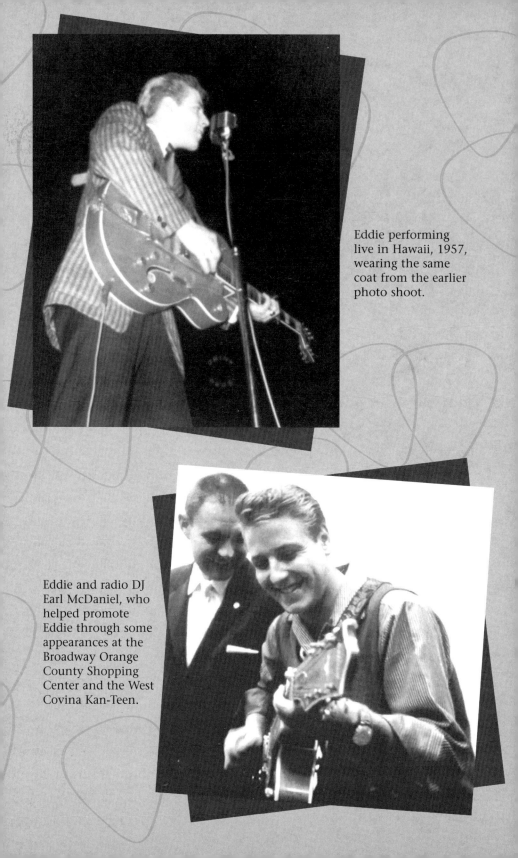

Eddie performing live in Hawaii, 1957, wearing the same coat from the earlier photo shoot.

Eddie and radio DJ Earl McDaniel, who helped promote Eddie through some appearances at the Broadway Orange County Shopping Center and the West Covina Kan-Teen.

Eddie playing the drums, Goldstar recording studio.

Me, 16 years old, playing drums on a gig with the Emperors, at a teen canteen, 1966.

Eddie and Sharon Sheeley during a lighter moment at
Goldstar recording studio.

Eddie and Sharon
taking a walk for
the camera.

crawled out the tiny window. He ran down the alley, naked as a jaybird. That moment made me realize how, suddenly, what seemed important to you one minute, in a blink of an eye can become instantly irrelevant, and that all that really matters in this life are the people whom you love. And I loved my Mom. I'd been frustrated with her, but I loved her. I loved her a lot. Taking Dad to her place was a violation of her trust. By the time I reached my twenties, I had a much more mature sense of Mom and her motivations. She was a true rebel and a fun-loving, forward-thinking person. She was a great jitterbug dancer and an amply talented singer—a remarkably gifted lady. She always wanted to be one of the gang instead of a "parent." She was fun to be around and was very accepting of people. Mom did the best she could in some very difficult circumstances. She was so hungry to be accepted and loved that she made some poor choices at times. But she was courageous and strong—as well as loving and protective of us kids—in ways that I didn't see as a child.

I once told Mom, "I love you, but I don't respect you." That statement, at the time, was appropriate. But it's not how I came to feel. She was never able to let go of the regret she felt about my disappointment in her. Although I told her many times that I felt differently, she was too hard on herself to accept my forgiveness, and I was too blind to see that I kept her away emotionally on some level. I learned a lot from Mom, and I don't think any parent could love their son more than she did me.

And I loved Dad, even though he continually disappointed me. Dad used to set up times for us to go hunting; I loved to go shooting with him. He'd set these trips up—usually it would be on a Friday or Saturday night. When I was playing, I would usually have a gig, so I'd just stay up after the show. He'd say he'd be over at 2 in the morning to pick me up. So I'd be ready to go, have all my stuff packed in the living room, and sit up until 4:30, when I'd finally crash. And he'd never show up. Next day I'd call around to all the bars. I'd find him and fume, "Why didn't you call me and tell me you weren't coming?" I was fed up with how unreliable he was.

Once when I was fifteen and a half he took me to Goldstar studios and had me cut a bunch of Eddie's tunes. I could sing, but I had a voice like Mickey Mouse. I didn't want to be there, and I definitely didn't want to be doing that. For all I knew, these were the engineers who worked with Eddie. I didn't want them comparing me with Ed. I wasn't happy, and I didn't feel good about what we were doing. I was supposed to just stand there without a band and do these songs. So I did it, and did it, and did it—it was repulsive to me. Listening to those songs now, I find there's no feeling in them, just playing, a terrible representation of what I was capable of at that time.

I had such respect for Dad's talent and heart. He was so troubled about something. I think it was about belief in himself. He was gifted, handsome, and smart, yet he would always wind up off track. I didn't like the way he was treated by his family. Dad was a quiet sort of guy with tremendous inner strength. He had something about him that was real powerful, but he didn't connect with it. I realized that on some level he was counting on me to carry on in a way that he couldn't. It was a confusing notion for a kid like me to have to sort through.

At Nellie's house, I had the front bedroom. I'd decided to construct my own studio there, so I had cut a hole through the closet to an adjacent bedroom and put a window in it. The other room was going to be where the band guys would be, and my bedroom was where the equipment was. In my bedroom I had two Voice of the Theater speakers, which each stood about four feet tall, three feet wide, and two feet deep, leaving room for little else. I had the two tape recorders that Dad used to have in his studio, all of my gear.

One night, Dad came over; I was standing in the doorway to the band-playing room talking to him. He wanted me to move into Hollywood with him, so we could seriously pursue the music business together. It was one of the few times my father ever reached out to me, and I knew it was difficult for him. I loved the idea of working on music with Dad—he was a great songwriter, and I had a lot of respect for his talent. But I hated his drinking. I hated his temper—he could just snap. The discussion began to get heated.

He kept pressing me, and I kept telling him, "Dad, it just looks to me that all it's going to be is me hanging with you, and you drinking. We'll pull chicks in—'Bobby is the young musician guy, he'll pull in the chicks'—and you'll have the booze, and we'll just party with chicks and drink, and that's what our lives will be about. That's not the vision I have for myself. I don't drink and I don't smoke; I hate being around it. The smell of the stuff is foul on my clothes. And when you're drinking, man, you're not yourself. You're angry and belligerent; you're hard to be around. And half the time I don't know if you're even going to show up or not. Usually it's because you're drinking. Why would I want to mess my life up like that?"

It was heartbreaking for him to hear me say those things. But finally I was speaking my mind, what I felt in my gut, how his drinking had ruined our lives already. Why would I want to keep doing that? He was furious. At one point he grabbed me by my shirt—just like you see the guys in the movies do—pulled my face close to his and yelled, "You're nothing but a punk!"

I grabbed his hand and powered it down with all my might—I felt like I had the strength of Superman. I hurled back, "There's one thing that I'm not and that's a punk, and don't you ever call me that again!" I didn't even cuss.

As his arm came down he taunted, "Go ahead, hit me! Hit me!" Flecks of spittle landed on my face.

"I don't want to hit you," I roared back, almost in tears, "I love you! I'd love to do the music business with you, but I can't stand your drinking. It destroyed your life with Mom and us, it broke this family up; it messed up Eddie's life; and it messed up Grandpa's life. Who do you know that it didn't mess up their life? I'm around it enough in the clubs. I don't drink, and I don't want to hang out with a drunk!"

It was a sad, sad time for both of us.

By the time I was eighteen, I'd developed a pretty solid reputation as a guitarist, working in bands and studios around southern California doing live shows and tons of demos. Although I'd played on the Bob Eubanks single, it wasn't until 1968 that I made my professional recording debut on a major label, recording a tune that I co-wrote on a record by the Knack. Not to be confused with the later "My Sharona" group of the same name, the Knack was a pop band touted as the next Beatles, even though the Beatles, of course, were still going strong at the time. This is the first group I threatened to quit if they mentioned my relation to Eddie in the band bio. By mid-1968 I'd hooked up with another LA-area group, the South, featuring some of the area's most highly respected players, including guitarist and vocalist Don Preston, who later worked with Leon Russell and Mad Dogs and Englishmen, and bassist and vocalist Casey Van Beek—Nellie's neighbor—who later played with Linda Ronstadt and the Tractors. I was still only eighteen when I joined the group—not old enough to play most of the places we worked— but I was able to find enough fake IDs to get away with it. We did a lot of recording, an album for A&M as the South, and then another for Stax Records under the name Still Rock. Stax, located in Memphis, Tennessee, wanted to make us their house band to take the place of Booker T. and the MGs, but we didn't want to leave California.

I did some recording with a group called the Formula 5 for disc jockey Wolfman Jack's production company. Top session players and stars like Delaney and Bonnie—the husband and wife duo whose band at various times included Eric Clapton, Dave Mason, Duane Allman, Leon Russell, Rita Coolidge, Jim Gordon, Bobby Whitlock, and Carl Radle—used to come to our club dates to listen and sit in. Delaney asked me to join his band, telling me I was the best guitarist he had heard since Duane Allman, certainly quite a compliment. I knew that if I joined Delaney and Bonnie, I would be guaranteed tremendous exposure, following in the footsteps of guys like Eric Clapton.

But I had been approached several times by Kindred, a rock band that shared management with the hit-making vocal group Three Dog Night and with Steppenwolf, arguable inventors of heavy metal with their defiant biker anthem of 1968, "Born to Be Wild." And I was part of a studio-session group at the Producers Workshop in Hollywood, a group that included guitarist Ben Benay;

bassist Emory Gordy, who'd go on to play with or produce Emmylou Harris, Steve Earle, Roy Orbison, and George Jones; drummer Dennis St. John, who'd later work with Neil Diamond, Carole Bayer Sager, and the Band; and keyboardist Spooner Oldham, who'd played with Percy Sledge, Wilson Pickett, and Aretha Franklin and who'd later work with Neil Young, Bob Dylan, and Jackson Browne.

Kindred was persistent. I recommended to them some great players; they'd decided that only I would do. Since they were already signed to Warner Brothers and had tremendous touring and recording potential, I decided to join them, recording a pair of Kindred albums in 1971 and 1972 and touring throughout America and Canada opening for Three Dog Night.

Through our shared management connection, I soon got a call from Jerry Edmonton, the drummer from Steppenwolf. They wanted me to join their band. I stayed for three albums and four years as the group's lead guitarist, one of its songwriters, and a co-lead and backing vocalist. Toward the end of my tenure with "the Wolf," I received a call from the Flying Burrito Brothers, the country-rock outfit founded by Gram Parsons and Chris Hillman of the Byrds. They needed a guitarist for a two-week tour. I went down to the rehearsal hall, jammed with the group, and found myself a Burrito for the next fourteen months. Like Uncle Ed in his brief lifetime, I have played with a plethora of artists—from obscure to superstars—and try to take something of value away from every musical experience. I would also try to leave having given my absolute best to bring their dreams into reality.

In October 1957, Eddie joined "The Big Show." Boasting such established names as Little Richard and Gene Vincent, as well as Alis Lesley, "the female Elvis Presley," the package tour was the first all rock 'n' roll extravaganza to visit Australia. The rock-starved crowds were receptive and rambunctious; every single date was sold out.

Though he was a virtual unknown in Australia, Ed was thrilled to be performing alongside his idol, Little Richard, and his new pal, Gene Vincent.

While in Australia, Ed ran into Warren Flock's brother, who was there with the U.S. Navy. Eddie was excited because he could get American cigarettes off him from the navy ship, so he was invited to all the shows. Warren's brother was thrilled, Flock told me, because there was a lot of sex going on at the offstage parties. It was almost a game. The revelers would turn the lights off, and by the time the lights came back on they were all supposed to be nude. It was quite a time. Eddie had to be under a doctor's care to get himself back in shape after that trip, Flock recalls, because he was worn out from all the partying. Eddie would later enthuse about all of the beautiful women he'd met in Australia.

Without a backing band of his own, Ed was accompanied by Australian rocker Johnny O'Keefe's group, the Deejays, as he sang his few Liberty singles and filled the rest of his set with covers of other pop tunes, like Charlie Gracie's "Butterfly," "White Sports Coat," and the country chestnut "Gone." He soon learned to incorporate some of the showbiz antics used by his cohorts.

Night after night, the headliners engaged in a friendly competition, Little Richard and Gene Vincent each trying to best each other in both set length and stage shenanigans. Despite his infirm leg, Gene would ricochet across the stage, torturing his mike stand—leaning on it, tossing it, spinning it about—and his band of merry hooligans would follow suit. At one show, husky teenage drummer Dickie Harrell hurtled headlong off a grand piano over the stage and into the band pit. Little Richard would cause riots at gig after gig as he tore his clothing from his body and tossed the shreds into the audience, eventually necessitating police intervention as kids sparred for bits of Richard's flashy wardrobe.

"...Screaming teenage admirers of an American Negro rock 'n' roll exponent, Little Richard, dragged him across the footlights and trampled him in a mob on the floor of Newcastle Stadium at the latest Big Show last night," reported one newspaper. "It was rock 'n' roll night and one of the most riotous in the stadium's history.

Against a background of non-stop noise attendants had to remove an over-excited teenager's foot from Little Richard's face before they could help him to his feet and rescue him from the mob."

A grand piano was badly damaged when the drummer in a 'musical' combination known as Gene Vincent and his Blue Caps stomped over the top of it and leaped off stage, over the footlights, beating a side drum under one arm. A side door of the stadium was smashed in. Footlight protection plates were pulled down when teenagers rushed forward to catch handkerchiefs thrown out by a 'singer' called Eddie Cochran. Cochran first used the handkerchiefs to mop sweat from his face.

Little Richard virtually invited himself to be dragged off the stage at the second performance of the show. He had been onstage only a few minutes before he peeled off the coat of a blue costume, akin to a pair of pajamas, he was wearing. 'Singing' bare-chested in his pants, with the top of his underpants showing and removing his red-and-white shoes he appeared to tear small pieces from the coat and threw them into the audience.

Later, he threw a belt and gestured as though about to throw a ring and watch. When he quivered and rolled and dropped to the floor near the footlights during the initial 'songs' teenagers reached across the footlights, apparently trying to help themselves to pieces of his pants.

A tug-o'-war, which at first seemed jocular, then began between the teenagers on one side and the members of Little Richard's band on the other for possession of the perspiring 'body.' Two girls scrambled on to the stage from the audience, evidently to help get the 'singer' over the footlights, and before stadium attendants could get through the mob, Little Richard was lying on the floor in front of the stage being trampled.

It was a night of feet stamping, whistling, yelling, audience-participation clapping and singing, essentially juvenile. There were the assorted spectacles of a pretty girl suddenly putting two fingers in her mouth and letting out a shattering whistle at one of the artists and of a girl standing less than ten feet from the stage inspecting Eddie Cochran minutely through a pair of field glasses.

On the October 4 date of the two-week-long tour, the show stopped at an outdoor arena. Forty thousand screaming teens shoehorned into the venue to witness the rock 'n' roll mayhem. That night, Russia launched Sputnik, the world's first artificial satellite; the Communists had beaten the Americans into orbit.

Richard was stunned when he saw the big ball of fire course directly over the stadium. Surely it was a sign, he thought. It made no matter how big a star he might be—he must save himself from his own damnation. So he stood up from his piano, vowing to forever after forsake show business for God.

The next day, as the musicians were in the bus departing on the vehicle-carrying ferry to the next city, Richard made his decision known. No one believed him. To prove his conviction, he tore off his sparkling diamond jewelry and threw it into the river behind the boat. Then he gave away the rest of his showbiz trappings, with Gene Vincent ending up with several of his flamboyant suits. Richard soon boarded a plane for religious seclusion in America, leaving half a million dollars' worth of cancelled Australian bookings in his wake—and "The Big Show" at an abrupt end.

Ed had invited to Australia with him singer and rhythm guitarist Ron Wilson, a Bell Gardens Music Center regular who'd introduced Ed to Warren Flock. "Bubba, you got to go with me," Ed had said to Ron, trying to persuade him to make the trip down under. "We'll take you down to Crest Records, and we'll press five hundred copies, and we'll air them down there and let 'em play 'em for a couple of weeks on the air. You go with me and you go on and you warm 'em up for thirty minutes, then I'll come out." But Wilson turned Ed down; he'd just returned from two years in Korea and had no desire to leave the country once more. After Ed's Australian stint concluded, Wilson went by Ed's house for a visit. Mom Cochran leaned over and squeezed his cheek and tsk-tsked, "You should have gone to Australia with him!"

Granny knew Wilson well, as he'd been a pal of Eddie's for several years. When Ron first met Ed, he and his folks were living in a small house trailer with a bedroom in the back, a small kitchen in the middle, and a little couch out front that folded out. Ed and

Ron would sit on that couch and practice. They were just kids, Ron about fifteen or sixteen, Ed three years younger. Grandpa Frank, Ed's dad, would come trudging home from work around midnight, but he insisted that the boys continue playing. "You've got to go to bed, right?" Ron would ask him, not wanting to overstay his welcome. "No, no, no," Grandpa would say patiently, "you guys play. It won't bother me." And he'd trudge off to bed. Granny would stay up and make the boys munchies. According to Granny, Eddie and Ron never ate enough.

Eddie jetted back to the States in mid-October to join the second leg of another traveling package tour, eight days of Irvin Feld's "The Biggest Show of Stars for '57." The bill also included Chuck Berry, Fats Domino, LaVern Baker, Paul Anka, the Everly Brothers, and Buddy Holly. The tour was grinding—no one artist performing more than two or three songs per show, with the musicians dozing on buses during long night hauls to the next city. From mid-October to late November the "Show of Stars" made its way from California up through the Pacific Northwest to Canada, back down to the Midwest, across New England, and down to the mid-Atlantic, playing over forty dates in as many days.

"...Man, Daddyo, they really broke it up in the Arena of the Municipal Auditorium last night," wrote one reviewer of the package in the *Kansas City Times* in November 1957 in an article headlined, "Rock 'n' Roll a Delight, Crowd Shouts, Stomps Through Performance."

> When Eddie Cochran wiggled and shouted through "You Say You Love Me but You Can't Come In," he wasn't far from the truth. There were [thousands of] cats there, and you couldn't have gotten many more out on the floor.
>
> It was the largest gathering of rock 'n' roll stars here since last April, when the same troupe appeared. Now they're on another tour, coming here from Wichita Falls, Texas.
>
> Things were quiet up to showtime, 10:30 o'clock. Then Chuck Berry bounded onto the stage with "School Days," and that crowd suddenly looked as if it must have taken its Asian flu shots with juke box needles.

The pace got hotter when Buddy Knox, Don Lanier, and Jim Bowen fired up "Rock Around the Clock." Lanier's bass fiddle became so lively with the beat that he wound up wrestling it on the stage floor.

Things were going fine until some square threw a bottle at The Drifters. After that dancers were hampered by the big boxes police shoved through the melee, gathering empty jugs.

Squealing for all their teenage worth, the crowd greeted Fats Domino in his shiny maroon tux. Even the upper deck spectators went into the aisles when Fats broke out with "My Blue Heaven."

Wilt (the Stilt) Chamberlain, all-American basketball player from the University of Kansas, wandered in and was mobbed by the mass of bobby-soxed signature seekers.

Almost everybody who is anybody in rock 'n' roll was there. Harold Cromer, the emcee, introduced LaVern Baker, Clyde McPhatter, Frankie Lymon, The Crickets, The Diamonds, Paul Anka, and Paul Willams.

The crowd moaned when Cromer said The Everly Brothers wouldn't appear. Don Everly had the flu, Comer said.

Otherwise, man, it was a real smash.

Eddie, confident, casual, and clever, took the often-grueling show business routine in stride. He eschewed the flashy garb of other rockers for a more accessible image—one with great appeal to young women, typically performing in tweed sport jacket, tie, and loafers. He rarely loitered backstage awaiting his cue; he had things perfectly timed so that when it was his turn to perform, he'd typically stride in directly from the street, shed the coat tossed nonchalantly over his shoulders, pick up his guitar, and walk straight onstage. When his set was through, he'd walk offstage, pick up his coat, and coolly exit the building.

Jody Reynolds, who worked often with Eddie, found Ed's down-to-earth attitude refreshing. Though onstage he was unstoppable, Jody found him totally unaffected by his fame. While the two were playing in San Francisco on a bill of twenty-five acts, Ed, with a couple of hits under his belt, was easily the shoo-in for top of the ticket. But Ed said, "I want to go on first. Then Jody and I are going out." Jody wound up opening the show, with Ed following him. Jody was amazed because Ed could have gone on twenty-fifth and closed the show. From that moment on, Jody knew that Ed was no phony, that he didn't take himself too seriously. Ed did his songs, then the two singers hit Market and First Streets and stayed out all night exploring San Francisco. They both liked to eat, and they were like kids in a candy shop among the smorgasbord of restaurants in big cities like Frisco. Eddie ate everything while they were in town, Jody recalled. He ate steak and potatoes, he ate fish once, he ate country food like his momma cooked. He ate chili with mustard and ketchup in it, and cheese and black olive pizzas.

Any show Jody did with Ed turned out to be an adventure, the two sneaking from the venue and living it up in town. Ed didn't give a care about when he went on. And if he wanted to leave early, even if he was at the top of the bill, he would go on earlier, and let someone else have his time slot so he could go have fun.

Fun for Ed was often mischievous. At one show in Australia, Warren Flock recalls, Eddie and some of the other male performers went to a lingerie store and bought boxes of ladies panties that had the days of the week embroidered on them. They brought the panties onstage with them when they came out for their encore, throwing them to the shrieking girls in the audience who dove for the suggestive loot. A live radio broadcast was being beamed from the show. The interviewer couldn't really describe what the musicians were doing that had so incited the crowd, so he fibbed a bit, going with the tamer line, telling listeners that the rock 'n' rollers were merely tossing handkerchiefs. Flock loved hearing Eddie tell his tales from the road, which were pretty comical at times. Ed would even crack himself up recalling his playful antics.

Bobby Charles, from *Town Hall Party*, got a kick out of Eddie's stories, as well. He can recall a particular time in 1957 when Ed visited him at a gig.

"Mr. Charles!" Ed chortled with mock propriety.

"Mr. Cochran!" Charles reciprocated. "Let me ask you this," Bobby continued, "Do you perhaps have a jug in the car?"

"As a matter of fact I do," Ed said grandly. "Are you a jug head?"

"Guilty as charged, sir," Bobby replied. "Lead the way."

So the two went out to the car and passed Ed's whisky bottle back and forth. Ed told Bobby all about making *The Girl Can't Help It* and the different people he knew, like Little Richard and Charlie Gracie. Eddie raved about Charlie Gracie's mother's Italian cooking. He also mentioned one party he went to, also attended by Natalie Wood, where the people behaved in an unseemly manner, drunken and disgusting.

Strong friendships—like that of Ed and Gene Vincent—were often forged on the punishing package tours, and by the time the "Show of Stars" pulled into New York City for a Christmas-season run at the Paramount Theatre, Eddie had become quite close with Buddy Holly and the Everly Brothers.

Buddy Holly had launched his career doing country music, eventually adding R&B numbers to his set after meeting Elvis Presley. He recorded early rockabilly sides in Nashville, resulting in the 1956 Decca singles "Blue Days, Black Nights" and "Modern Don Juan." After assembling the Crickets and recording in Norman Petty's New Mexico studio, Holly found himself with a Number One hit in early 1957, "That'll Be the Day."

Like Eddie, Holly and Petty experimented in the studio, toying with double-tracking, used on "Words of Love," the follow-up to "That'll Be the Day"; varying forms of echo, as on "Peggy Sue," a second gold-selling Top 10 hit; and close-miking techniques, which would eventually become commonplace in the industry. With the Crickets, Holly enjoyed another Top 10 hit with "Oh, Boy!" issued in October 1957.

Like most everyone who met him, Ed genuinely liked Holly. Less than two months after wrapping up the "Show of Stars" tour, Ed and Buddy were traveling together once more on a nearly three-week tour of major American cities. Buddy was not much older than my uncle, and the two had plenty in common, including their adoration of Ray Charles. Ed found Buddy's natural good-naturedness refreshing and his song writing impressive;

Buddy admired Ed's guitar playing and his winning way with the girls. The two became close on the road, singing, playing, partying, and laughing when they weren't onstage.

Ed also had tremendous respect for Don and Phil Everly, who were professional musicians even before their teens, trained by their accomplished guitarist father Ike. They used to vocalize with their family on radio broadcasts in Iowa. The pair made a brief foray into country music in the mid-'50s with a single for Columbia, but eventually wound up at Cadence, which released their "Bye Bye Love." Invested with the duo's trademark tight, two-part harmonies and modern pop sensibility, and propelled by a Bo Diddley-ish beat, the song just missed the very top spot on the music charts in 1957. A remarkable three-year string of classic hit singles for Cadence would follow, including "Wake Up Little Susie," "All I Have to Do Is Dream," "Bird Dog," "('Til) I Kissed You," and "When Will I Be Loved." As young stars of great skill and uncompromising musical standards, it was inevitable that Ed would find friendly kinship with Don and Phil.

Joe B. Mauldin of the Crickets recalls Eddie also developing a close friendship with LaVern Baker; the two shared a keenness for practical jokes. One night on the "Show of Stars" tour, Ed helped LaVern pull off a prank on Paul Anka. Seems LaVern—like just about all the other musicians—had heard just about enough from Anka about his many successes, and she thought he needed to be brought down a few notches. So LaVern purchased a jar of Vaseline and added to it a healthy amount of black charcoal powder, and then she enlisted some of her fellow musicians to help her carry out her plan. One night, after the show played a hockey rink, LaVern, Ed, and their cohorts caught Paul and stripped him near the showers. They covered him with the blackened Vaseline and emptied a feather pillow onto the gooey stuff. Paul Anka, teen idol, had effectively been tarred and feathered! The stunned Anka was left to shower with cold water—no hot water was available at the rink—then make the trip to the next town in a freezing tour bus. No harm was intended, and Anka took his tarring with great humor, though Joe B. recalls that Paul didn't brag nearly as much during the rest of the tour. Anka went on to become one of the most successful pop singer/songwriters of all time.

On the tour, most nights after a show would end up with a party in one of the performer's rooms. It would be wall-to-wall girls, with Ed—quietly strumming his guitar—their main attraction. One night, the party got a little out of hand, with close to thirty teenagers, including most of the musicians, crammed into a single hotel room, drinking, smoking, singing, and laughing. The hotel manager, accompanied by a burly house security officer, burst into the room and demanded everyone leave. One by one they all filed out. Ed was last. As he passed by the barrel-chested house dick, his wry sense of humor got the better of him. "You wouldn't be treatin' us like this if Eddie Cochran was here!" he muttered as he walked out the door.

Dovetailing with his "Show of Stars" appearances was the release of Ed's fourth Liberty single, a reworking of "Twenty Flight Rock," coupled with "Cradle Baby," an innocuous rocker. More polished than its original with backing by the ubiquitous Johnny Mann singers, the new "Twenty Flight Rock" still retained the urgency of its filmic forebear. "Good enough rocker for teen tastes, pop and country," wrote one reviewer of "Cradle Baby," who then applauded the new "Twenty Flight Rock" with "Cochran rocks this rockabilly in Presley fashion. Good job all around. Can do okay." Yet the single, like the two before it, was a commercial failure, this time not even penetrating the charts. It was no doubt a blow to Ed, who'd been working tirelessly on the road and on radio to promote his new outings. And it was another setback for Liberty, which, by the end of 1957, due to corrupt sales management and poor book-keeping, was nearly bankrupt.

By hiring music-industry mover and shaker Al Bennett, former-ly of the Dot label, Si Waronker was able to save his company. Bennett, a savvy businessman with an uncanny ability to sell, relied on his relationships within the music industry to maintain Liberty's distribution and to move millions of records, most notably the label's 1958 novelty tune "Witch Doctor" by David Seville. Within the first six weeks of its release, the single sold nearly three million dollars, effectively erasing Liberty's onerous debt load and giving the company its first Number One hit.

On January 12, 1958, Eddie was back in the Liberty studio with Guybo, this time joined by Earl Palmer, a first-rate session drummer hired by Waronker. Earl had kept time for Little Richard and Fats Domino, among others. Ed's experiences with the wilder and woollier of rock 'n' roll's earliest stars—controversial rebels like Little Richard and Gene Vincent—seemed to have rubbed off. He now employed a rougher, gruffer vocal attack, which he put to effective use on another of Granny Cochran's favorites, the driving "Jeannie, Jeannie, Jeannie," a tune originally penned as "Johnny, Johnny, Johnny" by fellow Liberty artist Rick Page and her husband, George Motola, a music industry jack-of-all-trades. Transformed into "Jeannie, Jeannie, Jeannie" by disc jockey Jimmie Maddin, Ed decided to give the tune a try, launching a vital transformation from innocuous teenage popster to rollicking rock 'n' roll renegade.

Though Waronker was open to almost anything Eddie wanted to do in the studio, he hedged any bets on Ed's tougher sound by coupling "Jeannie, Jeannie, Jeannie" with the Mann-backed pop-rocker "Pocketful of Hearts," recorded around the time of *Singin' to My Baby*, for Liberty's first release of 1958. Though reviewers hailed Eddie's "exuberant delivery" of the "catchy rockabilly" and noted that the "torrid new release" had Cochran "wailing in an exciting manner" in a "subdued Little Richard style," "Jeannie, Jeannie, Jeannie" again failed to lure buyers, just squeaking onto the charts at Number 94.

In February, Ed was booked onto another package bill, playing with the Coasters and Frankie Lymon. Ed was a huge fan of Lymon, a young male soprano who in 1955, at the age of thirteen, had a huge hit with his group the Teenagers, "Why Do Fools Fall in Love?" More hits—"I Want You to Be My Girl," "I Promise to Remember," and "The ABCs of Love"—followed before Lymon went solo in 1957. He was now on the road promoting his current single, "Goody, Goody." A date was scheduled in Honolulu, Hawaii, and Ed and Jerry Capehart jetted to the islands.

"Rock 'n' roll is changing," Ed told newspapermen in Hawaii. "I think it will keep on changing. But the heavy beat will always be there."

Ed "goes out 'with different girls'," is "5 feet 9 inches, I guess," and handles his money by putting "what I don't invest... into an account," noted one publication, and it quoted Eddie's response to his supposed resemblance to Elvis "what's his name" as, "The way I figure it, that everybody has a little of his (Presley) style when singing rock 'n' roll. I don't really sound like Presley."

Of his visits to Hawaii, Ed said, "I've been here about three times. The first time, I was playing guitar with Lefty Frizzell's group. I stopped over en route to Australia for the second time... Man, I dig it (Hawaii)! If I didn't live in California, I'd be living here."

Ed and Lymon had instantly bonded, with Ed taking the kid with the penchant for candy bars under his wing. After the show in Honolulu, unbeknownst to Jerry, Ed and his new under-age sidekick threw themselves a party. Bounteous liquor loosened inhibitions, and it wasn't long before the pair were supremely sloshed, laughing uproariously and staggering out onto Ed's hotel room balcony.

Over the course of their little soiree, they'd gathered quite a collection of champagne glasses, and the pair began hurling them one by one into the glittering blue swimming pool below. Shards of glass piled up like crystalline snowdrifts on the cement surrounding the pool, and it soon became difficult to distinguish whether the sparkles in the water were gentle trade-wind ripples or bloodthirsty bits of crystal catching the moonlight.

The next morning Ed awoke with a terrible hangover—and Jerry to an understandably disgruntled hotel management. A kiddie swim class was to have taken place that morning; it could have easily turned into a blood bath. Now the pool had to be drained and all of the tiny, transparent slivers carefully removed. When Ed sobered up and realized what he'd done, the terrific danger he'd created for others—children, no less—he was filled with shame.

Jerry hustled Ed off the islands just hours shy of his arrest. The Hawaiian newspapers had a field day with the story, running angry headlines about the hot-shot rock 'n' roll stars' outrageous party. Ed was sick about the incident. He and Frankie were just having fun—stupid, thoughtless fun. But he knew he had no one to blame but himself. On the flight home, Jerry lectured him about how he must conduct himself carefully, how he must keep his drinking under control now that he was in the public eye, particularly as a rock 'n' roll artist. Jerry didn't want Ed to jeopardize all he was working so hard to attain. Ed promised he'd never do anything like that again.

Upon Ed's return from Hawaii, Liberty issued its second Cochran release of the year. March's "Teresa" was a return to the sweet Ed sound, honeyed with a female backing chorus, about which one critic thought, "Comes thru [sic] for okay results but flip may be stronger." Backed with "Pretty Girl," a Cochran/Capehart collaboration more akin to "Jeannie, Jeannie, Jeannie" that inspired a reviewer to predict, "It can get action," the single tanked. The new Liberty ploy of pairing pleasant pop with Ed's more aggressive emergent sound foundered again.

In late March, Ed joined his pal Gene Vincent at the Capitol studios in Hollywood to lend a hand with Gene's fourth album, *A Gene Vincent Record Date*. Since Ed lived in the area and was such close friends with Gene's band members that he was practically a Blue Cap himself, he sat in on four of the five days of the Vincent recording sessions. He lent a bass voice to the layered doo-wop backing of "Git It," crawling into the cave of sound baffles the musicians had constructed in the middle of the studio to vocally anchor the high harmonies of Paul Peek and Tommy Facenda, and Gene's sweet falsetto. Other cuts featuring Ed included Gene's "Teenage Partner" (which Ed arranged for him), "Peace of Mind," "Lovely Loretta," "Somebody Help Me," "The Wayward Wind," and "Now Is the Hour."

Ed palled around with Gene and the Caps outside of the studio as well. He and teen Blue Cap drummer Juvey Gomez got to know each other pretty well while recording. Ed was impressed by fashion-forward Gomez's sense of style, asking him one day, "Where'd you get those shoes?" after admiring the kid's crazy moccasins. Eddie had a shoe fetish, and with his small feet—delicate, like his hands—he was able to buy display models or custom samples of nearly any type of footwear. So Juvey and Ed made several clothes shopping excursions around Los Angeles.

After Gene's album sessions were complete, Vincent and his band began shooting *Hot Rod Gang*, a rock 'n' roll exploitation flick that starred John Ashley, another of Jerry Capehart's management clients. Capehart was the associate musical supervisor on the film, and members of Ed's future backing band—Dick D'Agostin and Gene Riggio—accompanied Ashley in one of the film's singing sequences.

Ed also attended parties that Gene Vincent held in his hotel room every evening while he was in town. Gene and the Blue Caps had moved to the Knickerbocker Hotel in Hollywood after staff at their first hotel, fed up with the noise, the vandalism, and the ceaseless stream of girls coming in and out of the rooms, had asked them to leave. Stars like Johnny Cash and Bob Luman would drop by, as well as John Ashley, Lefty Frizzell, and Ricky Nelson, the baby-faced star of TV's popular *Ozzie and Harriet* who idolized Vincent and had a double-sided million-seller in 1956 with "I'm Walkin'" and "A Teenager's Romance."

In early 1958, Nelson scored another hit with the ballad "Poor Little Fool." Unusual in its omission of a chorus, the song was composed by a sixteen-year-old named Sharon Sheeley, a star-struck kid from Newport Beach, California, with big songwriting dreams. Sharon was a gutsy girl who'd already dabbled in fashion modeling and had stumbled into a friendship with Elvis Presley. It was Presley, in fact, who encouraged her to give song writing a try when she was fifteen. He was in Hollywood to make his first film, *Love Me Tender*. Like every other girl in the world, Sharon was there, below the Knickerbocker Hotel, one face in a thousand hoping to catch a glimpse of the most handsome man she'd ever seen. Spying her from the balcony, Elvis sent one of his buddies down to ask Sharon and her sister up to his room. She reminded him of his big love in high school who'd stood him up for the prom, he told her—the one he always liked that got away. Sharon and Elvis talked and quickly became good friends.

Though he was only twenty, to the fifteen-year-old girl Elvis seemed an old and wise man. In their conversations, they discussed her future, her goals, her ambitions, about which she was unclear. Elvis convinced her that if she really wanted to do something, then she shouldn't just talk about it, she should go out and do it.

"What would you like to do?" Elvis asked her.

"Well, I write good poems," she mused. "I always get A's in school for writing poems."

"Then put a tune to those poems," he urged. "Go ahead, try it."

So she did. Her first shot out was "Poor Little Fool," whose words and music she wrote in her head, not being an instrumentalist or a singer. She knew it was perfect for Ricky Nelson. But how could she get the song to him? It so happened that the Nelsons had just bought a house in Laguna, about ten miles from where Sharon lived in Newport Beach. Sharon arranged a meeting with Nelson by staging an automobile breakdown in front of his house. Feigning car trouble, Sharon asked for assistance; Ricky Nelson invited her inside to use the phone. While waiting for a tow truck to arrive, Sharon casually mentioned that she'd written a song for Elvis—which she hadn't—that he'd put on hold to record—which he hadn't. She played him the song, which she had recorded. He hated it, saying it was too fast. But his guitar player thought the tune had promise. "You know Rick," he said, "if you slow it down, it's really a good song." Still skeptical, Nelson said, "Well, we'll see. Maybe I can fit it on my next album and maybe I can't." That's the last Sharon heard of it until one day Nelson phoned her to say he'd just cut it. Nelson made the song his, taking it to Number One—and he made Sharon Sheeley a bona fide, sought-after songwriter in the process.

Although countless high-powered managers wanted Sharon as their client—the novelty of a female songwriter equaled big bucks in those days—it was Jerry Capehart whom the wily Sheeley chose to represent her. And she chose him for one reason only: he handled Eddie Cochran, the love of her life.

7

Sharon

WHEN *THE GIRL CAN'T HELP IT* hit movie theaters around the winter holidays of 1956, all the girls in Sharon Sheeley's high school were gushing about a guy in the film who looked just like Elvis, one Eddie Cochran. Sharon and her little sister, Mary Jo, didn't have the money to actually see the movie, so they went down to the theater and gazed at the posters to see what all the hullabaloo was about. She saw Eddie—handsome, side-burned Eddie—and it was love at first sight. If she once thought Elvis was the epitome of masculine gorgeousness, she now thought Eddie Cochran was the most beautiful man she'd ever seen. "When I grow up, I'm gonna marry him," she told her sister. "Yeah, right," her sister retorted. "You and all the other girls in the world." And from then on, that was Sharon's mission: to get Eddie. And she had to be in the music business to meet him.

Once "Poor Little Fool" had garnered her entrée into the music industry, Sharon became one of a tight-knit coterie of young adult music stars—Ricky Nelson, the Everly Brothers, Phil Spector, Jan and Dean, Johnny and Dorsey Burnette—who palled around together in Los Angeles. Friendly with the Everlys, Sharon—willowy, almost gangly, and just getting the braces off of her teeth—was introduced to Eddie one night backstage at a rock 'n' roll package show on which the musicians were all appearing. She was sitting in the Everlys' dressing room when there was a knock on the door.

"It's Cochran, open up," boomed a deep voice and in walked Ed. He joked around with Don and Phil, doing quick draws with his ever-present gun. Though he was polite to Sharon, he paid her virtually no attention, she remembers. She could've been a lampshade; it was, "Hi, how are you?" and "Goodbye."

But after Eddie left, Phil could tell the girl was thoroughly smitten.

"Forget it," he told her, "forget it, not that kid. Don't go for him, go for anybody else."

Sharon could not be swayed. Although it was a heart-stoppingly momentous occasion in *her* adolescent experience, Eddie quickly forgot their brief meeting. Four months later, Sharon re-met Eddie when "Poor Little Fool" was Number One on the charts. She was still a lampshade, she remembered, and it was still, "Hi, how are you?" and "Goodbye." But this time Ed said to her casually, "If you think about it, and you can write something for me, I'd love to hear it." Being madly in love, she ran home and wrote reams of songs, trying to create the perfect tune for Eddie Cochran.

The two would come face to face again in May 1958, when Jerry Capehart invited Sharon to his apartment off Sunset Boulevard to share a song with Eddie. Jerry was not there when she arrived, and she battled a near-debilitating case of nerves as Eddie opened the door and invited her in.

"I hear you wrote a song for me," he said, handing her his guitar and asking her to play it for him.

Neither a guitar player nor a singer, the stunned Sharon croaked that she didn't play. Eddie laughed his marvelous laugh, she recalled, and said, "Wing it, and I'll play behind you." So she squeaked out a few bars of "Love Again," a bittersweet ballad she'd composed especially for Ed. Her voice was so high from nerves that she could barely get the words out. Ed listened politely, then told her it really wasn't his kind of song. Crushed, Sharon burst into tears and ran out of the apartment.

Passing Jerry in the apartment hallway, she heard him scold Eddie, saying, "You just chased a million dollars out the door!" Ed, who'd only been teasing Sharon, followed her into the parking lot and apologized. Then together they put "Love Again" down on tape, Sharon creaking away with Ed playing under her. Two weeks later he recorded it.

Along with a second Sheeley original, the dolorous "Lonely," "Love Again" was waxed at the same session as another tune, a song Eddie'd written with Jerry Capehart the night before called "Summertime Blues." Now given virtually free rein in the studio by Liberty, Ed followed his studio-tech instincts—first laying down a basic track of Guybo's jouncing bass with himself on rhythm guitar and an unknown drummer, some forgotten fella from the union book, whom Ed had never used before and would never use again. Then Ed overdubbed a second track, his distinctive chugging guitar playing a now-legendary repetitive blues riff, along with his spoken authoritative vocal: "I'd like to help you, son, but you're too young to vote"—Ed's cynical Congressman in a vocal rip of Kingfish from *Amos and Andy*.

Handclaps were also added. Sharon had always wanted to do something on one of Eddie's records, and Eddie had promised her she could, she remembered. But since she didn't play an instrument and definitely couldn't sing, Ed told her she could clap on the record. After about an hour of Sharon doing everything in the world wrong while trying to get the clap track down, the engineer threw up his hands. "Come on, Eddie," he pleaded. "It'll take you five seconds to just go in there and get it down." But Eddie kept his word to Sharon, saying, "No, I promised her, and by God she's going to do it." After about an hour and a half, Eddie came into the booth with Sharon. He stood next to her and clapped, she followed his small hands, and together they did the handclapping. When she heard the playback, Sharon thought the song was terrific.

Al Bennett, now president of Liberty, heard a hit, as well. And he was right. Ed's sophisticated anthem of teen freedom versus adult responsibility just couldn't miss. "Lad who had a hit a while back with 'Sittin' in the Balcony' may have another one here with this driving effort," reported one reviewer. "He sings the infectious tune brightly. It could happen." And it did, racing up the charts the summer of '58, cracking the Top 10 to peak at Number 8, eclipsing what Sharon would always say was its A-side, her "Love Again." "Summertime Blues" introduced a new instrumental and vocal tension to rock 'n' roll's teddy bear–teen dreamery. Insistent, intelligent, and innovative, rife with teenage angst and adolescent ennui, the quintessential Cochran sound had been born.

That sound was to become highly influential, particularly to a generation of aspiring rockers thousands of miles across the Atlantic. Thanks in large part to American cultural exports, England was undergoing its own adolescent revolution. The universal struggle of teens around the globe—finding and maintaining one's identity in a hypocritical, antagonistic, and conformist adult world— was addressed in films like *Blackboard Jungle* and *Rebel Without a Cause* and in the forbidden music of American rock 'n' rollers like Presley, Richard, Holly, Vincent, and, ultimately, Cochran.

Loathed by parents and poo-poohed by the BBC—which banned Vincent's "Woman Love" for its supposed suggestiveness— stateside rock 'n' roll, beamed across Europe via Radio Luxembourg (in English only) in the evenings, became all the more attractive to British teens. As the dire financial straits of post-war Europe began to ease, British kids were able, for the very first time, to make purchasing decisions of their own. They snatched up blue jeans, 78s (and later 45s), and phonographs. And if they worked hard enough and saved carefully enough, they became the proud owners of their own British-built motorbikes, the finest in the world.

An entire youth subculture with the motorcycle at its core was starting to bloom in the United Kingdom. The shiny, hand-built machines with the evocative names—the Norton Dominator, the Triumph Thunderbird, the BSA Gold Star—were a teenager's gleaming talisman of independence, affluence, and power. Black leather jackets—protective gear for bikers—quickly became the wardrobe staple of choice for young males, paired with blue jeans and, for the more misanthropically inclined, the metal-studded belt inherited from the Teds, the first identifiable postwar youth subculture.

The Teddy Boys—named for their Edwardian-style dress of long, draping coats faced with velvet, ornately embroidered vests, drainpipe-thin trousers, skinny bootlace ties, and thick, crepe-soled shoes—was a group comprised largely of working-class youths, war babies brought up on rations, many without fathers, a deprived generation who acted out their disaffection through violence. Vandalism, gang fights, even murder, perpetrated by and among the Teds, had British authorities up in arms between 1953 and 1956, mirroring the concern over juvenile delinquency that was also reaching a fever pitch thousands of miles across the Atlantic.

The black leathers of the Rockers soon eclipsed the Teds, though it was certainly no relief to English parents. Marlon Brando's portrayal in *The Wild One* of the leather-jacketed Johnny, the bored and alienated youth whose motorcycle gang wreaks havoc on a sleepy midwestern town, awakened the rebel in many an English adolescent. Although the film was banned in the U.K. until 1968, British teens desperately drooled over their revered *Wild One* stills and posters and fashioned themselves after the coolest actor they'd ever seen. James Dean, who took Brando's disturbed but sensitive anti-hero to the next level with his three major motion pictures—*Rebel*, *East of Eden*, and *Giant*—was equally revered.

The Rockers, mostly working-class youths themselves, wholly identified with the American rockers, particularly Ed and Ed's pal Gene Vincent. Ed and Gene, like most of the early American rock 'n' rollers, came from the same humble, blue-collar beginnings as the Rockers. Ed and Gene were rebels too: Vincent, a motorcycle warrior with the limp to prove it; and Ed, an individualist who urged boys to eschew the adult world's petty tyrannies, to party while the folks are away, to dream of hot chicks and cool cars. And Ed and Gene stayed true to their rock 'n' roll roots, keeping the big beat alive as one by one the originators simply dropped out of sight—Little Richard to religion, Presley to the Army, and Jerry Lee Lewis to scandal.

Ed's intensity, his laid-back rebellion resonated with British teens. "Summertime Blues" climbed to Number 18 on the U.K. charts, and in 1970 a wildly intense, instrument-smashing, genre-bashing quartet of British Cochran fans—The Who—would make a worldwide hit and rock radio staple of the song. Other aspiring British musicians would take Ed and his music to heart, including the Beatles, the Rolling Stones, and Rod Stewart. He would even later affect those too young to have seen or heard Ed during his heyday; the direct rawness of his music and his simmering rebellion would ultimately inspire even punk rock revolutionaries like the Sex Pistols.

In the U.S., Eddie immediately hit the road in support of "Summertime Blues," playing concerts and making regional radio and television appearances across the country. In August he worked his way back from a TV appearance in Baltimore, Maryland, to appear at the Dick Clark–hosted "All-Star Record Hop" in Minneapolis with Jack Scott, Duane Eddy, Dale Hawkins, Bobby Hendricks, and Jody Reynolds, with whom Ed often talked about the Bible, God, and things spiritual.

Jody can remember a long conversation about spirituality on a flight to San Francisco. Johnny Burnette, the only guy Jody ever saw who was more afraid of flying than he was, was also on that flight and near tears with fright. "I shouldn't be afraid to fly because I'm covered by Jesus," Jody reasoned.

"Yeah," Ed chimed in, "I'm not afraid to fly, but I keep covered by Jesus 'cause I pray all the time."

But Eddie would never let anyone catch him praying, Jody noticed, although Ed told his pal he prayed all the time. Jody could see an intensely spiritual side to my uncle, who was raised as a Methodist. Not Hollywood new era, or New Age, or anything like that. Just plain old Christian spirituality. Whether he was stone sober or had had a couple, Ed believed strongly in Jesus Christ, Jody saw. Eddie believed in heaven. And he thought he was going there. "I fool around a lot and get in trouble," he once confessed to Jody. "But not a night goes by that I don't thank the Lord for my success."

It was back to the East Coast in September, stopping in Washington, DC, for a stint on WTTG's *Milt Grant Show* with Paul Anka, then on to more package tours in October, the first spotlighting Bobby Darin, Frankie Avalon, Clyde McPhattter, Connie Francis, the Coasters, Buddy Holly and the Crickets, Dion and the

Belmonts, and others; the second including Ritchie Valens, Eddie Fontaine, Rod McKuen, Jody Reynolds, and Troyce Key, whom Eddie had backed at a Warner Brothers session that summer during his continuous work as a studio musician for hire.

On one of these trips to the East Coast, Jerry had invited Sharon along. The manager was trying to foster a writing relationship between his star singer and his successful songwriter. Ed didn't appreciate Jerry's inviting Sharon, Jerry told me, because Ed felt her presence would cramp his style with the ladies. Ed simply didn't want Jerry making decisions for him regarding the female company he kept.

So Jerry was often left to escort Sharon around, and she wound up needing his help more than anyone had expected. In an effort to make herself more appealing to her major crush Ed, Sharon had left her glasses back home in Hollywood. Without them she was blind as a bat. Jerry recalled that in New York City, he was showing Sharon the sights one day when they passed by the mighty United Nations building. Sharon's eyes were so bad that when Jerry pointed the UN out to her, she couldn't even make it out. Another time, at the Park Sheraton Hotel, Jerry pointed Sharon out to the management, saying, "She's with us." The hotel staff lifted their eyebrows in surprise. After a few moments it dawned on Jerry; Sharon—dressed fairly provocatively in high heels and a tight skirt and blindly bumbling around without her glasses—looked a bit like a ditsy hooker.

On the same trip, at another hotel, Sharon was accosted by a house security guard who actually did mistake her for a prostitute. He came on to her pretty intensely, forcing his way into her room and threatening her. Terrified, Sharon rang Jerry's room for help. Eddie and Guybo were with Jerry at the time, and he ordered them to Sharon's room as fast as they could get there, telling them some security guy was assaulting Sharon. Ed was there in a flash, burst through the door, and floored the guard as they struggled. The guard tried to escape down the stairwell; Ed knocked him down the flight of stairs just as Jerry was coming up. Jerry held down the guard, who was begging for mercy and pleading for them to let him go. He didn't want to lose his job, he whimpered. Finally, Ed and

Jerry confirmed who he was, and eventually they let him go. Of course, Eddie coming to her rescue only magnified my uncle's hero status in Sharon's heart. But it also demonstrated the existence of some kind of relationship growing between the two—if only one of protector and protected at that point.

Ed's fancy, in fact, was fairly fickle at that stage in his young life. One night stands or a different woman in many a town were not uncommon for Ed. And the fruit of such commitment-less unions would come back to haunt both Ed and the family.

During one stay in Pittsburgh for a radio interview, Eddie got together with a young usherette from the Fulton Theater, a downtown movie house. She had seen Eddie's films and was a fan. She had called into the radio station during the interview and she and Eddie arranged to meet afterwards at his hotel, the Carlton House. Ed had asked if she might bring a friend for Jerry Capehart, but at the last minute, the friend couldn't come. So the young woman decided to go by herself. At the hotel she met Jerry, but he soon left, and she and Ed were alone together. Nine months later the young woman, who swore to be a virgin before her evening with Eddie, gave birth to a daughter.

When she phoned Eddie to tell him that he had a beautiful blonde daughter with green eyes who looked just like him, he denied even knowing her, let alone ever being with her. The woman hired an attorney. He contacted Ed but received the same response. He told his client that she had a very tenuous case, as it was basically her word against Ed's, since, in those days, there was no definitive paternity-testing technology available.

The young woman was devastated. In the '50s, you just didn't get yourself pregnant. She panicked, then wound up marrying her boyfriend, who raised the girl as his own. As part of the arrangement with her boyfriend, the woman agreed to put his name on her daughter's birth certificate instead of Ed's. The girl would, for all intents and purposes, be his child, and the woman also agreed that she would not have any contact with the Cochran family or ever tell her daughter of her paternity. After Eddie died, the young woman lived in constant fear that the Cochran family, seeking to hold onto a little piece of Ed, would come to take her daughter away. She would hardly let her little girl out of the house.

Eventually the girl learned of her paternity, and in recent years she made contact with the family. Another woman claiming to be Eddie's offspring has also come forward. Since there is now no sample from which to extract Ed's DNA to establish if, indeed, these women are his children, both women agreed to the next best thing, a comparison of their own DNA to determine if they could possibly be related. The results were impressive. There is a 99.98 percent probability that these two women—from different cities and different families, who heretofore had never known each other, whose mothers swore that Eddie was their father—are sisters. What this means for the Cochran family—emotionally, financially—is still being sorted out. But apparently Ed left a human as well as musical legacy.

To accompany him on short tours and his club dates in southern California, Ed began using Dot recording act Dick D'Agostin and the Swingers, who frequently backed a vast array of rock 'n' roll artists visiting the area, such as Johnny Otis, the Penguins, Jimmy Clanton, Jerry Wallace, Freddy Cannon, Jan and Dean, Bobby Vee, Skip and Flip, Sam Cooke, Ed Townsend, Ritchie Valens, Jack Scott, Jesse Belvin, Johnny Burnette, Trini Lopez, Lou Rawls, P. J. Proby, the Teddy Bears, Big Jay McNeely, and the Champs. Eddie's intense touring schedule with other acts allowed him to hear some fantastic bands, and he'd decided he needed a band of his own. He was a huge fan of Fats Domino's group, and Little Richard's combo simply knocked Eddie out. Both bands were incredibly tight and grooved together so naturally, as is the case with most ensembles who play together constantly. With a seasoned band, all sorts of arrangements and improvisation can arise that just aren't possible with a pick-up band.

Eddie wanted this same tight and cohesive sound. He wanted a group of musicians with whom to work exclusively, like Gene Vincent's Blue Caps and Buddy Holly's Crickets, like Fats Domino's and Little Richard's backing groups. So he set about assembling a more permanent backing band. Of course, his longtime friend and associate Guybo Smith was first choice for bass. On drums, Ed chose Gene Riggio from the Swingers, who'd become Liberty label mates. Pianist Jim Stivers was handpicked from a Long Beach nightclub, and saxophonist Jimmy Seals, later of '70s-rocking Seals and Crofts fame, also came aboard.

But the lineup changed often—advertisements around this period have Ed playing with everyone from "His Orchestra" to the "Swingsters" to the "Summertime Blues Boys," and by the end of the summer of 1959 Ed's band would be called the Hollywood Swingers—and it wasn't truly cemented until late summer when Guybo, newly married, decided to give up his road work. Ed asked pianist Jim Stivers if he would play bass, recruiting Dick D'Agostin for keyboard duties, plus the Swingers' Gene Riggio on drums, Paul Kaufman on sax, and Larry D'Agostin on rhythm guitar.

Dick played piano, but he could play guitar as well. He'd picked up the second instrument because the pianos that were provided by promoters and venues were typically out of tune and unreliable. They'd often be a quarter-tone sharp, making it tough for any vocalist who was already singing at the top of his range. From his first gigs with my uncle, Dick enjoyed working with Ed, who seemed so supremely confident with that 6120 in his hands. D'Agostin immediately found what so many other people have said of Ed to be true, that Eddie was such a tremendous talent—he played with such authority and intensity—that he made any musician want to play better. Dick also admired Ed's easy rapport with people.

Packed into a 1959 Ford Country Squire station wagon signed for by Jerry Capehart on the heels of the great success of "Summertime Blues"—Jerry found it perplexing that the Cochran family was unwilling to sign for Eddie—and hauling their gear in a U-Haul trailer behind it, Ed and his band headed for Montana, the first stop of a Midwest tour. Gene remembered that they were driving down the road with Jimmy at the wheel when Jimmy turned to Ed and said, "I guess now is as good a time as any to tell you. I don't play bass." He told Ed that he didn't even know how to play guitar, let alone bass, and that he didn't even have a bass guitar to bring along.

"Stop this son of a bitch!" Ed said, as Jimmy quickly brought the car to a squealing halt.

"Get out of the car, Stivers!" Ed demanded. A cowering Jimmy got out of the car and walked across the street as Ed got out of the passenger side. Expecting Jimmy to join him, Ed looked around for his reluctant bass player.

"Stivers!" he roared.

"Yeah?" Jimmy yelled from across the road.

"Get your ass over here!" Ed commanded. Jimmy did. Ed told him how it was going to be. "By the time we get to the gig, you will know how to play bass," he told Jimmy.

A bass was quickly purchased at the next town and Ed spent the rest of the drive teaching Stivers the basics. Stivers marked the neck of the bass with tape indicating all the fret positions. The first night, Jimmy tore his hands up from playing the foreign instrument. He grew blisters on top of broken blisters and was bleeding in some places. After Stivers's shaky debut performance, Dick D'Agostin made a suggestion. "Why don't we just make it easy and put Stivers on piano and me on bass?" he asked. So Ed quickly switched Jimmy back to keys and put Dick on bass, an instrument he could also play.

D'Agostin and the guys played a wide variety of places with Ed—flatbed trucks, on top of drive-in theater snack bars, on the pitcher's mound of a baseball field in Texas, on Indian reservations in the Southwest, in Quonset huts, at armories, women's clubs, and VFW halls, as well as elegant theaters and auditoriums. Crowd sizes varied, Dick remembers, at times venues being so empty one could shoot a cannonball through them and never hit any one—and at others the halls were packed with thousands of people. Ed and his band never knew exactly what to expect or how good a promoter was going to be.

Ed and the group played a big loop through the Dakotas, across the Midwest, and down through Texas and Oklahoma. One week they'd be freezing, the next they'd need short sleeves. But Eddie always made it fun for his players. He was intense and had a real drive, yet there would always be some practical joke brewing. When Ed was back in Los Angeles, he and Dad would both cop the Kingfish tone of voice and joke together about whatever was happening. It would keep people in stitches. One of them would start it, Dad or Ed, just a normal conversation, but in the Kingfish voice. It didn't matter what the conversation was about—they would do it in that voice and have friends like Johnny Rook rolling on the floor in guffaws. On and on they would go—Johnny would just sit there and wait for the next line to come out. It didn't have to be funny, it was the diction, the way they said it; it would have your sides splitting. Dad and Ed also used to do this thing where they would flap their lips with a "B" sound on just about any word. They'd say, "YaBBBBees, yaBBBBees," instead of "Yes, yes"—sort of a cross between Daffy Duck and Kingfish.

Eddie seemed always up for a good time, always looking for ways to make people laugh, but when playing, Dick notes, Eddie kept himself focused—and he always made the music fantastic.

From 1955 to 1957, Dick D'Agostin was the associate editor of *Modern Teen* and of *Dig* magazine, for which he wrote a dance column. He'd landed the job because in addition to his musical talent, he was also a rock 'n' roll dance champion in the state of California. All of the Swingers, in fact, were accomplished dancers, and it was their dance abilities—plus Dick's connections through *Dig*—that landed Dick and Gene Riggio in the Gene Vincent film *Hot Rod Gang*. Dancing became such an important part of the Swingers' live act, in fact, that once Dave Shriver joined the band, they incorporated a swing dance segment for Gene and Dave into Eddie's show. The young, dance-rabid crowds ate it up, and later, dance contests became quite popular at the local clubs and teen canteens. Swinging, jiving couples would compete all over Los Angeles and Orange counties, with the best kids turning up on TV dance shows.

Despite his early successes, Eddie was still reluctant to play the role of rock 'n' roll star. Dick remembers one time when Eddie had an interview planned with one of the local radio stations, but for some reason didn't want to do it. Dick knew the powerful influence deejays could have on a young talent's career. In those days radio was a different industry. It was alive and vibrant. The deejays had personality and cast their own signatures on their programs. They had the power to break a new artist because they believed in him, becoming part of an artist's team. Many deejays were so devoted to the music that they were almost part of the band—they partied with the musicians, kept the same crazy hours, and shared the same passion for the music—unlike today, with the conglomerate corporate head dictating what will or will not be played. Today's music industry is flooded with accountant and lawyer types without the same vibrant and magical appreciation for the art.

In Ed's day, many times the local radio station was a small frame house on the outskirts of town, easily recognizable by the transmission tower nearby. After so many tours, the musicians tended to get to know some of the deejays. A few times, in fact, Dick showed up unannounced at radio stations and crawled through a window to surprise whoever was on the air—scaring the hell out of a few of them.

Not wanting Eddie to miss any opportunity to market himself, Dick encouraged Eddie to keep the radio commitment he was so intent on blowing off. But Eddie rebuffed Dick, telling him that if it was that important to him, then Dick should do the interview. Since Dick had spent a fair bit of time around Eddie and knew quite a bit about him and his career, he thought he could pull it off. The interview went off without a hitch. Later, the deejay arrived at the show with a couple of ladies, bragging about having met Eddie earlier that evening. When Dick introduced Eddie as "the pride of Liberty Records," the deejay, with jaw dropped to the floor, realized he'd been had.

When Dick D'Agostin was drafted, Stivers assembled a new version of the Hollywood Swingers for Ed; the 1959 version included veteran drummer Gene Riggio, tenor saxophonist Mike Henderson, guitarist and baritone saxophonist Mike Deasy, and bassist Don Meyer.

Meyer would quit after only one week, following some band shenanigans on the road. Henderson, Deasy, and Meyer were sharing a room in a hotel on a hill. The two Mikes were entertaining some girls, while Meyer was trying to get some shut-eye on a roll-away bed. The mischievous Mikes decided to fold up the bed—with Meyer still in it—and roll it down the hall. Before they knew it, the bed was rolling down the hill. As the bed flew down the incline with Meyer kicking and screaming within it, legs sticking out one side, hands and head out the other—Jim Stivers ran to get Ed. "You gotta see this!" he told him.

Ed arrived just in time to see the bed crash headfirst into the curb, startling the hotel gardener. With Meyer's legs kicking on one end of the bed and his hands flailing on the other, the gardener finally managed to open the bed and free the flustered bassist. Meyer sprinted up the hill back up to the hotel. "I quit! I quit!" he raged. "I don't need this shit!" Dave Shriver was hired to take Meyer's place, and this lineup would accompany Ed on most all of his tours and TV appearances, plus recording sessions, from mid-1959 on.

In addition to playing the Troyce Key tracks, in the summer of 1958 Ed had also played on cuts for Bob Denton and Jerry Capehart, who'd scored a one-off deal for himself with the Dot label as Jerry Neal. In September 1958, when Liberty launched subsidiary label Freedom, Eddie contributed arrangements, guitar, and even bass to several of the upstart imprint's releases, including Jerry Capehart–produced singles by Johnny Burnette and the Four Dots. In addition to Ed and Sharon, Capehart at that time was also managing Burnette (formerly of the Rock 'n' Roll Trio, responsible for rockabilly gems like "Rockabilly Boogie" and "Train Kept a Rollin'"), the Four Dots, and actor and fledgling rock 'n' roll singer John Ashley.

How to follow Ed's strongest hit to date was of no doubt a prime concern to Liberty Records. Eddie and Jerry had been toying with a tune tentatively titled, "Let's Get Together," which, like

"Summertime Blues," relied on an infectious guitar hook and whose lyrics were a lively slice of rebellious teenage life, my favorite line being "… and the house'll be a-shakin' from our bare feet slappin' on the floor!" It seemed a perfect piece for Eddie's next single, so on October 10, 1958, drummer Earl Palmer was again recruited, along with Guybo on bass and Ray Johnson on piano, to join Ed at Goldstar. Again, Eddie assembled the track in layers, combining his newly defiant vocals, lashings of acoustic guitar, Guybo's locomotive electric bass, plus tambourine hits instead of handclaps to emphasize the beat.

"Let's Get Together" was good but didn't quite seem complete. Inspired, Eddie returned to the microphone and recorded another set of vocals, this time replacing the "Let's get together" that ended each verse with the more forceful "C'mon everybody," taken from the tune's opening line, "Well, c'mon everybody and let's get together tonight." The track was sped up just a hair to obtain a more raucously rocking effect, the title was changed to "C'mon Everybody," and Eddie had yet another hit—soon to be a rock classic—on his hands. Backed with the rock-a-ballad "Don't Ever Let Me Go," recorded in July at the RCA studio in Hollywood, "C'mon Everybody" was released the same month it was recorded.

"Eddie Cochran, the man responsible for the year's biggest 'summer' hit, 'Summertime Blues,' could have a huge fall-winter click in his follow-up offering 'C'mon Everybody,'" opined one reviewer. "Spirited rocker with Eddie assisting himself with some sensational guitar work. This lad is gonna stay in the big-time." "Side has a lot of drive and could grab coins," mused another. And though "C'mon Everybody" did climb to a respectable Number 35 on the charts, it was hardly the follow-up smash all had been anticipating, despite Liberty's best promotional efforts and Ed's live and televised appearances, including a slot on *American Bandstand* on November 24.

The single fared much better on the other side of the Atlantic, however, cresting to Number 6 in the United Kingdom after its January 1959 release. "C'mon Everybody" would later become a rock 'n' roll classic—providing the sound track for a Levi's jeans commercial in the late 1980s, and performed by countless rock acts, including U2.

Eddie returned to Goldstar before the year was out to record another destined-to-be-classic gem, "Nervous Breakdown." Co-penned with Mario Roccuzzo, an aspiring songwriter who worked at a Los Angeles music store that Eddie frequented, the tune evolved after a couple of beers at the apartment of a mutual friend, Corey Allen, best known for playing the character Buzz in the James Dean flick *Rebel Without A Cause*.

With a tipsy Roccuzzo feeding him lyrics, Eddie hammered out the song, another perfect sonic capsule of teen angst. As Eddie crafted it at Goldstar, "Nervous Breakdown," with its propulsive acoustic guitar figures, forceful bass, and winkingly demented vocal quality—Ed's sly sense of humor in full play—seemed a natural next single, the capper to Ed's "tough teen" trilogy. But for whatever reason, Liberty kept it in the can.

As 1958 drew to a close, flamboyant disc jockey Alan Freed— credited with popularizing the term "rock 'n' roll" with his 1952 "Moon Dog House Rock 'n' Roll Party" radio show—hosted an eleven-day concert extravaganza at the Loew's State Theatre in New York. Eddie joined an all-star bill that included Frankie Avalon, Chuck Berry, Bo Diddley, Gino and Gina, Jackie Wilson, Jo-Ann Campbell, Jimmy Clanton, Harvey and the Moonglows, Baby Washington, the Cadillacs, the Flamingos, the Nu-Tornados and Crests, Ed Townsend, and Inga. The first six days of the show were headlined by Johnny Ray; the Everly Brothers topped the final five.

Jerry and Sharon also went to New York. Although the press had already all but dubbed Ed and Sharon a couple, playing off the professional relationship of boy star and his girl songwriter, no romance had blossomed from the pair's moments together. Until New York. For Sharon, capturing Eddie had become her life's work. Her every waking moment was consumed with ardent thoughts of the handsome young singer with the chiseled jaw and deep-set eyes. She'd relentlessly pursued him—showing up at all his personal appearances, blowing her savings on eye-catching fashions, even bleaching her naturally very dark hair to an attention-grabbing platinum blonde. Frankie Avalon and some of the other young stars asked her out. But nothing seemed to work on Eddie. Until New Year's Eve.

Eddie threw a big party in his suite at the Sheraton while in New York. Everyone was there: Buddy Holly and the Crickets, the Everly Brothers, Buddy Knox. Alone in her hotel room, Sharon received a call from Guybo. Eddie would like her to drop by his soiree. Crushed that Ed didn't even think enough of her to invite her himself, Sharon scrubbed all the makeup from her face, brushed her hair into braids, bagged her fancy fashions for an old pair of Levi's, a sweatshirt, and tennis shoes, and reluctantly joined the party. As the last guest was departing, Eddie asked Sharon to stay, he wanted to talk to her.

When it was just the two of them, Sharon remembered, Eddie looked over at her and asked, "Are you in love with me?"

Sharon recalled that she almost died of embarrassment. She wanted to say, "Well, what makes you think something like that? I've only chased you for two years." Flustered, she instead replied indignantly, "You know, that's a very embarrassing thing to ask someone, and I resent that you would—"

But she said he interrupted her tirade with a simple, "Well, you sure better be because I'm sure in love with you."

No dates, never kissed, never held hands, never even shared a soda. Sharon was stunned. Eddie came over and sat next to her. And then they kissed for the very first time. For Sharon, it was like something straight out of the movies; she could hear bells ringing clear across Manhattan.

Sharon's recollections of her experiences with Ed fuelled a "Did Ed love Sharon?" debate. She had a way of remembering those days with a child-like charm, painting a world of rainbows and dreams fulfilled. Her stories sounded like movie script stuff penned for Disney, with perfect scenes perfectly played out. No surprise: a good songwriter at her best is a good storyteller. And Sharon knew how to craft a story. That does not, however, diminish the sincerity of her experiences.

"Will you marry me?" she remembered Eddie asking her.

"You bet," she answered. Then her curiosity got the best of her. "When did you first know that you were in love?" she asked, dying to know which of her fabulously fashionable, extravagantly expensive outfits had done the trick.

"The first time I ever saw you," he replied.

She said she had to fight her compulsion to beat him over the head with her shoe.

"You made me chase you for two years! I made a fool of myself in front of everybody in the industry!" she fumed with exasperation.

"I had to be real sure," she recalled him telling her, a mischievous twinkle in his eye. And that was it. Eddie and Sharon were now officially an item.

In addition to his radio work and live package shows, Alan Freed was also promoting rock 'n' roll around Hollywood: in 1956 he appeared in *Rock Around the Clock*, a slightly fictionalized account of how he discovered western-swing-turned-rock 'n' roll act Bill Haley and the Comets. By the time of the New York all-star concert, Freed had wangled a deal with the Hal Roach studios in California to produce *Johnny Melody*, a rock 'n' roll movie featuring several of the artists playing the Loew's State Theatre. Footage—which would eventually open the film—was shot, depicting Ed performing alongside Chuck Berry, Ritchie Valens, Jackie Wilson, Jo-Ann Campbell, Harvey and the Moonglows, the Cadillacs, and the Flamingos.

Back in California on January 17, 1959, Ed headed to Goldstar to record material for the *Johnny Melody* sound track. His newly intense sound continued to evolve with the latest Cochran/Capehart collaboration, "Teenage Heaven," a clever adaptation of the country standard "Home On The Range." With canny lyrics once again taken straight from the teen experience—expressing every adolescent's wish for less school, no hassles, and grown-up goodies like a phone of one's own—the tune was conceptually in line with Ed's run of "reality teen" rockers.

But whereas "Summertime Blues" and "C'mon Everybody" centered around a distinctively rhythmic guitar riff, "Teenage Heaven's" boogieing sound, with its jangling Chuck Berry-esque guitar intro, was more expansive, its slicker production punched up with saxophone honks and wails from Plas Johnson. Johnson similarly contributed to the attitude-dripping "My Way," swapping stinging solo licks with Ed, who played the roughneck rebel who snarls that he was "born a tiger, I always had my way, nobody's going to change me, this or any other day."

The affecting ballad "I Remember"—like "Teenage Heaven" and "My Way," another Ed and Jerry co-composition—also evidenced Eddie's continuing development as a vocalist. Sung with great poignancy, the cinematically melancholy tune, strummed on the Martin guitar belonging to my Uncle Bill, Ed's brother, was his finest take on a ballad yet. The acoustic also figured into the crafting of "Rock 'n' Roll Blues"—a mediocre piece of pop in no way befitting the newly forceful Cochran musical sensibility—which Eddie gussied up with some studio trickery. Overdubbing the guitar atop a slower rendition of the song, the final result, when played back at normal speed, gave the tinkling sonic impression of a harpsichord.

"Teenage Heaven" and "I Remember" were selected for inclusion in *Johnny Melody*, so Liberty paired the two songs as a single and released it later that month. Although Ed was filmed singing both songs, the "I Remember" footage was ultimately edited out of the movie, issued not long after the single under the new title *Go, Johnny, Go!* A fairly typical rock 'n' roll exploitation flick with a flimsy story line following the travails of singing star-to-be Johnny Melody, played by Jimmy Clanton, the film also starred Alan Freed and Sandy Stewart and was redeemed by its many musical performances. Eddie, clad in a cardigan, turned in a rather low-key, if typically confident, performance of "Teenage Heaven" in the film, at one point removing his guitar to dance with it.

Eddie hit the promo trail yet again in early 1959, working both "C'mon Everybody," which still seemed to have some legs, and "Teenage Heaven." On January 17, he was in snowy Cincinatti,

Ohio, playing an appreciation concert for local radio and television personality Bob Braun. More than sixty-five hundred kids braved the city's snow-bound streets to see Ed, along with June Valli, Jerry Vale, Jack Scott, Jackie Dee, Dale Wright, and Bill Parsons. In an interview after the show, Ed reaffirmed his dedication to his genre, saying, "No other music is closer to the people or more expressive than rock 'n' roll."

Ed had flown to Cincinatti from Philadelphia, going in with fellow rocker Jack Scott to rent a small twin-engine Commander. Jerry Capehart was traveling with Ed, Scott's brother was accompanying him. It was extraordinarily cold and the passengers shivered on the floor, trying to sleep. At one point, Scott woke up to find Jerry in the seat next to the pilot. There was some problem with the heat in the plane and Jerry, a former wartime pilot, was trying to assist, scratching ice from the instruments. The Commander pilot made an emergency landing at a small airport, but as there were no services open there, he took off again. It was so frigid in the tiny plane that the passengers' body heat kept fogging up the instruments. Finally, the pilot, veins bulging in the back of his neck, put down in a small airfield, frosted with drifts of blowing snow. The group, exhausted from fright, spent the night there, sleeping on benches inside the building.

Television appearances including another *Bandstand* gig in March, concert performances, the radio circuit—Eddie worked tirelessly behind his latest disc. Touring was a constant, with the musicians trekking as far north as Canada and as far south as Texas, with particular attention paid to the Midwest, an especially strong sales territory for rock 'n' roll records. The pace on the road was brutal, the group having just enough time after leaving one job to drive all night long to arrive at the next, set up the stage, change into performance clothes, and close the show. After the show was over, they changed back into their street clothes, put their instruments in their cases, piled the gear back into the station wagon, and then tore out to the next gig, arriving just in time to do it over again.

The group rarely slept in a motel; the car more often than not served as their motel on wheels. They bathed in the bathroom sinks at each venue. When they were afforded the luxury of a motel, it was three or more guys to a room. They'd attempt to steam the wrinkles from their show clothes by running hot showers. One day Gene Riggio had tried to steam the group's "steel" jackets, their smart sport coats of silver lamé. "What's that on the back of your coat?" Jim Stivers asked him later. It was rust.

Whenever Ed and the band hit the road, they always made sure to pick up Gene Riggio last. His mom was a gifted cook, and she always sent the boys on their way with bellies bulging with spaghetti. It became a tradition. They all loved her sauce; she never used hamburger, she stripped the beef from a roast.

After they'd eaten, they'd all pile into the station wagon, Ed always taking the front passenger seat, where he'd put his feet up on the dashboard and doze. Dave Shriver would usually do all the driving, earning him the nickname "Driver Shriver." Gene Riggio would lie in the back behind Dave and Ed, followed by road manager Denny Thompson and Mike Deasy, with Jim Stivers and Mike Henderson in the very back near the tailgate, next to the ice chest. Ed always wanted a can of beer when he woke up. With seven young men shoehorned into a station wagon, privacy was necessarily a non-issue. Belching, farting, illnesses—it was all shared. Even parasites were passed around; just about all the guys contracted crabs a few times on their concert jaunts.

When I first hit the road as a professional guitarist, I quickly found out what Eddie's life as a touring musician must have been like. On one tour with Kindred, we drove from Chicago to Los Angeles with no hotel stops in between. Straight through. There were seven of us dozing in a station wagon. At one point, I was awakened by a loud noise to my left. I looked up and saw the massive tire of an eighteen-wheeler scraping against the side of our car. Our bass player, at the wheel, had nodded off for a few seconds and had drifted into the side of the tractor trailer.

One night with the Flying Burrito Brothers we had to drive five hundred miles after a gig in a raging snowstorm. We pulled in to town in time to set up the gear, do a quick sound check, jump in the shower, grab a bite, and play the show. Then we packed up, turned around and drove five hundred miles back, pretty much the same way we came, right back through what the blizzard had piled up for us. We barely made the next show. Our pedal steel guitarist "Sneaky" Pete Kleinow usually drove, while we played cards. I'd deal. The bets were small, but they would really build up. Sneaky would usually wind up losing more often than not; driving and playing was a real handicap for him, but the adrenaline probably kept us alive.

We would play cards till we got too tired, then we'd sleep. Every now and then one of us would check on Sneaky to make sure he was doing all right. We often did twenty-nine cities in thirty days. Many times the hotels were not the best—one of the guys even got scabies once. It's a wonder we all didn't get them because we were in such close quarters all the time. You really get to know each other on those tours. Still, it's a rough way to go, as I'm sure Eddie quickly realized.

One night when Eddie and the band were on the road, the band got busted for possession of bennies, the pep pills Benzedrine and Dexedrine. Several of the band members had been using them, as did many of the traveling musicians of the day. Rushing onto the stage straight off a several-hundred-mile haul from their last gig, they'd need a little pick-me-up to perform at their best. Although none of the band members recalls seeing Eddie using the uppers, Gene Vincent bassist Bill Mack remembers that Eddie turned him on to bennies while the two groups were playing together in Canada, along with Bill Justis, the Champs, and others. Stivers bought the stuff. And Eddie would say, "Hey Jim, give this guy something," when a fellow musician needed to wake up to get through a job or stay awake to drive.

As Stivers solidified his position with the band, it was natural to have him assume road-manager duties. A natural boxer and brawler, he was a streetwise kind of guy. He taught the fellows in the band a few techniques, just in case any trouble presented itself. He even gave them a code phrase—"Hey, Rube!"—to use for trouble, which would bring everyone running to sort out whatever came up. The band had gathered at Jimmy's house one time, Gene Riggio recalls—Mike Deasy, Mike Henderson, Gene, and Dave Shriver. "In case anything happens on the road," Jim told the fellows, "I'm gonna show you a few things."

Actually, Jim was no stranger to trouble. Jimmy told me that at one point he was doing some dirty work for some mob types. He'd follow his prey into the men's room, and once the guy was at the urinal and definitely occupied, Jimmy would grab him by the head and slam him into the porcelain in front of him, knocking the guy out cold. Then he'd give the sap a beating he'd never forget. It was supposed to get the poor guy's attention for the people to whom he owed money. They wanted his full attention next time they talked to him, and Jimmy's handiwork usually did the trick. Jimmy traveled in some pretty tough circles, so for him, something as simple as obtaining controlled substances was a piece of cake.

I remember when I was fourteen and playing in the band Benny and the Midnighters, who later became Thee Midnighters of regional hits "Land of a Thousand Dances" and "Whittier Boulevard." We were playing some pretty rough areas—East Los Angeles, Boyle Heights. One night I was stunned to see one of the local guitar players shooting up with heroin. Just right there, out in the parking lot, in full view of everyone. The other guys in the band, who were all older than me, pulled me away and tried to distract me, but I was shocked.

I'd never used drugs. I was scared of them, truth be known. Bennies, reds or downers, pot—they were all very popular while I was coming up. One night in Salt Lake City my band had been up thirty-six hours straight. We were really beat. The rest of the guys took some uppers for the show, then after our performance we all hit the sack, exhausted. Next morning I woke up refreshed; the rest of the guys were completely haggard. They didn't sleep well at all after the beanies. To me, it was just another confirmation not to get involved with the stuff. I didn't think I'd like what I would become if I got involved with drugs. I was afraid I'd lose control. And I didn't want anything to interfere with my life the way prescription drugs and alcohol had done in Mom and Dad's lives. I saw how out of control my family had been. I saw how different my dad became when he drank too much. Later I saw how his alcoholism killed him and how it had helped to destroy his life. And so, to this day, I've never done drugs, and I don't drink alcohol.

Audiences across the country adored Ed and the band, though some reviewers, try as they may, just didn't get it. "Every hipster in town was hopping last night at the rock 'n' roll dance featuring Eddie Cochran and the Summertime Blues Boys," wrote a Topeka Daily Capitol reporter in July 1959.

> As far as those jumping teenagers are concerned the night was way out. But Eddie is different, you know, like I mean, he is in solid, a real cool cat.
>
> The 21-year-old singer and his band are on a tour of the Midwest and appeared at the Municipal Auditorium Friday.
>
> Cochran also made a short appearance at the Jayhawk Theater Friday. His latest movie, *Go, Johnny, Go*, in which he is a guest artist, opens there July 23.
>
> The young Oklahoman, who got his first role in *The Girl Can't Help It*, says he would rather perform rock 'n' roll music than any other kind.

"No other music is so close to the people. It let's [sic] them show their emotions."

Topeka teenagers gave vent to their emotions for sure.

The band stepped to the stage in a neat set of threads, which translated means in gold dinner jackets. With a yell of wild Indians, the kids grabbed their chairs and charged the stage.

Like it was crazy, dad, the snapping fingers, stomping feet and heads rolling back and forth, eyes closed, with the rhythm of a serpent ready to strike.

And did they dig Eddie Cochran?

"Oh, yes," sighed Paula Collins, 13. "He has been one of my favorites since his very first record, "Sitting [sic] in the Balcony."

Another avid admirer could only express her appreciation thusly: "Yeeeeoowwww!!"

Cochran opened with "Come on Everybody [sic]" and everybody did. Those who hadn't cooled it at the foot of the stage were rocking and rolling in the back.

Why they call it 'rock 'n' roll' came through at that hop—they rocked, full skirts flying, and they rolled, their heads, hips, and bodies.

Cochran winked at a feminine fan. She swooned. Her friends giggled enviously.

The young guitarist impressed this observer, uninitiated in jive and jargon, that he would never be a soothing crooner like Frank Sinatra. But neither is he an Elvis Presley.

He strummed his guitar vigorously. He sang, his head thrown back, at the top of his voice. His body shook, rattled, and rolled.

His singing and the music had a faint resemblance to a civilized form of hog calling. But perhaps we just aren't hip.

Another night while out on the road, Ed and the band played a show in the same town where there was a gas station robbery. The next morning, as the guys were heading out to the highway, they stopped to fill up the station wagon. Not long after they'd gotten back on the road, they were pulled over by police. Seems the gas station attendant, noting the huge wad of cash belted in rubber bands from which road manager Denny Thompson peeled off bills to pay for the gas, had called the cops, sure that the band was responsible for the robbery the night before.

Gene Riggio, who'd been sleeping on pillows in the back of the wagon, was petrified; Ed's .22 and his .45 Colt Buntline, which he carried with him at all times, were tucked deep underneath the pillows. That Buntline was a powerful and dangerous gun, Gene knew, as he'd shot it one time and never touched it again. (That one shot had been a virtual explosion, with lead, powder, and sparks flying everywhere, the earth-shaking blast downright deafening.) The cops cleared everyone out of the wagon and started making their search from the rear. Geno's spot was way up toward the front, and he remembers that they had the car configured so that the rear of the wagon was completely flat. He slept with his nose facing the back of the front seat, where the driver and Ed were sitting. Dave was next to him, Jimmy Stivers between the humps, and then Mike Deasy, Mike Henderson, and the ubiquitous beer chest. "Oh my God, don't let them find the guns, please don't let them find the guns," Geno prayed silently, as he didn't know whether Ed had permits for the weapons, and if he did, whether they were valid in that state. Often on their road trips they'd get off the side of the road and start shooting.

To Geno's relief, the police concluded their search, never finding the guns. The band's story had checked out, and after signing some autographs for the daughter of one of the officers, the guys were let go.

Daughters were a particular favorite of Eddie's while on the road. After one gig at the Surf Ballroom in Clear Lake, Iowa, Gene Riggio was coming out the backstage door when Eddie said in that Kingfish voice, "Now, Geno, you gots to go out there and you gots to get me a girl!" "Hey I'm Catholic, " Gene was thinking as he walked out the door, and just then, a beautiful chick approached. "Is Eddie back there?" she asked. "Sure, go right ahead," Gene said, grateful for the out to Eddie's request. He sent her in. "Geno, that was a fox!" Ed enthused later, never knowing that Gene didn't find her, she walked herself right in.

Audience response to Eddie in the live-concert setting was overwhelmingly positive, but from town to town there was always the odd troublemaker. Eddie took them in stride. At one snowy Midwest show—Gene remembered it as the Surf Ballroom in Clear Lake, Iowa, although Dave says it may have been somewhere in Kansas—Eddie admonished a heckler with, "Hey, buddy, come speak to me after the show. There's a lot of people who paid good money to be here." The burly malcontent decided to take Eddie up on his offer.

As the band was loading its gear back into the trailer, the heckler appeared. He was a big guy with bulging arms and a couple of buddies to back him up. He was wearing a white shirt with a white silk vest, white pants and white buckskin shoes—he looked like a glass of milk, according to Gene.

"Can I help you?" asked Jim Stivers, who was helping Dave Shriver pass equipment to Gene Riggio in the trailer.

"I'm gonna kick that kid's ass," the heckler said.

"Who?" Jim asked.

"That Cochran guy."

"He's not here," Jim told him.

"Don't gimme that shit," the heckler said, "Cochran's here and I'm gonna kick his ass."

Just then Ed, wearing his dark brown overcoat, walked around the front of the car.

"I'm Cochran," he told the troublemaker. "What can I do for you?"

"I'm gonna kick your ass," the bully hissed.

"Now wait a minute, are you sure I can't talk you outta this?" Ed calmly asked him.

"No way," the heckler frothed, "I'm gonna kick your ass!"

Within the blink of an eye from under his coat Ed whipped out the Buntline, muttered, "Well, I guess I'm gonna have to kill you," and proceeded to fire just to the right of the guy. Sparks flew from the muzzle—the shot sounded like a god damned cannon going off.

The color drained from the brute's face, and a dark yellow stain quickly spread across the front of his white trousers, down his pant leg, and into the snow; the heckler, frozen in his tracks, had pissed his pants.

Awed at what Eddie had just done, Dave began hastily tossing the cases into the trailer. "We gotta get outta here!" he shouted. "David, you're hitting me with this stuff!" Geno yelled back, ducking the flying gear. They finished loading and locked up the back; the band jumped into the car and tore out of the parking lot.

"You know what, Eddie?" Mike Deasy said after a few moments. "It's a good thing we left when we did."

"Why, Mike?" Ed asked.

"Because I was really startin' to get pissed," Mike winked.

When I was a kid, Granny used to let me take that Buntline up to Deep Creek to do some shooting. I used it to punch half-inch holes in old car hoods like they were made of cardboard. That gun really had a kick; it was so powerful. I've tried to tell people that that thing was dangerous—lead and powder came out everywhere from between the cylinder gap and the barrel. It sounded like a cannon—scary.

Johnny Rook remembers being frightened—after first being greatly amused—by Eddie's antics with the Buntline. Once when he and Ed were shooting up in the desert, Ed asked Johnny to put a can on his head. He wanted to do a little target practice. Johnny, as gleefully drunk as Eddie, thought it a splendid idea and happily complied, balancing a tin can on his noggin several yards away from Ed. "Stand still," Ed instructed his friend. "Okay," Johnny gladly obeyed. Then Ed pulled out the Buntline and took aim. Or tried to; Johnny can remember Ed waving his arm back and forth. "That's okay," Johnny thought to himself at the time, "Shoot that son of a bitch off my head!" Mercifully, Ed never did shoot the gun. Johnny never thought a thing about it—until he sobered up and realized just what could have happened out there in the desert. But he recalls the incident with chuckling fondness now, musing that if there is a God, he was looking after the two of them that day.

Reviews of "Teenage Heaven" were largely favorable, critics enthusing: "The chanter is at his r&r best as he contemplates all the pleasures found in a 'teen's paradise.'" "[A] contagious ditty that moves along at a dandy jump clip." "Cochran should coast to a high position on the charts with this strong side... it appears a sure winner." "This bumptious rebellion will capture the crowd under age twenty, when both life and melody are viewed simply, and beat and rhythm are a lot more important than grace and subtlety... good for dancing, hoping [sic] and swinging." Despite the critical raves, Ed's promotional efforts, and the release of *Go, Johnny Go!*, sales figures were not as enthusiastic: "Teenage Heaven" penetrated the *Billboard* charts for just a single week, reaching a dismal Number 99.

Also appearing in *Go, Johnny Go!* was seventeen-year-old singer Ritchie Valens, the first Hispanic rock star, with whom Eddie had developed a strong friendship on their shared concert bookings. The two often socialized offstage as well, indulging their mutual love of music and Mexican food. Valens grew up in the Los Angeles suburbs, and, like Eddie, was playing guitar by the time he was in junior high school. Also an ardent fan of Little Richard, Valens was discovered in 1958 by producer Bob Keane, who signed the guitarist to his Del-Fi label. Valens's first single, the brash "Come On Let's Go," made Number 42 on the charts. He'd recorded Sharon Sheeley's "Hurry Up," but it was the pensive "Donna" that took him to Number Two in 1959. The song's flip, "La Bamba," was equally beloved, and truly innovative, sung entirely in Spanish.

So when news hit on February 3, 1959 that Valens—along with another of Ed's pals, Buddy Holly—had been killed when their private plane crashed in the midst of a Midwest tour, Eddie was devastated. Holly and Valens—along with J.P. Richardson, aka the Big Bopper of "Chantilly Lace" fame—had appeared at the Surf Ballroom in Clear Lake, Iowa, as part of the Winter Dance Party

Tour, also featuring Dion and the Belmonts. Reticent to climb once more aboard the unheated tour bus in the frigid weather conditions, Holly chartered a tiny private plane to take him, along with Waylon Jennings and Tommy Allsup, who were backing Holly on the package show, to the next tour stop. At the last minute, Jennings surrendered his seat to Richardson, who was plagued with the flu. Valens won Allsup's seat in a coin toss. The plane went down shortly after takeoff. And teenagers around the globe grieved.

Publicly, Eddie attempted to funnel his grief into the recording of the song "Three Stars," a loving tribute to his fallen fellow rockers, which was penned by a young disc jockey at San Bernardino radio station KFXM. But, take after take, he was unable to get through the tune without breaking down in tears. He was eventually able to get a serviceable take in the can, but Liberty opted not to release it. The song would not be heard by Ed's fans until 1966, when it was released in the U.K., followed by an American release in 1972.

Privately, the deaths of Buddy Holly and Ritchie Valens took an immeasurable toll on Ed. Jerry had always been adamant about Eddie not flying the small charter planes so convenient for road-weary rock 'n' roll stars, practically forbidding him to ever step foot aboard "one of those Spam cans." As a former air force pilot, Jerry knew they were dangerous and flimsy, and that the pilots were often not the best. If only Eddie had warned Buddy. Now it was too late.

I remember I was on a gig when I heard about Ricky Nelson's plane going down in 1985. Andy Chapin, who'd played keyboards with me in Steppenwolf for a while, was also on that plane. He was a real sweet guy, and his sudden and needless death just tore me up. I called Granny from the gig to talk with her about it. If anyone could understand the pain of tragic loss, it would be Eddie's mom. Andy's death just brought up again all those wrenchingly sad feelings about losing Eddie.

Several years later I received a call from John Kay of Steppenwolf. My good friend Jerry Edmonton, drummer with the band, had been killed in a car accident, John told me. Following Andy Chapin's death, Jerry had gotten to know Andy's widow, and after a few years, they'd married. It was heartbreaking to me, not only losing Jerry but also watching what Andy's window had to go through, burying two husbands. The old familiar ache of Ed's death had returned.

I recently lost another old friend on TWA flight 800. A few days before, I was attending the Chet Atkins Appreciation Society convention in Nashville. I ran into my old friend Marcel Dadi. He was the "Chet Atkins of France," an amazing guitarist and a wonderful person. He said he wanted to talk to me, wanted to know if there was a time when we could get together. I invited him to dinner with some other friends later that night. He came by and spent about and hour and a half discussing my producing a CD of his work. He had heard some of the production work I did on some CDs for Adrian Legg, one of which had won "Best Acoustic Guitar Album of the Year" honors in *Guitar Player Magazine*. I was blown away with the offer; Marcel was an amazing talent. Chet himself had produced Marcel in the past, and it was an honor to be considered to work with him in that capacity. A few days after the convention I was making calls to prepare for the CD project when I heard the news on TV. Flight 800 to Paris had gone down. I had a sick feeling in my stomach remembering that Marcel wasn't leaving until a few days after the convention. Within a couple of hours I got a call from Michael O'Dorn, another great guitar player, who also had been at that dinner with Marcel and me. He confirmed my worst fears. Marcel was on that flight, and there were no survivors. I was simply devastated.

It was then, nearly four decades after Ed's death, I came to the realization—so simple it seems a cliché, but so incredibly painful to abide—that losing someone you care about is something you never, ever get over. You learn to live with it, to live around it, to bury it beneath the floorboards of your heart. But it is never completely gone.

Eddie knew this as well. With the passing of Buddy Holly and Ritchie Valens, my usually happy-go-lucky uncle was utterly devastated. He refused to listen to any of his late friends' records. For months he'd spend free moments holed up his room, playing the blues on his guitar. Granny was worried sick about him. She phoned Ed's pal Johnny Rook, who worked the graveyard shift at Douglas Aircraft in Culver City by night and pounded the Hollywood pavement looking for acting work by day. "I think we sure could use you right now," Granny told him.

Johnny went over to the house. He found Ed in his room. All the blinds were pulled, and Ed was sitting up against the top part of the bed, with a pillow behind him and the guitar on his lap. Johnny sat silently across from him on a chair. Ed just kept strumming his guitar, real soft—pickin' on it, pickin' on it, and pickin' on it—tears brimming his reluctant rock star eyes. After about twenty minutes, he put the Gretsch down. He walked over to Johnny, put his arms around him and hugged him. "Johnny," he said quietly, "if anything like this ever happens to me, I want you to take care of Shrimper."

Some time after Buddy and Ritchie were killed, Eddie showed up late for a recording session. The band had been waiting there for quite some time, on the studio's clock. Ed pulled up and Jerry ran over to him.

"Where have you been?" he asked.

Eddie was sitting in the station wagon with a beer between his legs, drunk.

"What does it matter, Dad?" Eddie muttered. "I won't be around long any way." Jerry sent Eddie home and cancelled the session.

8
Liberty

ON FEBRUARY 7, 1959, just four days after the deaths of Buddy Holly and Ritchie Valens, Eddie put on a relatively happy face and appeared on television's *Town Hall Party*, the Los Angeles–area musical variety show on which he and Hank Cochran had appeared in late April 1956. Joined by Dick D'Agostin and the Swingers—on this date comprised of Dick D'Agostin on piano and backing vocals, Paul Coffman on sax, Gene Riggio on drums, either Larry D'Agostin or Dave Oster on rhythm guitar—plus Guybo on bass, Eddie performed seven songs, both his own—"C'mon Everybody," which he sang twice, and "Summertime Blues"—plus his takes on "Have I Told You Lately That I Love You," "Don't Blame It on Me," Chuck Berry's "School Days," "Be Honest with Me," and "Money Honey."

April 2 found Eddie back at Goldstar, this time working on a locomotive instrumental that again borrowed that infectious Bo Diddley beat. Co-written with Jerry, the tune "Guybo" was named for Ed's longtime buddy and musical cohort. Liberty, in its attempts to position Eddie as a vocalist, obviously had no interest in issuing instrumentals from their answer to Elvis Presley, so the track would not see wax until late summer of 1959, when it was released by Silver Records. A new label owned by Sylvester Cross of American Music, to which both Ed and Jerry were still contracted, Silver may have been created for Ed's myriad other projects, with Cross being assured he'd get a piece of anything in which Ed had a hand.

Of course, any of Ed's work released on any label other than Liberty would have to be credited to another name, so the pseudonym the Kelly Four—probably a nod to our family's Irish heritage that would ultimately become the Hollywood Swingers' name—was chosen for the single. Ed produced both sides: the guitar-layered "Guybo," re-recorded on August 25, and its flip, "Strollin' Guitar," another textural instrumental with a twangy, almost western feel recorded August 26. It was an impressive instrumental debut for Ed—albeit under a fake name—and was critically well received.

Ed's interest in instrumentals is evidenced by his labors on several others throughout 1959, one titled "The Scream" after vocal overdubs were added to Ed's basic track in 1962 or '63; the drumless "Hammy Blues," reminiscent of "Guybo" and "Strollin' Guitar," which Ed co-composed with my dad; the Halloween-titled "Have an Apple Dearie," and "Jam Sand-Witch," both waxed in October, perhaps with a seasonal novelty release in mind; and "Fourth Man Theme," a rip on Anton Kara's "Third Man Theme." None of these tracks would ever be commercially available during Ed's lifetime.

Silver would release a second Kelly Four single in 1960, "Annie Has a Party," coupled with "So Fine, Be Mine," most likely recorded in late 1959 and produced by Ed. Ed also contributed to other Silver releases during late 1958 and 1959, including those by John Ashley and the Four Dots (recording under the fictitious moniker the Voices of Allah); Jerry Stone with the Four Dots; and Jewel Akens and Eddie Daniels, recording under their first names. For other labels, Ed continued to work as a session musician, turning up on Jay Johnson's "Walk the Dog" and Barry Martin's "The Willies" and "Minnie the Moocher" on Freedom, and on his pal Baker Knight's "Just Relax" for Coral. In 1959 he recorded aspiring songwriter Maurice Cash McCall's "Jelly Bean" and "Don't Bye Bye Baby Me," the backing tracks to which were released on the Era label, with a doo-wop vocal group added, and credited to the Tigers.

On April 23, 1959, Ed worked out a pair of tunes at a session at United Recorders. Penned for Ed by the husband and wife team of Bill and Doree Post, who also recorded for Crest Records,

"Weekend," with its femme backing chorus, could have easily slipped into the realm of fluffy pop. But fueled by Eddie's burning vocal—punctuated with his comical Kingfish-ish routine—and urgent, acoustic guitar chords, the insistent bass work of either Guybo or Dave Shriver, and Gene Riggio's driving drums, "Weekend" was yet another stellar addition to Ed's musical compendium of the teenage experience. Surprisingly, Liberty did not release the tune until after Ed's death. The doughy ballad "Think of Me," also recorded at the session, did suffer from the drippy female backing and could never be considered Ed's finest work.

For his next Liberty release, his tenth single for the label, Eddie recorded what would become yet another classic. Written by my dad and Sharon Sheeley, "Somethin' Else" chronicled the woes of a teen without a car cool enough to get the fine-looking girl. Dion of the Belmonts had actually inspired the song, Sharon remembered, when, spying Eddie and Sharon walking down the hall on their fateful New Year's Eve in New York City, he yelled out, "Hey, Cochran, she's somethin' else!" Sharon jotted the line down on a matchbook and wrote the song that same night. Aware that Eddie's idol was Little Richard, she thought she would be very clever and nick the drum riff from Richard's "Keep a-Knockin' But You Can't Come In." "He'll automatically have to like that one," Sharon thought of her masterpiece. As recorded by Ed at Goldstar on June 23, 1959, the tune was downright tough—brashly defiant vocals, propulsive bass, crashing drums, another rock 'n' roll triumph of spare intensity.

For years, Sharon was proud that she'd gotten away with her great drum riff theft. Then one day, after Eddie's death, a drummer friend sat her down and showed her that the two songs' beats were nothing alike. As keen a musician as Eddie was, he would've noticed in a second if it was the same riff, it dawned on Sharon. She had been miles away in her stab at the Richard riff, but in her head, she'd actually pulled it off.

There are other sides of the story, as well. According to Dave Shriver, Dad was pissed that Eddie had given Sharon part of "Somethin' Else." She didn't write it, he'd insisted. And then there's

Jerry's assertion that he wrote the last verse and simply didn't take credit for it. All of them—Dad, Sharon, Jerry—were great songwriters, and I wish they had sorted it out back then, instead of harboring resentments that festered for decades.

Liberty paired the track with "Boll Weevil," Eddie's likable take on the classic folksong, which he personalized with the concluding lyric, "If anybody should ask you who it was that sang this song, say a guitar picker from Oklahoma City with a pair of blue jeans on." The line only served to perpetuate lore that Ed was actually an Okie, not a Minnesotan, but it gave a rustic charm to the chorus-sweetened rock 'n' roll ditty on which Dick D'Agostin played piano. He remembered that he and the band would often do a session with Eddie, then wind up backing other people who happened to be in the studio that day. They did so many sessions, they lost count of who and what they did. Sometimes they would recognize something they'd hear on the radio as a tune they'd played on, having completely forgotten about the session, just one of countless many.

The single received favorable reviews, with *Billboard* opining that "Cochran could bounce back onto the charts with these strong efforts. 'Somethin' Else' is a moving rocker that is given a rhythmic chant. 'Boll Weevil' is a rockabilly adaptation of the traditional folk tune." "Somethin' Else"—which he performed on another *American Bandstand* appearance—did indeed put Ed back on the charts, where the single crested at Number 58 during its eight-week residency. In the U.K., however, the disc reached Number 22, making clear Ed's burgeoning fan base in England and environs.

On August 10, 1959, Ed was scheduled to appear on saxophonist Johnny Otis's televised musical variety show. The program, broadcast live, came on at 6 p.m. About 4:30 that afternoon, Ed swung by his pal Ronnie Ennis's house. He asked if Ronnie wanted to go with him down to the TV studio. Ronnie declined—he had some things to do—but assured Ed he'd catch him on the show. Ed took off. At 6 p.m., Ronnie turned on his television. Otis's show came on, and the announcer ran down the list of performers, including "special guest star Eddie Cochran." Ronnie watched the entire program—and no Eddie. He started to worry about his buddy—had something happened to Ed on the way to the studio?

Just as the show was ending, there was a knock at Ronnie's door. It was Ed.

"What the hell happened?" Ronnie demanded.

"I got down there and that S.O.B. started jumping in my face about me being late for rehearsals," Eddie related. "So I walked out."

Seems Ed didn't think much of Otis to begin with. On Otis's radio show he'd made a habit of announcing that Ed would be appearing at the El Monte Legion Stadium without ever arranging any dates with Ed or Jerry. Just to save face, Ed would play the unscheduled concerts.

"And then he had nerve to start cussing me because I was late for rehearsals?" Ed fumed to his friend. "Who does he think he is?!"

Ronnie thought Eddie's walkout was hysterical, and he broke down laughing. Ed soon joined him.

In August, along with his Silver instrumentals "Guybo" and "Strollin' Guitar," Ed also tried his hand at a trio of blues tunes while at the Goldstar studios. Eddie was no stranger to the blues, he admired the genre greatly and was friendly with blues legends Lowell Fulson, who penned "Reconsider Baby," and with B.B. King. Ed would often join King and Fulson on the latter's front porch in Los Angeles for impromptu jam sessions.

At Goldstar, backed by Jim Stivers on piano, possibly Dave Shriver on electric bass, and Gene Riggio on drums, Ed and Jerry's own snaky "Eddie's Blues" featured wiggling tremolo-dipped riffing, banjo-esque rolling, and blisteringly swift single-string guitar runs from Ed, handily illustrating just how comfortable and capable he'd become with virtually any musical style. The pair's "Chicken Shot Blues," with the same backing musicians, was similar in its lowdown atmosphere and no-holds-barred attitude, particularly in Ed's solos. Sleepy John Estes's "Milk Cow Blues," which Elvis Presley had recorded in 1955 as a raucous rockabilly mover, was kept lean and langorously lowdown with Ed's snarling vocal.

It was with Ed's demos of these blues songs that I'd first built my guitar skills as a kid. Don't ask me how I wound up with the tapes—probably my dad had them lying around the house—but I listened to them over and over and learned everything I could off of them. And it was "Milk Cow Blues" that I played at that school talent show, my first public performance at age twelve and a half.

My down-to-earth uncle, more interested in making music than living a glamorous rock star's existence, was still working tirelessly as a session man for other acts as well. He shared his August 25 session with singer and songwriter Darry Weaver, providing guitar and most probably bass for three of the less-than-stellar vocalist's tunes. The August 26 date that produced "Strollin' Guitar" also yielded another vocal-less blues, titled simply "Instrumental Blues," plus the Hal Winn ballad "Little Angel" and Ed and Jerry's "My Love to Remember" from the Cochran Brothers days.

A few days later, Ed revisited Goldstar with Stivers, Shriver, Riggio, and saxophonists Mike Henderson and Mike Deasy to wax "Hallelujah, I Love Her So," penned by Ray Charles, one of Ed's favorite performers. Maintaining the bluesy tone of the prior sessions, the group pounded out a dozen playful takes of the tune, Ed's mischievously phrased, growl-garnished vocal and blistering guitar solo buttressed by the honking horns, tap-dancing piano, and skipping rhythm section. The final take was chosen as Ed's next Liberty single, paired with "Little Angel," and released in late October, 1959—with a few horrifying additions.

Unbeknownst to Ed, the songs' masters were handed over to Tommy "Snuff" Garrett, Liberty's first A&R (artists and repertoire) representative. Garrett's vast knowledge of pop music and growing feel for what makes a hit were formed at Dallas, Texas, radio station KLIF. After a year in Hollywood during his teens, he moved back to Texas where he eventually landed a job as both a disc jockey and a TV host. Garrett desperately desired to be involved in the business end of music, however, so he was thrilled when he finally scored a gig as a local promotion man for Liberty.

Garrett blossomed during his years with the label, branching out from promo into production and eventually becoming the head of A&R. In that capacity, to create recordings with the widest possible commercial appeal, Garrett advocated the use of grand orchestral arrangements and lavish backing vocal choirs. This formula he applied to Ed's latest output, swathing "Hallelujah, I Love Her So" with slick and swooping strings and adding frothy choral backing to "Little Angel." Ed was horrified.

But reviews were not unkind. "Cochran belts 'Hallelujah,' the great Ray Charles tune over a gospelish arrangement that includes strings," *Billboard* wrote of the single. "It's a standout side, and a likely winner. 'Little Angel' is also on the spiritual order, and it's also accorded a smart warble." "Cochran...should head right back for hitsville with his newest Liberty effort," enthused another critic. "It's a sensational thumping-rock-string [sic] of the great Ray Charles-penned 'Hallelujah, I Love Her So.' Watch it zoom. On the under end the chorus and ork ably assist Eddie as he emotionally knocks out a hip-swinging rock-a-ballad romancer tabbed 'Little Angel.' Also bears watching." Though Snuff Garrett productions for other Liberty artists were successful for the label—particularly those of Johnny Burnette and Bobby Vee—Ed's eleventh Liberty single didn't even make the American charts. In the U.K., the record reached a respectable Number 22.

Throughout the fall of 1959, Liberty's promotions department tied in Ed's personal appearance tour of the Midwest with Liberty distributors in key markets to plug his current single "Somethin' Else." Again, he and the Kelly Four—still being billed in some venues as Jim Stivers and His Hollywood Swingers—were on the road, braving the elements and the audiences. On September 10, in Hot Springs, South Dakota, Ed was mobbed by eager autograph-seeking fans backstage at the City Auditorium. Radio station KOBH had arranged the show after a poll of its listeners determined that Ed was that area's favorite male singer.

At a September 25 show in Williston, North Dakota, nearly two thousand teenagers waited patiently for their idol, who was held up by thick, red mud that had deluged the highways due to torrential rain. At one point, the trailer got stuck in the mire; the band, including an ill Gene Riggio, was forced to get out of the station wagon to push the vehicle free. Gene lost a shoe to the muck, and climbed back into the car. Stivers at the wheel raced the engine, drenching the others in the sludge.

Eventually a big rig came by and offered the boys some help. The rig driver hooked them up and pulled them out of the mud enough so that they could follow him in his wheel tracks. It was on that same ill-fated trip that they discovered they had crabs. Dave Shriver fronted the money to buy the medicine to get rid of the little critters. But the guys didn't realize they had to wash and treat their blankets, so they all got re-infested. Dave never did get his money reimbursed.

But they did ultimately make it to the gig, mud and all. Crusted in the rusty red stuff from their filthy flattops to spoiled suede bucks, the band finally hit the stage about 11:50 p.m., with some of the kids who'd hung around that long actually helping the band load their gear into the venue. But the "dance session" was closed fifteen minutes later due to state laws prohibiting teenage dances after midnight. Ed and the band felt awful for letting the kids down, but they really needed the box-office money to make it to their next date.

Dave Shriver negotiated with the concert promoter: The band would not have to return the ticket take for their fifteen-minute show if they would return to nearby Chadron, Nebraska, the following week and play a full-length concert for free.

And so they did. In Chadron, on October 3, Ed's twenty-first birthday, he was presented with a twenty-pound birthday cake, a key to the city, and a trophy proclaiming him the "Number One Male Singer in the Seven State Area of KOBH," the South Dakota–based radio station responsible for both that date and the Hot Springs gig.

Ed's pal Johnny Rook was now in Hot Springs, working as a deejay, for which he'd become quite famous. Ed had actually had a hand in getting Johnny into radio. He and Johnny were having dinner one night with Jerry Capehart and Si Waronker at the fancy restaurant inside the El Dorado Hotel in Los Angeles. Tennessee Ernie Ford dropped by their table, and in the course of the conversation, Johnny explained how Burt Lancaster had gotten him into acting, not that it had amounted to much. Roles were getting harder and harder to find. In fact, just about the only thing Johnny was doing at that point was helping Eddie, making the rounds to the radio stations trying to get his records played.

Well, had he ever considered going into radio? Ernie Ford asked. Johnny hadn't ever really thought about it. It didn't sound like such a bad idea, so Johnny decided to drop by a couple of stations to see if he might be able to russle up some work. But when he admitted his lack of experience to the radio brass, he was quickly shown the door. Dejected, and with his showbiz options seemingly exhausted in southern California, Johnny went back home to Nebraska. From his Midwestern turf he still kept up with the radio and records industry, reading all of the trade magazines. His dad, who worked for the railroad, couldn't have been less thrilled with his son's interest in the entertainment business. Why didn't he just get a real job down at the railroad? His mother was more sympathetic. So when Johnny saw in *Cash Box* an item about a station up in New Castle, Wyoming, that was looking for a disc jockey, his mom drove him all the way there one day after his dad had left for work. The station hired him, and Johnny Rho became Johnny Rowe, also known as Johnny Rook, radio personality.

A week after Ed's birthday bash in Chadron, Ed made his third *American Bandstand* appearance of 1959. Joining singer Sammy Turner, vocal trio the Isley Brothers, and vocal-instrumental quartet the Fireflies, he eschewed the more-current "Somethin' Else" for his first Liberty hit, the far tamer "Sittin' in the Balcony."

Purporting itself to be rock 'n' roll's most steadfast proponent, *American Bandstand* was actually becoming the music's slyest enemy. With the luminaries of rock 'n' roll—Elvis Presley, Little

Richard, and Buddy Holly—out of the picture, the void was filled by the homogenized likes of Bobby Rydell, Frankie Avalon, and Fabian, recording for Dick Clark's Philadelphia-based record labels, as well as crooners like ABC-Paramount's Paul Anka and Atlantic's Bobby Darin, all of whom appeared regularly on *Bandstand*. The fresh-faced and wholesome singers—boosted by the highly influential television program—proved eminently palatable to the American public, and their limp, saccharine pop tunes began to swamp the pop charts.

Dick Clark, raking in over a half a million bucks a year through his TV show salary, ownership in music corporations, and gratuitous "composer" royalties, did not appear bothered in the least about authentic rock 'n' roll's apparent decline. "I don't make culture," he'd later say. "I sell it."

And trouble was brewing in the American music industry as well. As radio had emerged as a vital component of the making of a hit, record companies, greasing the wheels of commerce, began secretly paying disc jockeys on the side. It started out as the simple giving of gifts—hi-fi stereos, free merchandise that could be converted to cash—but by the late 1950s an organized system of direct cash payments was firmly in place. Dubbed "payola," the illegal practice was first brought to the public's attention on November 19, 1959, when, in the course of a congressional investigation into the rigging of daytime quiz shows, the New York District Attorney's office served subpoenas on several record companies, ordering them to hand over their books for investigation. Heads within the popular music industry began to roll.

Among the first to go was Alan Freed, rock 'n' roll's staunchest radio friend and the most visible disc jockey in the business. Over the years Freed had amassed a small fortune from his salary at New York's WABC radio, to which he'd moved after leaving WINS; his concert promotions; and record company kickbacks. When Freed refused "on principle" to sign a statement saying he'd never received money or gifts to promote records, he was promptly dismissed from WABC, as well as from television station WNEW, which aired his rock 'n' roll dance show. Freed would die within a few years, pickled in alcohol and ruined by payola and income tax indictments.

Hearing dates were set for the House Legislative Oversight subcommittee of the Commerce Committee to investigate the misuse of free records, payola to disc jockeys and other radio station personnel, payola to record company A&R men, chart rigging through dealer payola, kickbacks at every level of the record industry, and conflict of interest between music and broadcast interests that used radio to promote their own products.

And although clean-cut Dick Clark enjoyed ownership in some thirty-three record companies, a management firm, and a record-pressing plant, and at the time of the hearings held copyright to 162 songs, many of which he helped to popularize on *Bandstand*, ABC stuck by the show's host. The investigating committee simply ordered Clark to divest most of his music publishing and management holdings.

The payola scandal sent a chilling pall across the American music industry, and for an artist like Eddie Cochran, more interested in music than money, it surely must have been disheartening.

STEP THREE: *Endings*

9

U.K. Tour

THEY CALLED IT "A Fast-Moving Anglo-American Beat Show." British rockers Georgie Fame, Billy Fury, Billy Raymond, Joe Brown, and the Tony Sheridan Trio. American rock 'n' roller Gene Vincent. And Eddie Cochran.

The first all rock 'n' roll program ever to tour the United Kingdom—when Bill Haley, Buddy Holly, Jerry Lee Lewis and a few others had played across the Atlantic some time earlier it always had been as part of a variety package—was assembled by Larry Parnes, England's crown prince of promotion. He set the first brick of his empire in 1956 when he stumbled across Tommy Steele in a London coffee bar and went on to make him a star. Since then he'd amassed an entire stable of golden boys, virtually interchangeable young singers he rechristened with "power" showbiz monikers: Along with Fury, there was Vince Eager, Johnny Gentle, Dickie Pride, and Lance Fortune.

Parnes created the artists, and they endowed him with great wealth. As the chief supplier of talent for the hugely popular television music show *Oh Boy!*, which had aspiring musicians across Britain glued to the tube every Saturday night, Parnes was enormously influential.

He was also quite shrewd, quickly realizing a consumer demand for American pop stars in the U.K. In 1959 he attempted to bring Elvis Presley over; when that proved impossible, he thought of

Gene Vincent. He was able to negotiate a fair price: fifteen hundred pounds a week, six shows a week, for four or five weeks in the first part of 1960. But after booking Vincent, Parnes got an uneasy feeling that it would probably be best if he added somebody else to the bill. He'd been reading about Eddie Cochran, the up-and-coming American singer and guitarist whose half dozen U.K. singles had been going over quite well. He also knew that Eddie and Gene had toured together in Australia and had done some recording together also. It seemed like a perfect fit. So in just a few days Parnes had booked Ed quite reasonably as well, at two hundred fifty pounds a week plus expenses. He felt reassured.

Jerry Capehart, on the other hand, did not. California booking agent Norm Riley, who had a less than scrupulous reputation, had arranged the American performers' British debut. Riley had apparently told Capehart that Jerry would be accompanying Ed on the U.K. tour, but when it came time to dole out the plane tickets, Jerry was left out in the cold. In England, Riley took to calling himself Ed's manager. Jerry was livid.

It had become evident, however, by this time that Ed was drifting away from Jerry. Perhaps the constant criticizing of Capehart by Ed's friends and family had finally gotten to Ed. Perhaps Jerry—now well ensconced in his own career as producer, songwriter, and manager to many artists—didn't have the time to devote to Ed anymore. Or perhaps Ed, now keenly confident in his own abilities, simply outgrew Jerry.

Ed, I'm sure, was finding it more and more difficult to contend with some of Jerry's more irksome traits, like his manager's tendency to color the truth. Jerry's attitude toward Ed's increased drinking may have played a part, as well. Jerry told me that Ed's drinking had gotten so bad that he decided he would never imbibe while around his client any more. Ed's drinking became such a rub between the two of them that Eddie began to do his best to avoid Jerry's disapproving looks and antagonistic comments, keeping himself less and less in Jerry's presence when not recording, and more and more out carousing with his buddies and my dad. And although at times Jerry was brilliant, the not-so-brilliant times seemed to come more often. Sure, Eddie loved Jerry, even called him "Dad." And Eddie once punched my father for badmouthing him. But Ed and Jerry's relationship was definitely becoming more and more strained.

I was about fourteen when I first met Jerry. Dad had taken me to Hollywood to shop some songs. We were walking down Sunset Boulevard, Jerry was about fifty feet ahead of us. Dad and Jerry recognized each other at about the same time and they ran up to each other, embraced and cried. I didn't know what was going on. I'd always heard what a jerk Jerry was, how he'd ripped Eddie off and stuff. And here they were, my dad and Jerry, hugging and crying in the middle of the sidewalk. I realized, yet again, that what my dad said did not necessarily match what my dad did. Jerry told us that he was managing Glen Campbell, who was a great guitarist. "But he can't carry Ed's guitar case," Jerry said, obviously still a fan of my talented uncle. For all of the family's badmouthing of Jerry, I could see that there seemed to be a genuine affection between Dad and Jerry.

I would get a taste of Jerry's confounding nature when we went into the studio together to record my solo album *Private Edition*. I was doing a vocal on "Somethin' Else," and had just finished a take on the line "She's sure fine lookin' man, she's somethin' else." Jerry jumped up in the booth and shouted, "No, no, no! I told you not to do it that way! Do it like I told you!" I thought I'd sung it just fine, so, unbeknownst to Jerry, I proceeded to play back my performance to discover what it was he was not happy with. I mouthed the lyrics as that line—which sounded perfectly fine to me—went by. He thought I was recording. When I stopped the machine, Jerry jumped up and said, "That's it! That's what I've been tryin' to get you to do all along!" The performance that was unacceptable on first listen was now apparently exactly what Jerry'd been looking for all along. I was thoroughly exasperated and mentally put another checkmark into the "I can't always trust Jerry's word" column.

Not long after that I was in the booth overdubbing some guitar on another song when Jerry stopped me. He thought he heard something odd. I rewound the tape and played it back. "There, right there," he said. I marked the position on the auto-locator and proceeded to scrutinize every track until I had exhausted every possibility—every note, every sound, on every track was just as it should be, and Jerry agreed. Still, during listen after re-listen, every time that passage of the song came up Jerry would say, "Right there." Remembering the annoying "Somethin' Else" incident, I decided to test Jerry. I rewound the tape to a previous but duplicate part of the song—a portion of the recording that had already passed Jerry's muster. But sure enough, once more Jerry said, "Right there!"

I was fuming. I stood up. "You son of a bitch!" I exploded. "You haven't heard that problem for fifteen or twenty minutes! Once you started looking for it you never heard it again, but you were too consumed by your ego and fear of having been wrong that you let me waste all this time searching for a non-existent sound!"

I pounded the wall in frustration. "Why do you waste our time with nonsense like this?" I implored him. I pleaded with him to stop the mind games that seemed to always get in the way of real creativity. "What is going on?" I asked him. "How do you ever expect me to trust your judgment when you do such asinine stuff?"

Jerry broke down in tears. "I'm afraid of losing you like I lost Eddie," he sobbed.

And I finally began to understand. Jerry was so intent on keeping you from finding out that you didn't need him that he would do and say the most ridiculous things. And I'd eventually discover that anyone who knew him experienced this side of Jerry. He was so intent on winning your love and confidence that he regularly undermined it. He simply didn't realize—or couldn't accept, for whatever reason—that we already did love him. I could finally comprehend the nature of Ed's and Jerry's relationship because I was experiencing the same thing. All of us—Jerry and Ed, Jerry and me—we were definitely more like family than simply business associates or creative collaborators. We got under each other's skin, we had the power to break each other's heart, we needed the tolerance and foresight to let each other grow.

And I'm sure that's what was starting to happen with Eddie and Jerry around the time Ed left for England. Their roles were shifting, and it was becoming uncomfortable. Whether they could admit it or not, they each needed their independence—like a child learning to separate from its parents, or a brother finding an identity outside of his sibling. And though there was no official parting of the ways, Ed and Jerry surely knew things were going to have to be different. Their roles were being redefined by the vagaries and necessities of life. And so, Jerry did not accompany Ed to the U.K.

British tour promoter Larry Parnes didn't like to leave anything to chance. Every tour he put together was analyzed and strategized like a military campaign, with maps and charts and demographics and attendance statistics. After the first week of shows in late January, Parnes's hallowed numbers assured him; he was sold out for the entire tour. Of course, having a pair of new records out from Gene didn't hurt things any, nor did the fact that Ed's "Hallelujah, I Love Her So" had cracked the U.K.'s Top 30 and would ultimately peak at Number 22.

Before Ed's arrival in England on January 10, 1960, he'd completed another session at Goldstar, with Snuff Garett and Si Waronker behind the board. It had been decided to team Ed with some different players, and so drummer Jerry Allison and guitarist Sonny Curtis from Buddy Holly's backing band the Crickets were brought in. Guybo remained on bass. The Crickets, Garrett's fellow Texans, had just moved to Los Angeles on New Year's Day; now, just a week later, they were hunkered down with one of their late boss's closest friends, laying down a trio of tracks in a new studio using new recording techniques. Unlike the Nashville sessions the Crickets were used to, where the band encircled a mike and simply played, at Goldstar the musicians were separated by baffles, to achieve a more pristine sound quality. Without being able to see one another, the players' timing was off. Ed was pressed for time himself, needing to depart in a few hours to catch a midnight plane to London. He took charge of the situation, rehearsing the band and finally getting the three songs onto tape despite Waronker's constantly eyeing his stopwatch and stopping the band for tempo fluctuations.

Sonny Curtis remembers that although Snuff Garrett was indeed present at the session, it was actually Waronker who was producing, putting the players through the hoops and saying, "The tempos keep drifting!" Curtis—who played an orange Gretsch guitar on the session, with the the "G" brand on the body and half-moon markers on the neck; Ed played the Martin D18—was not savvy at all at that point in his career when it came to recording, he recalls, having had—in Clovis, New Mexico—only a bit of studio experience, which he now calls "real loose and weak." In Clovis, tracks weren't even counted off; here at Ed's session, Si Waronker was there with his stopwatch, motioning up and down with his hand to keep time. Curtis thought Ed probably wanted to smack him, and recalls Ed finally saying to Waronker, "Leave us alone; let us pick!"

"Cut Across Shorty" was a rousing revisiting of Ed's country roots, a revved-up rock 'n' roll read of the tune also cut by Carl Smith. Sharon Sheeley's "Cherished Memories," a sentimental romancer, which with its frothy choral backing could have easily drowned in maudlin depths, was transformed into a jaunty doo-wop ditty, thanks largely to Allison's martial drum beats. "Three Steps to Heaven," written by my Dad and Ed, was originally demoed in June 1959. The version cut on January 8, 1960 was essentially the same, with a minor reshuffling of verses. Propelled by Ed's acoustic strumming and Sonny Curtis's single-string chord arpeggios, the mid-tempo tune recounting a recipe for romantic bliss was full of gentle hope. And though reviews of "Three Steps to

Heaven," backed with "Cut Across Shorty," issued in March 1960, were largely complimentary, the single only limped to Number 108 in the American charts before dropping off altogether, although it eventually fared well in England and Europe.

Besides working in one last recording session, Ed had paid a visit to his old pal and former musical partner Hank Cochran before departing for the U.K. Hank hadn't yet left for Nashville; after the Cochran Brothers' split, he'd been up north for a time doing the *California Hayride* himself, then returned with his wife and kids to Bell Gardens, where he played a club at night and watched his kids during the day.

One evening there was a racket at his front door. It was Ed. He was holding two bulging sacks of beer, one in each arm. "Damn, chief," Hank said, delighted to see his old buddy, "C'mon in!" Ed was driving his Country Squire station wagon, and after Ed caught up on Hank's news—he was leaving for Nashville in a week—said hello to Hank's wife, and hugged the kids, the two climbed into Ed's car and drove around, reminiscing and draining the cold brews.

After a few frosty beverages, Hank said to Ed, " You know, I am so proud of you and what you've done. Man, with all that's been goin' on with you, what have you got planned next?" "I'm going to England," Ed told Hank, sounding a bit bemused. "I'm a damned star in England." "Well, hell," Hank said, "you've always been a damned star. Just nobody knew it!"

Hank was just a few short years away from becoming a star himself, thanks in no small part to a sassy broad with a voice as big as all outdoors, Patsy Cline. She would make a hit of Hank's "I Fall to Pieces," and when she was searching for a follow-up to her smash hit "Crazy," penned by the then-unknown Willie Nelson, whom Hank also brought to world recognition, it was Hank who would hand it to her. One day, as he was sitting at his desk at Pamper Music, wracking his brain for a song fine enough to follow "Crazy," the number one jukebox record of all time, he pulled out one of the drawers. He noticed a picture of an old girlfriend, who was now with someone else.

He got to thinking about that girl. After a few minutes of pondering, he concluded, "Well, at least I got her picture, he's got her, I guess. Everything happens for a—." The song leapt up and grabbed him. He scribbled it down as fast as the words came to him, then snatched up his guitar and strummed out the tune. It all fit perfectly together.

He phoned Patsy. "I've got it!" he gushed.

"You got what?" she asked.

"I got that damn song we've been looking for!" he told her.

"Well, bring it on over here," she said, "and stop by the liquor store and get us a bottle."

His was a dry county, so Hank drove all around Nashville to find a store that was still open. When he arrived at Patsy's he had a quart of whiskey and guitar in hand. They went into the kitchen, put the bottle in the middle of the kitchen table, and sat down. Patsy twisted the top off, threw it down, and took a nice, little drink. She handed the bottle to Hank. He took one just a little bit better. He handed the bottle back to her and she took a bigger drink.

"Sing the sombitch," she said.

So Hank sang his new song, "She's Got You."

Halfway through, tears started rolling down Patsy's cheeks. By song's end, Hank was crying.

"Ah, damn," she said when he was through. "That's it, you son of a bitch."

Patsy took another swig. So did Hank. And he played "that sombitch" again and again.

Soon Dottie West came by. "Hand me that bottle," Dottie said, to Hank's amazement. He didn't think Dottie even drank. She downed a giant swallow, and so did Hank and Patsy. Then it was more singing, and more crying.

Patsy phoned her manager and sang the song to him; he started crying on the other end of the line. And she phoned her producer Owen Bradley and sang it to him, Hank accompanying her on his guitar. "Where did that kid find that?" the stunned Bradley asked when they were through. He set the session for the very next day, and Patsy cut it. On playback, Bradley's entire office was in tears. Hank had himself another hit.

Eddie was met at the airport in London by a throng of his enthusiastic fans, and he barely had time to rest before he was put to work, appearing at a reception thrown for him by his British record label in London and rehearsing in Manchester for the first of two spots on *Boy Meets Girls*, another popular television program produced by Jack Good, of *Oh Boy!* show fame. Because a mutual musicians' exchange could not be worked out—the number of British players visiting the United States had to be the same as the number of American players visiting the U.K.—Eddie was without a backing band. So for his *Boy Meets Girls* performances, Ed was joined by guitarists Joe Brown, Eric Ford, and Brian Daley; saxophonist Red Price, bassists Alan Weighall and Bill Stark; drummers Andy White and Don Storer; and the Vernons Girls on backing vocals.

Virtually all who met Ed were impressed. Sixteen-year-old Sheila Bruce of the Vernons Girls went completely to jelly, so gorgeous did she find my uncle with his blond hair, tanned face, and brown leather bomber jacket like what the American Air Force pilots wore. Singer Marty Wilde, host of *Boy Meets Girls*, thought Ed the most beautiful man he'd ever seen in show business, and beyond the cosmetic dazzle, found him to be a likably charming outlaw sort, a Billy the Kid with a guitar. Ed's two appearances on Wilde's television show were quite successful, with his performances of "Hallelujah, I Love Her So," "C'mon Everybody," "Somethin' Else," "Twenty Flight Rock," the Presley-popularized "Money Honey," and "Have I Told You Lately That I Love You" earning resounding applause and screams from the teenage studio audience.

For the U.K. tour, which would commence on January 24, Eddie was to be accompanied by Marty Wilde's band, the Wildcats, and rehearsals with the group soon got underway in a club in London's West End. A Wildcat appointment book notes a rehearsal with Eddie Cochran on Tuesday, January 19, 1960, from 11 a.m. to 4 p.m. at Richardson's, a practice space. The following Friday, the 22nd, the book notes, the band rehearsed with Gene Vincent. The following Tuesday, January 26, two days after Ed joined the tour, the Wildcats again rehearsed with him, this time from 11 a.m. to 5 p.m. at the Metro in London. After another rehearsal with their bandleader Marty Wilde, the group flew to Glasgow, Scotland, on February 1 to join the tour on its week stint at the Empire.

At the Wildcats' first rehearsal with Ed, when guitarist Big Jim Sullivan arrived, Ed was already there. Eddie opened his guitar case and pulled out his instrument, the beautiful orange Gretsch. He sat down and launched into Chet Atkins's version of the Birth of "The Blues." Sullivan was completely knocked out. He was a huge Atkins fan, and Eddie was playing exactly like Chet. There was hardly anyone in England at the time who could pull off the fingerpicking style, and to hear a young player like Ed do it so well, with so little apparent effort, was amazing.

When Ed then pulled out his rock riffs and his blues licks, Sullivan and the other Wildcats simply stood slack-jawed, utterly awed. They'd all expected Ed would be good, as they'd heard his records, but they'd never heard another guitarist play anything like the handsome American.

"How'd you get your start?" guitarist Tony Belcher asked.

"I used to be a session player," Ed quipped, "then I got greedy and started to sing."

The Wildcats wanted to learn all they could from Ed, and my uncle was more than happy to oblige them. To Jim Sullivan, and later on the tour to, Joe Brown, he imparted new knowledge regarding string bending. The young British guitarists were not aware of variously gauged strings—in England, guitar strings were guitar strings. At the Bell Gardens Music Center back in California, all of Eddie's string gauges were scribbled onto a piece of paper up under a cabinet; Eddie would order his strings from the store while he was in England. He used V. C. Squier strings, the only manufacturer for years that made individual gauges. Eddie showed the English guitarists he worked with how to use lighter strings to make bends easier and runs swifter, suggesting banjo strings for the first two, a normal second guitar string for the third, and so on. He even assisted Wildcat drummer Brian Bennett, showing him how to play more syncopated rhythms and provoking him to think of new ways to use the bass drum.

I remember hearing that Eddie was disappointed with his choice of amplifiers while in England. Eddie tried a Selmer and borrowed Big Jim Sullivan's Haco, then settled into a Vox AC30. Tony Belcher was using a Vox AC15 with mixed results. Once, while playing in the coastal town of Blackpool, Belcher failed to realize that his amp had a step-down transformer and that the voltage at the venue was lower. The band launched into a number with Marty Wilde, and suddenly the audience started laughing. Tony wondered why but kept playing. Then the rest of his band burst out laughing. And then Marty Wilde turned around and started laughing. "What's happened?" Tony wondered. Then he turned around to see plumes of smoke billowing from his amplifier. He didn't think it was so funny, especially when he had to have the transformer rewound when they returned to Bournemouth—it cost him half a week's wages.

The tour was a screaming success from its very first date at the Granada Theatre in Ipswich, where Ed and Gene were reunited. "It's great to be here in 'Hipswich,'" Ed told the eager crowd with a sideways switch of his hips, immediately endearing himself to boys and shrieking girls alike. Tony Belcher remembers that Eddie looked particularly impressive onstage, wearing his red shirt and black leather pants and swinging his guitar around. Assuming the role of rockin' rebel seemed quite natural for him. He'd often just start a song and the band would join in, and he switched the order of the set from show to show according to how the audience was reacting.

At each venue, the musicians played through the house public address systems, but with all of the screaming they usually couldn't hear a thing, Belcher recalls, so they largely played by feel. They'd rehearsed and gotten all of the song tempos down, so they knew how they went, and they followed the drums. Their amps just weren't powerful enough to overpower the eager audience's din. And distortion was definitely a no-no. If the guitar players started to get feedback, they'd move away form their amps, opting for a cleaner sound instead.

Tony Belcher played a Maton hollowbody guitar, and Big Jim played a Gibson ES 345 with a custom L5 neck, a very rare instrument. Jim remembers that Ed really liked that guitar. Although Ed will forever be identified with that beautiful amber red 6120, it's clear to me from many conversations with friends that he was evolving on many levels and paying close attention to which guitars could facilitate his ever-developing style. Those old Gretsches were notorious for the necks coming off due to faulty glue joints; I have three of them and every one has needed the neck reset. And although Eddie modified his Gretsch with a Gibson P90 pickup in the front position, Big Jim remembers that Eddie mostly used the back or treble pickup. I suspect that he couldn't always go for strictly the best tone; he needed to cut through the roar of the crowd, as well as overcome an under-powered amp.

The authority with which Eddie played—his profound self-assuredness—also captured the interest of the British musicians. He knew exactly how he wanted things to sound. Brian Bennett remembers that he liked the drums up close to him. Ed had a great sense of time, and taught the drummer how to syncopate the kick drum, a forward-thinking style that would soon come into vogue.

The package played Coventry, Worcester, Bradford, and Southampton before heading up to Scotland for the week's run in Glasgow. Dubbed "the death place" in the concert business, Glasgow was a rough town for performers. The crowds were generally unruly and would hurl bottles at the stage simply for the hell of it, whether they liked the show or not. Typically pretty-boy singers with the sexiest images were the ones who'd bear the brunt; Glasgow blokes didn't go in for the warblers who made their girls all hot and sweaty. Billy Fury had a tough time of it—whiskey bottles went whizzing and his band eventually deserted him, leaving him to muscle it out onstage alone. But the Americans made it through the week unscathed. Eddie closed the first half of the show, the crowd going wild for "Summertime Blues," "C'mon Everybody," and "Twenty Flight Rock," though the Scots loudly protested when he mistakenly chatted about being in England.

The show moved back down to England, stopping at Sheffield, London, Taunton, and Leicester, then returned to Scotland to play Dundee. On February 7, in Sheffield, the *Star* newspaper hosted a buffet for Eddie, Gene, and Vince Eager at the Green Room, a posh restaurant just above the Gaumont Theatre, where the show would spend a week. Carole (née Ward) Commander, Paul Anka fan club secretary for the paper's teen section, was assigned to interview Ed. In the background, his "Hallelujah, I Love Her So" was playing. She was taken with my uncle's good looks; she silently admired his flawless complexion and ash blond hair. She hadn't expected his hair to be so light; the Brylcreem must have darkened it in the photos she'd seen, she assumed. And she was surprised by his breezy charm and natural friendliness—he was so down to earth, so easy to talk to, and he made her feel so relaxed. Quite different from Gene, whom she found very quiet, difficult to get through to, and nearly impossible to size up.

She caught Ed's show later in Manchester, and was thrilled as he started with his back to the audience, then whipped around with his guitar as he ripped into "Somethin' Else." He was dressed in an orange-ish shirt open at the collar and dark leather trousers, and he wore makeup, his eyebrows and lashes darkened. He was every bit a star. Eddie had taken to wearing stage makeup even during the day on many occasions. The whole band used to wear it for the shows. They would sometimes forget to clean the makeup off; red-necked truck drivers would pull up beside them and think they were all homosexuals.

Ed recorded a pair of appearances on the BBC radio show "Saturday Club"; he performed songs on February 16 for the program that aired March 5: "Milk Cow Blues," "C'mon Everybody," "Hallelujah, I Love Her So," and "What'd I Say," the 1959 Ray Charles jewel with which Ed had been alternating opening and closing his act while in England. "If you listened to any of [Charles's] discs, you'll understand what I mean when I say that he has the most exciting beat sound I've ever heard—or am likely to hear, for that matter," Ed opined in one British paper, hoping to turn the U.K. kids on to one of his favorite artists. "Ray's music isn't

strictly rock 'n' roll. It's more rhythm and blues, with spiritual over-
tones. I don't consciously try to copy him. I simply set out to gen-
erate the same exciting feeling that he produces when he sings."

Most nights Eddie would start his set with "Somethin' Else," the
Wildcats recall, ending with Ray Charles's "What'd I Say," although
he'd often shuffle the song order depending on the audience. He'd
always try to involve the crowd, getting them singing along on call-
and-response type passages. The sets were loose and spontaneous,
the band keying off Eddie, following him as he launched a song.
And Ed was a true showman, vamping on the intro to "Somethin'
Else" with his back to his fans, who were tense with anticipation,
and falling to his knees on the repeated choruses of "What'd I Say"
during his finale, taking his bows then leaving the stage as the band
continued the chorus. When the audience was teased into a suffi-
cient frenzy, he returned to the stage to riotous applause.

The package tour stopped in Leicester on February 18. To the
exhilarated kids in the audience, the Americans were the most exciting thing they'd ever seen. Others thought the show a disgrace. One
reviewer harrumphed, "on to the stage at De Montfort Hall last
night stepped a young man wearing black leather trousers, black
leather motorcycling jacket and black leather gloves. He grasped
the microphone as if it were the last straw, threw it into the air,
then with an expression of agony on his face, bellowed into it."

> The audience went frantic. The girls jumped up as if they had sat
> on a hot iron and the boys clapped and whistled.

> This was Mr. Gene Vincent.

> An American colleague of his on the same bill had exactly the
> same effect on the crowd. When Eddie Cochran, dressed smartly
> in gray skin-tight leather trousers, a pink shirt, and silver lame
> waistcoat, contorted himself in various positions, the girls went
> even wilder.

> Now I am no square...I can appreciate a tune with a foot-tapping
> beat as much as anyone. But last night's exhibition of 'talent'
> sickened me.

> It was not so much the singing, because there was so much
> yelling going on I could hardly hear it, but the fact that these

"singers" seemed to get such immense enjoyment out of leg-kicking, face-pulling, and making the youngsters scream.

I cannot believe this is true entertainment. A clown making funny faces would have got the same results from small children.

Then why do these idiotic teenagers behave in such a ridiculous fashion?

After watching that show I am still no further nearer the answer. I didn't feel at all like going hysterical!

The way in which they shrieked, jumped up, and ran to the stage in a desperate effort to touch their idol was pathetic as well as slightly disgusting.

I can only hope that last night's audience were not typical of Leicester's young people.

On February 23, Ed again performed "Hallelujah, I Love Her So," along with "Somethin' Else" and "Twenty Flight Rock," on "Saturday Club," and he played guitar for Gene, who also appeared on the earlier program, as he sang his latest U.K. single, "My Heart." During the show, broadcast March 12, Ed and host Brian Matthew chatted about Ed's ability to play other instruments, his ambitions—"To be successful," Ed simply stated—and future tour plans. The current tour would end on April 17, Ed said, when he would fly back home for a ten day rest, then return to the U.K. for ten more weeks of touring.

Ed, along with Gene, also appeared on *Boy Meets Girls* again, playing abbreviated renditions of "Hallelujah, I Love Her So" and "Twenty Flight Rock" and superb reads of "Summertime Blues" and "Milk Cow Blues." The program aired on February 20. He played guitar for Gene's two numbers, "My Heart" and "Dance in the Street," and they both joined Marty Wilde, Billy Fury, and Joe Brown for a raucous finale of the blues classic "My Babe."

On February 21, Gene and Ed played the Wembley Arena in London as part of the Poll Winners Concert put on by the magazine *New Musical Express*, and on February 27 the pair were again seen on *Boy Meets Girls*. This time Ed experimented a bit, taking on the big band swing of "I Don't Like You No More," written by singer

Teddy Randazzo, with whom Ed had previously toured. A punchy version of Chuck Berry's "Sweet Little Sixteen" followed, as did a gleefully impromptu take of the Big Bopper-penned "White Lightning" by both Ed and Gene that had the studio audience howling. Ed performed "C'mon Everybody" on the "Parade of Pop" radio show the following day.

Then it was on to Stockton-on-Tees; Cardiff in Wales; and Leeds, Birmingham, Liverpool, Newcastle, Manchester, and London. It's been rumored that in Leeds Eddie fell into the orchestra pit, and when he got up said, "Did I kill any of them damned fiddle players?" But Big Jim Sullivan assures me that it was Vince Eager, not Ed, who fell while doing something like "Whole Lotta Shakin' Goin' On." Seems during rehearsal, the orchestra pit had been elevated to the stage level and Vince had hopped over the footlights onto the raised platform. Later during the performance, Eager once again hopped over the footlights, thinking the pit was still at stage level. It had been lowered, however, and Eager wasn't able to see that past the blinding footlights. He made a terrible crunch as he crashed to the ground, but then a hand came over the pit wall; he hauled himself up, and continued his song.

The reception was the same all over. Screaming fans filled the theater seats during the concerts, then streamed from the halls afterward onto the streets in rabid search of their rock 'n' roll idols. It soon got to the point that after the shows, decoys resembling Ed and Gene had to be sent out to distract the shrieking mobs while the musicians made their getaway.

Ed and Gene shared rooms on the road, as well as a penchant for mischief and a taste for alcohol. Jack Good, who also wrote about music for *Disc* magazine, would sometimes have to wake them up. Ed and Gene would share a double room with one on each side of the bed, snoring away with a whiskey bottle between them.

One day Ed decided to play a joke on Gene. While Gene was in the bathtub, Ed took Gene's leg brace and hid it atop the wardrobe in their hotel room. Then Ed and Hal Carter went out to do some shopping and autograph-signing. When they returned a few hours later, the hotel was in pandemonium. The hotel manager was furious and ready to phone the police. Seems Gene, when he couldn't find his brace, exploded, threatening to sue the hotel for a million dollars because someone had stolen his brace. Eddie thought it was a gas, but he apologized to the manager, then went up to make things right with Gene.

Another time, during a rare break in the tour, Gene received from the States an advance copy of his new album *Crazy Times*. Eager to let Eddie take a listen, he put it on their record player. During one song, the needle stuck in the groove; Gene's hiccupping passage repeated again and again. "You know, Gene," Ed smiled playfully, "that's the greatest track yet!"

Eddie's drinking increased even more while he was in England. He had already garnered a reputation at home among his peers; Sharon told me that Don Everly once asked her, "Why are you dating that alcoholic?" Bobby Darin asked her the same question, she said. While Gene used alcohol to numb the ceaseless pain of his crippled leg, my uncle seemed to use it to numb the ache of missing his home. For a young man who'd never lived anywhere but in his mother's house, the long weeks in a foreign environment—particularly a relatively dismal one like wintertime England—took their toll. Back home, Eddie was accustomed to having a nice cold beer, but in England the beer was always served warm. Tour manager Hal Carter remembers Eddie saying in his Kingfish drawl, "You can stop boiling the beer now, it's done!" It was his way of jokingly complaining about something he missed so much.

Post-war England was not the most hospitable place for Americans used to hamburgers, Cokes, and milkshakes anytime they got the hankering. Even into the early '60s, the country was still in an almost impoverished state, lacking most of the comforts of home in the United States. Air conditioning and heating were rare, fast or convenience foods were unheard of, the black-and-white television service was limited to two channels, and everything, including restaurants, bars, and hotels, seemed to shut down by ten or eleven at night. Just locating a bottle of Jack Daniels was a tremendous undertaking.

Add to that the bone-chilling cold, and for young Americans who came to the U.K. to tour, it was certainly no vacation. Ed—desperately homesick and missing his mama's cooking—would mutter to Hal, "Goddamn, I'm never going to get home! I'm going to freeze to death in this country!" To Jerry Allison of the Crickets, who'd arrive in the U.K. to tour with the Everly Brothers, he said, "If I'd known you guys were coming over here I'd have had you bring me a bottle of American air!" And to Sonny Curtis, also on board with the Everlys, he asked, "Why didn't you bring us some American Coke?" Alcohol, it seemed to Ed, was the best way to keep his cool and stay warm.

The stress began to get to Ed. In Leeds, he broke down in tears after speaking to Granny on the phone. He telephoned her almost every day he was in England, sometimes talking for hours and racking up enormous phone bills. That night he was particularly upset and just wanted to go home. He had had enough. He was drinking and drinking, and by the time Hal Carter came to pick him up to take him to the show he was drunk as a lord.

Hal started pouring black coffee into him at the hotel, then loaded him into a cab and continued the coffee infusion at the venue. Then he lay Ed down on the floor in the dressing room, his leather laundry bag tucked under his head. He looked like he was on a slab in the morgue.

When it was almost Ed's turn to perform, Hal dressed him in his show clothes, hung his guitar around his neck. and wheeled him out onto the stage. With the Wildcats behind him, Ed pulled the show off, managing to stay standing for a good twenty minutes. But when he went down on his knees for his finale, he couldn't get back up.

The curtains closed and Hal ran out and stood Ed back up; the curtains reopened and Ed went into the song again. Again he slid to his knees and again he couldn't get himself back up. The curtains closed, Hal ran out and propped Ed back up, and the curtains opened again. And Ed went into the same song one more time, sliding down and getting stuck on his knees. After all was said and done, Ed never remembered doing the show.

When Sharon Sheeley arrived in England, she was a welcome reminder of home. Their relationship was not unlike any young romance, heady and intense, with its fair share of turmoil. Though Sharon's feelings for Ed were well known, many of my uncle's friends wondered whether Ed really reciprocated her emotion. Certainly they spent time together when they could, working around Ed's full schedule. But Ed was a young, virile man working in a field full of temptation. Sharon remembered Eddie once saying, "Honey, I'm just not ready to settle down."

As much as they cared for each other, Ed and Sharon still had moments where they just couldn't take any more. One night back home while the Everlys were staying at the Hollywood Hawaiian hotel, Ed and Sharon, Jerry Allison, Ronnie Ennis, and Don Everly piled into Ed's car. They were heading out to Ed's house so he could demonstrate some of his impressive quick-draw techniques, for which he'd developed quite a reputation. At the first traffic light Don bailed out of the car, saying Ed was driving far too fast for him. The quartet then continued to Ed's house.

Ed was the quickest draw around. He'd have you stand in front of him with your arms at your sides bent at the elbow, and your hands pointing as if you were aiming a pair of six-shooters at him. Then he'd have you clap your hands together as soon as you saw him reach for his holster. But Ed would always beat you—you'd find the six-gun between your hands. He'd have his gun out and ready to fire before your palms ever met. As a kid, I was in awe of Ed's nimble way with guns. And it seems all Ed's pals were too.

Ed would play "guns" with my cousin "Little Ed," Red and Glo's son, too. Eddie would razz Little Ed something terrible, Johnny Rook remembers, picking the kid up and throwing him over his back. Johnny never saw anyone else pay much attention to Little Ed, a cute, shy kid who reminded Johnny of Opie from the *Andy Griffith Show*. Eddie would play with Little Ed. There was a stairwell just outside the back porch of the Priory Street house in Bell Gardens. Eddie would go out the side of the house and Little Ed would run like hell and hide down in the stairwell. Eddie would pull out his "gun," fingers pointed like a piece, and aim at the boy.

He'd make a dramatic production of pretending to shoot him, complete with "Pow! Pow!" shot sounds. Then he'd blow the fake smoke away from the barrel of his fingers.

After Jerry Allison, Ronnie, and Sharon had gotten their fill of Ed's gun tricks, everyone piled back into the car. Feeling feisty after his firearms performance, Ed tore out for Hollywood. On their way back, Ed and Sharon got into a heated discussion, which turned into a downright argument. Sharon demanded that Ed let her out. So he did. He pulled over on the 101 freeway—in Boyle Heights in East Los Angeles, certainly not the best part of town—and said, "There you go." Sharon got out. "Now what do I do?" Sharon thought to herself. Surely Ed and the guys would come back for her. She hid in the bushes, just to show them. But they never came by. Sharon had to call the hotel for somebody to come get her. Granny had taught Ed never to argue with a lady.

But when Sharon arrived in England, Eddie introduced her as his fiancé to Duane Eddy, also in the U.K. to tour. Sharon was thrilled to be with Ed again, but she wasn't too pleased about having to share him with Gene. Eddie was very protective of Gene, she noticed. It got on her nerves sometimes, as she and Gene just didn't like each other. It was obvious to her that Gene was jealous of her relationship with Ed, that he resented terribly that she'd come over, that she was taking his beloved Eddie's attention that he was so used to having all to himself.

And Sharon resented Gene. She'd flown thousands of miles to be with the man she loved; she really wanted to spend some time with him alone without having Gene around twenty-four hours a day. Gene, with his painful leg and his drinking, was always upset about one thing or another; he was just a miserable person, Sharon thought. And Ed, well, he had to do quite a balancing act. He was torn between keeping her happy and keeping Gene from wallowing in his sorrows, which could sometimes turn suicidal.

Big Jim Sullivan recalls Gene as an ornery, vicious sort who carried a knife around with him and wasn't afraid to use it. A few times he'd walked to the back of the tour bus threatening to stab somebody, but with so many musicians aboard to contend with, his threats never really amounted to anything. I later met a fellow who'd worked with Gene in England. He asked him how he'd gotten along with the brooding rocker. The guy showed me his right hand, adorned between the first two knuckles with a half-moon scar. "Do you see that scar?" he asked. "That scar is from Gene's teeth!"

Jet Harris of the Shadows, another British band, remembers that he, Gene, and John Leyton, an English actor-turned-pop singer, once shared a dressing room. While Harris was applying some stage makeup, he heard a click behind him. It was Gene, and he had a gun pointed right at him.

"Harris, it's your turn!" Gene said.

Harris did the first thing that came to his mind; he grabbed Leyton and put him in front of him. Harris, like most everyone who'd had similarly unnerving experiences with Vincent, never could tell if Gene was serious or kidding. It all depended on how much whiskey the Jekyll-and-Hyde Vincent had consumed. Harris went on to become great friends with Gene, referring to him as a "sweetie," but emphasizes that Gene was a man possessed after a few drinks. That's why Harris weaned Gene off the hard stuff and down to the milder pints, a feat about which Harris—who himself eventually gave up drinking—was especially proud.

Sharon cherished her moments with Ed. But, not surprisingly, people often got confusing messages about the couple. Eddie was clearly a hit with the ladies. And Sharon was clearly a hit with the guys. She once showed me some very personal love letters from Billy Fury. He was obviously quite enamored with Sharon, and she used to try to make Eddie jealous by flirting with Fury. But it didn't have the effect she sought; Eddie used to encourage Billy and Sharon, supremely confident in the knowledge that he was Sharon's only real interest.

Eddie always had an air of genuine confidence. Under it all, however, he was very insecure on some level. It was as though he didn't feel he deserved all the attention. Those who were really close to him never understood where that insecurity came from. Eddie was formidable in so many ways; how could he not feel he deserved the world?

The conflicting stories from friends, family, and associates about Eddie's love for Sharon versus his continuing liaisons with the ladies made for some very different opinions of the couple's commitment to each other. Some people would see Eddie trying to distance himself from Sharon, maneuvering in hotels to keep her room at the end of the hall or, more preferably, on a different floor. Others would see his pride and happiness when she was with him.

My mother—a true romantic who was also very insightful—always told me that Eddie loved Sharon much more than Dad or his pals thought. Perhaps their relationship was not too unlike that of my parents. Dad played around with lots of ladies, too. Did it mean he didn't love my mom? Not a chance; Dad loved Mom forever. Were they like two lions at each others throats? Yes. Did they do just what it took to make the other one crazy? Absolutely. But, in the end, were they crazy about each other? For sure. Love is not necessarily the way we have been taught, and Eddie's shenanigans with other ladies didn't rule out deep and sincere feelings for Sharon.

To Sharon, Ed was the obvious star of Parnes's Anglo-American package. But when the idea of changing the marquee to Ed as headliner was broached, Ed would always say absolutely not. He wouldn't hear of it. He knew that Gene wouldn't be able to handle it, that emotionally Gene could not endure the blow of having his best friend's name put above his. And Eddie didn't even care. It just wasn't that important to him. He preferred to make mischief with Gene, getting themselves thrown out of hotels with their pranks. One night they collected all the shoes that hotel guests had left in the hallway to be polished and chucked them down the laundry chute. Next morning, Ed, Sharon, and Gene walked smartly out of the lobby, the only ones in the whole building wearing shoes—a dead giveaway. Another time they crammed hotel guests' shoes into the fire extinguisher compartments dotting the hallways or lined them atop the partitions placed in the entries of each hall. Most of the shoes looked alike, the style of the day for the typical businessman being the brogue. Tour manager Hal Carter is sure that more than one businessman left with shoes the next day that were the right size but didn't match.

Other nights, Ed and Gene would have a few drinks, then go around knocking on hotel room doors at two in the morning. The groggy guest would open the door, and Ed would say grandly, "Ready, Mr. Vincent?" Gene would answer, "I'm ready, Mr. Cochran," and they'd sing in giggling unison, "My old man's a dustman, he wears the dustman's hat," from the current Number One hit by Lonnie Donegan. Then, bang! They'd slam the door.

Crickets Sonny Curtis, Joe B. Maudlin, and Jerry (J. I.) Allison met up with Eddie in England as well, where they were backing up the Everly Brothers. They flew out of New York at night and arrived in London early in the morning. After checking into the Cumberland Hotel, Jerry said, "Man, we ought to go see Eddie." Since Jerry had the address of the apartment on Jermyn Street at which Ed and Gene stayed on the rare nights they were not on the road, they paid the pair a visit. Ed and Gene were still up, having been partying all night long. Sharon was in the bedroom asleep. After hanging out for awhile, the Crickets returned to the Cumberland. Soon their phone rang—it was a twelve-year-old fan calling to ask if he might have Sonny Curtis's autograph. Curtis was happy to oblige, and mentioned that he'd just come from seeing Eddie Cochran. "Man, oh man," the kid gushed, "Would I ever love to see Eddie Cochran!" So Curtis gave the boy the address and instructed him to tell Eddie that he was a friend of Curtis's. The kid went to the apartment and was lavished with both Eddie's and Gene's autographs. Curtis wasn't surprised—he always thought Ed was an unassuming kind of guy, more of a picker than a star.

Despite all the carousing with friends, though, Sharon and Ed were able to find a little time for themselves. They'd take 3 a.m. taxi trips around London on sightseeing expeditions. They'd visit Buckingham Palace, where Ed was intent on making the stoic guards in their tall black hats smile. And they'd steal quiet moments at the hotel playing music, she on the piano, he on the guitar.

But the merciless tour schedule that had Ed and his fellow performers hopping from one end of the United Kingdom to another in no logical order—Parnes would wring as much work as he could from his performers' weekly salaries—was wearing on all of the musicians. When Jack Good—who'd become quite friendly with Ed—visited Gene and my uncle at their hotel room in Manchester, he found them both in bed.

Ed—who'd good-humoredly taken to prefacing most of his conversation with Good with "Good Lord, Holmes" and whom Good called "My dear Watson"—was suffering from insomnia and strained eyes. He was hardly the madcap fellow Good had once seen taking a bath dressed in a belt, straw hat, and a pair of sunglasses. Gene was recuperating from pneumonia and pleurisy. Joe Brown had practically lost his voice, and Billy Fury was not feeling well, either. Good doubted that either Ed or Gene would be able to make the show that evening. He was wrong. They were superb.

After performances from the Tony Sheridan Trio, Brown and Peter Wynne, Ed took the stage. Good was stunned by his act; far from showing signs of strain, Ed was the most dynamic Good had ever seen him, actually making the most of his malady. Ed crouched with his back to the crowd as the Wildcats whipped through the first dozen bars of "What'd I Say." With his first words to the song, there was an audible gasp from the audience as Ed swung round to face them. He was clad in light tan leather trousers, a turquoise shirt, a shimmering silver vest—and a pair of dark glasses. He looked fabulous. And outrageous. He used the shades as a prop during that first song, making a great play of pulling them from his handsome face, like a stripper teasing a bar full of sailors.

Making the most of his deep, graveled voice—at once irresistibly sexy and radiating total control—my charismatic uncle, as he typically did when he performed, moved gracefully, almost elegantly across the stage, churning his guitar like the wheels of a train. During his solos, he'd lift a foot just off the floor and glide across the stage and back by twisting his other foot sideways. "Cochran is the toughest, ruggedest [sic] exponent of rock," Good wrote in *Disc*. "How he makes that music swing. He punches it over like a singing Rocky Marciano, and the whole audience was knocked out."

British teens were knocked out at every stop on the concert tour. In the audience at the Liverpool Empire in mid-March were four lanky teenagers with their hair greased back coolly from their foreheads—John, Paul, George, and Stu. They'd formed an amateur band of their own, the Silver Beetles, though they were still searching for a drummer. The scruffy boys loved Ed and Gene's music. When Paul was first introduced to John between sets of a church party gig that John's former group, the skiffle band the Quarry Men, was playing in 1957, he'd showed off by reeling off Ed's "Twenty Flight Rock." The four lads now included the song in their set list, along with Gene's "Be-Bop-A-Lula," the first record Paul had ever purchased, plus favorites memorized from Radio Luxembourg, tunes like Chuck Berry's "Maybellene" and "Roll over Beethoven," and Fats Domino's "Ain't That a Shame."

At the show, the audience reaction was astounding, something rarely before seen in uptight England. Teenage girls were actually caressing their private parts as they screamed at the American performers; their response to Ed's fierce beauty and Gene's tortured splendor was purely sexual. As fledgling rock 'n' rollers themselves, the phenomenon was inspiring. But as fans of Ed and Gene, it was also exasperating. As the insistent screams of the female fans threatened to drown out his American idols, John Lennon yelled furiously at the shrieking girls to shut up.

Back in London, Keith Goodwin of the *New Musical Express* dropped by Ed and Gene's flat at the Stratford Court Hotel in Oxford Street. The two still weren't feeling their best—Gene was still mending from his pneumonia and Ed had not yet licked his insomnia. But they were in excellent spirits, the new record by teenage American songbird Brenda Lee apparently giving them a lift.

"It's been pretty tough these last few weeks," Eddie told the reporter as Lee's sultry single "Sweet Nuthins" reached its end on the phonograph behind him.

"But everybody's been real good to us," Gene added, "and that's how we got on our feet again so quickly."

Goodwin had hardly settled himself in a chair before the two were singing the praises of Brenda Lee, giving "Sweet Nuthins" spin after spin.

"What a voice!" Gene raved. "It's unbelievable for someone so young!

"Listen to that drive," Ed chimed in, "isn't she great?"

They chatted with Goodwin a bit, telling him of their immediate plans, that they'd be returning to America in a few days for a sorely needed ten-day rest. Then they'd be back in Britain for another string of one-night stands and then a summer-season stint at the coastal resort town of Blackpool.

Gene was noncommittal about his trip to the States, saying only, "I've got some business to attend to." Ed was more forthcoming. "Well, I have some TV shows and stage dates lined up," he said. "Also, I have to attend talks for a film which I'll be making later in the year. This is very important to me, since it'll be my first dramatic acting role." Other press accounts mentioned an appearance for my uncle on *The Ed Sullivan Show*, scheduled during his American hiatus.

The three conversed casually and at length about the merits of Ray Charles, Brenda Lee, Josh White, and other American stars, Gene and Ed going about their daily business as the reporter tried to get questions in where he could.

How did they find British audiences, Goodwin wanted to know. "They were real good to us. But, I don't think they're quite as demonstrative as in the States," Ed said, apparently oblivious to the scandalous behavior he'd instigated amongst his female concert-going fans. "Over there, they often go nuts even when you're just announcing a number. But in Britain, they're somewhat more reserved and polite."

"I found that they went more for my wild rock songs than my ballads," Gene added. "But on the whole, they weren't too different from American audiences. They scream a lot and clap and get excited just like Americans. I guess audiences are pretty much the same the world over."

What did they think of the fans they met, the reporter wondered.

"I loved them," Gene said. "They're very devoted and very friendly, and it was a pleasure to meet them. But so many of them just don't look like teenagers. They seem so grown up in the way the dress and act."

"I love them, too," Eddie said. "Their loyalty is amazing at times. For instance, we saw the same fans at theaters all over the country. They must have traveled miles to see us."

"Did they ask for souvenirs?" Goodwin queried.

"Well, yes," Gene answered. "But most of them are happy just to shake your hand and have a little chat with you. I liked that. Mind you, I gave away quite a lot of souvenirs. American dimes seem to be the favorite with the fans."

"And guitar picks," Ed added. "I've handed out a whole stack of them. Shirts, too. Now and again, a fan asks for one of my shirts as a keepsake, and I don't like to say no. Also, on an average, we signed between 200 and 300 autographs each week."

"How about working conditions in Britain?" Goodwin asked.

"Right off, I must tell you that I've been far more tired here than in the States," Ed said, picking up a pair of dark glasses. "Why? Probably because we've had so little time to relax. People are always calling on us between shows—not that I'm complaining about that—and when we're not working, we're traveling."

"Traveling, I would say, presents the biggest problem of all," Gene explained as he lathered his face with shaving cream. "Most of our journeys are by train. Now, I don't want to offend anybody, but I must say I don't like British trains. They're not comfortable, there's no way to relax; traveling just becomes boring and sometimes unbearable."

"What about theaters?" Goodwin asked.

"Fine!" Gene exclaimed. "No complaints there. We've played some good places and have always been treated very well."

"I agree with Gene," Ed said. "But I would say that I prefer doing one-night stands as opposed to whole weeks at one theater. It's just that I like a change."

The reporter wondered what they thought of Britain as a country.

"Are you joking?" Gene chuckled, between strokes of his razor. "So much of our time has been taken up traveling that we really haven't had time to see the country! But seriously, I like it here, and would like to spend a lot more time in Britain in the future. I've thoroughly enjoyed myself."

Eddie, who had now donned the dark glasses and was strategically positioned in front of a small sunlamp, agreed. "More than anything else, I enjoyed the people—they're real nice and they've made us feel at home. On the other hand, I'm not crazy about your food. I miss home cooking a lot, and right now, I'm so homesick that I feel I just have to get back to the States for a few days."

Goodwin's interview with Gene and Ed was published in the same issue of the *New Musical Express*, April 15, Good Friday, that also ran an open letter from Buddy Holly's mother, expressing her thanks for support over the last year since her son's sudden and tragic death.

10
Catastrophe

SOMETHING ABOUT EDDIE was different.

Sharon first noticed in Manchester, England, during the show's run there March 28 through April 2, 1960. He went though a silent change, so subtle that only those who knew him very well were able to pick up on it. When they'd arrived in town, Ed had made her go to a record shop and buy all the Buddy Holly records she could find. This, from the guy who'd refused to listen to a Holly tune since Buddy, Ritchie, and the Big Bopper had died. When she'd returned, arms loaded with vinyl, he sat for hours in front of the record player in their hotel room, listening to his late friend's music over and over. "Isn't that making you sad?" Sharon asked him. "Why are you doing this?" "It doesn't make me sad anymore," Ed told her, "it's gonna be all right now." There was a sense of mystery, Sharon thought, a feeling that he knew something that she didn't, that started there in Manchester.

Not long after, one evening after midnight, Sharon was startled awake by the sound of loud screams. She tossed on her robe, dashed to the top of the stairs at the Milverton Lodge in Manchester where they were staying, and looked down. Eddie was pounding his fists on the hotel manager's door. When he opened it, Eddie—pale, drawn, and still sleepless—grabbed him by the lapels of his robe and shook him violently, screaming over and over again, "I'm gonna die, my God, and nobody can stop me! Nobody can stop it!"

Sharon and the hotel manager could do nothing to allay his fears; a doctor was eventually called who gave him some sedatives.

Some of his fellow musicians, like Wildcats drummer Brian Bennett, noticed a dark melancholia descend over my uncle toward the end of the tour. Early in the tour, Ed had visited Blackpool by the seaside, where he had his palm read by Gypsy Rose Lee. She had a premonition that he wouldn't return home. Publicly, he didn't seem to let the dark prediction bother him. But privately it disturbed him greatly; Sharon knew he had nightmares about it. Ed's sense that he was going to die young—keenly heightened in England—had always puzzled his friends. I think it's ironic that one of Eddie's favorite songs during his days with Chuck Foreman—at the very start of a career gloriously bright with promise—was "Live Fast, Love Hard, Die Young, and Leave A Beautiful Memory." The tune was written by the brother of Johnnie Berry, Ed's old girlfriend, and it was a big hit for Faron Young.

Ed managed to keep up a chipper face for his fans and the press, though, breezing through interviews like the one for *New Musical Express*, done in London with Gene. And he tried his best to wrangle a birthday surprise for Sharon, who turned twenty on April 4. That day he turned his entire wage packet over to Pat Thompkins, the road manager filling in for Hal Carter, who was still in Manchester with Joe Brown and Billy Fury; they were working on *Wham!* a new television program of Jack Good's. "Patrick, will you do something for me?" Ed asked. "Take this. Use whatever you need. Get the biggest cake in town and have 'Happy Birthday Sharon' written on it." Thompkins couldn't keep the secret, however, and Sharon insisted they go together and buy a small cake, plus a present for Eddie, a blue corduroy shirt.

The run at London's Empire Theatre in Finsbury Park, April 4 through 9, was originally to have been the final engagement of the tour for the United States-bound Ed and Gene. But the early shows had been so successful that another five-night stand of concerts was added at the Hippodrome in Bristol. On Friday night, April 15, Sharon phoned her mother, telling her they would definitely be heading to the airport after Ed's last concert the following night.

Janet Redfern on stage gives Eddie key to city of Chadron.
Eddie holds trophy naming him #1 singer voted by listeners
of KOBH, October 3, 1959.

Eddie and his 21st birthday cake. To Eddie's right,
Mrs. Redfern, Janet Redfern, Denny Thompson
(Eddie's road manager), and John Rook.

Eddie, October 3, 1959, signing autographs for admiring fans, in Chadron. Johnny Rook behind Eddie.

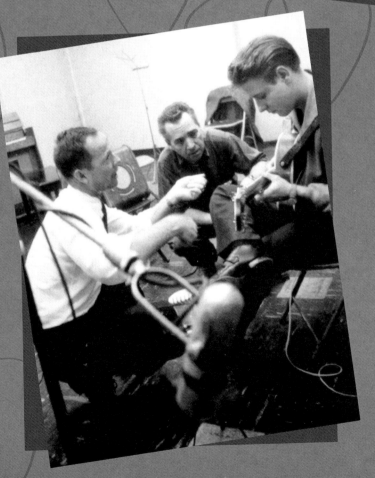

Left to right: Jerry Capehart, unknown, Eddie discussing details during session.

Eddie at the NME Pollwinner's concert, 1960, UK.

Bob Weir and me, live, January 1979, Knott's Berry Farm Cloud 9 Theater, with Ibanez -Tama Allstar Band featuring Billy Cobham (drums), Alphonso Johnson (bass), and Steve Miller (guitar).

Carole (née Ward) Commander, interviewing Eddie, February 7, 1960 in the green room, Gaumont Theatre, Sheffield, England.

Carole (née Ward) Commander, getting a hug from Eddie, February 7, 1960 in the green room, Gaumont Theatre, Sheffield, England.

My four-shot
promo, 1981

Eddie having fun on the phone,
at the Decca Reception,
January 1960, UK.

Eddie displaying his charming
smile, Decca Reception,
January 1960, UK.

Boy Meets Girl television show: Eddie, Gene Vincent, Marty Wilde.

Eddie, *Boy Meets Girl*, January 1960.

Newspaper clipping of Eddie's funeral. Granny in center, Dad behind her, Gloria to her left; next row back, left to right: Hank (Pat's husband), Grandpa, Richie Valens's mom, Little Ed Julson.

SINGER BURIED — Mrs. Alice Cochran, mother of rock and roll singer Eddie Cochran, weeps over the casket of her son who was killed in an auto crash 10 days ago in Bath, England. She is shown being comforted by relatives. Standing behind them (second from left) is the singer's father, and Mrs. Conception Valenz, whose son, singer Richie Valenz, died in an air crash last year. About 250 persons attended the graveside services yesterday at Forest Lawn Memorial Park in Cypress.

My lovely daughter Bree, 20 years old, picking up her new golden retriever.

Bree, dancing and having a great time, as usual.

Eddie in England, looking towards the heavens.

"Put on the beans and cornbread, Shrimper!" Ed told Granny when he made his daily call. "I'm coming home!"

The bill in Bristol featured Dean Webb, Tony Sheridan and his threesome, Georgie Fame, Billy Raymond, and Peter Wynne playing alongside Ed and Gene.

On the morning of April 16, Thompkins delivered plane tickets to Ed and Gene's hotel room. Sitting up in bed, they ripped open the envelope.

"Take a look, boy," Eddie crowed. "Real genuine tickets to the USA!"

Gene grinned, and with a couple of whoops they tossed the tickets in the air. For the rest of the day, about all they did was sit and look at those tickets.

On the final night, the Wildcats, Marty Wilde's band that had backed Ed the entire tour, were called away to London to accompany Wilde, who was substituting for an artist who'd fallen ill on "Sunday Night at the Palladium." Despite the less-than-stellar backing of British musicians called in at the last minute, Ed's final performance thrilled the excited crowd at the Hippodrome. Sharon watched from the wings as Eddie strode on to the stage in complete darkness. As the music started, a single spotlight beamed tightly and brightly—on Ed's butt. He was wearing a pair of tight red leather trousers, and he was suggestively gyrating his hips. For conservative England it was downright wicked, outrageously sexy. And the crowd went wild for it.

Johnny Gentle, another of Parnes's power-named singers, took an ailing Dean Webb's place on the bill. Gentle had driven to the theater and was returning to London after the show. Eddie tried to catch a ride for his California-bound party with Gentle, but Gentle's car was already full. Although the trio's plane was not scheduled to depart until one o'clock the following afternoon, Eddie was intent on making the journey back to London that evening. The train, cramped and uncomfortable, would no doubt have had Gene complaining the entire way. And they didn't start running again until almost four in the morning. So a car was hired. Eddie was determined to keep his appointment with destiny, a fact not lost on me more than four decades later.

The cream-colored Ford Consul driven by nineteen-year-old George Martin left the Royal Hotel in Bristol around 11 p.m. It had been used for a wedding that day, Martin explained, and was still littered with colorful confetti. Gene climbed into the backseat first, then Ed, then Sharon, and Pat Thompkins sat in the front passenger seat. Martin headed southeast to Bath, then east toward London. Though he wasn't attired in the bowler, pin stripe trousers, and umbrella he'd playfully promised Jack Good he'd be wearing on his arrival in the States, Ed was delighted to finally be on his way home. To prove it, he belted out a few bars of "California, Here I Come."

Soon the car fell silent, its occupants gazing out at the dark, deserted streets blanketed in thick fog and the black trees whizzing by as the car hurtled through the night. Sharon knew Ed was in a hurry to get to the airport, but she worried that they were going dangerously fast. "Why are we going so fast?" she asked Martin. "Don't you think that we should slow down?" The engine's hum, and his trusty alcohol, soon lulled Gene to sleep. It was almost midnight. Pat Thompkins leaned over to fish a fresh pack of cigarettes from the travel bag at his feet.

Suddenly, Martin lost control of the vehicle. The car spun backwards, careening with explosive impact into a concrete lightpost. Lives were changed—and ended—in an instant.

The Consul skidded for fifty yards before coming to a halt, its rear end a mangled mass of twisted metal. Bodies lay crumpled on the wet grass, now festively adorned with bits of confetti. At exactly midnight, the streetlights went out. Ed's white guitar case gleamed in the moonlight.

Sharon lifted an eyelid. A dark and silvery world slowly spun into focus. Gene was kneeling beside her, rubbing his left shoulder. Sharon tasted blood in her mouth. She felt cold, wet, and heavy. She tried to stand up, tried to move, but there was nothing to move. She was completely numb. She panicked. What happened? Where was she? Where was Eddie?

She looked at Gene. "Where's Eddie?" she demanded, her voice a hoarse whisper.

Gene's eyes were wide. "Oh, he's fine," Gene drawled nervously, trying his best to sound comforting. "He's sitting in the car having a cigarette. He's just shook up is all."

At that moment, Sharon knew that Ed was either dead or dying. If he wasn't, he'd be there at her side, not Gene. He wouldn't be relaxing in the car while she was laying on the grass out here—wherever here was—bleeding to death. She prayed, motionless and silent, shattered on the ground. She prayed to God with all her might, Please, please don't let Eddie leave me. And then she passed out.

Next thing she knew she was holding Eddie's hand. She could barely see him through the fog. He seemed to be sleeping. He looked so beautiful. Was she dreaming? A stranger's face parted the silver murk. He was wearing a uniform. A siren shrieked above her, painfully bright lights assaulted her eyes.

"Something told me you two were in love," the ambulance driver told Sharon, "so I locked your hands together, miss."

"Thank you," Sharon whispered.

And then she prayed to God not to let her go back under. If she did, she knew she'd never see Eddie again. Her lids fell. And she never saw her beloved again.

When the ambulance reached St. Martin's Hospital in Bath, Eddie was alive but "deeply unconscious," according to one of nine doctors called to his bedside. "Our efforts kept him alive much longer than he might have lived otherwise. But there was simply nothing we could do to save him. He never regained consciousness." Eddie, just twenty-one years old, died of severe brain lacerations at just after four o'clock Easter Sunday afternoon, April 17, 1960.

For most of my life I could not fathom why Ed's death had such a profound effect on me. Ten-year-old boys weren't supposed to react with such emotional ferocity, such head-banging intensity, as I did to the passing of an uncle whom I dearly loved, but barely really knew. Nearly forty years later I would learn the answer. It would be the most painful lesson of my life.

Bree's day started early that spring day in 1999. My daughter— Breeannon Mikalia Cochran, second-born of our four children and the oldest of our three daughters—had a class at Cumberland Institute for Wellness Education, a school of massage therapy and related fields in Nashville, Tennessee, not far from our home. She'd recently finished her courses in massage therapy and was now taking an extended course in cranio-sacral massage. She was a gifted healer.

I was so proud of her. She graduated from high school at age sixteen and worked three jobs while in her first year of college. Though she was only twenty-one, she'd already developed then soundly beaten a severe drinking problem. She'd gone back to school while still holding a full-time job. She'd really turned her life around. We were so excited for Bree's future.

"I love you!" she chirped to her mother and me as she ran out the door that morning to catch a ride with her boyfriend. Within seconds she came bounding back inside the house. She knew we'd be attending a music industry benefit that day, and that this would be her mother's first event at which she'd distribute her new business cards as a Reiki healer—one who channels the universal life force energy for the purpose of healing—and herbologist. She wanted to wish her mom good luck and tell her she loved her again.

At about 3:30 p.m. or so, while at the benefit with Rita, I got a call from Bree. Her boyfriend and his dad were going to a hockey game that night, and they would be leaving straight from school. She'd be without a ride, unless I could bring her the keys to her car, which she'd left parked at Cumberland the day before. Could I please bring her her keys, Bree wanted to know. I had a gig lined up right after the benefit. If I brought Bree her keys, I'd have to leave that moment—I was on one side of town, our house was on another, Nashville was in another direction, and my gig was in still another.

"Are you sure you can't work it out another way?" I asked her.

"No, Dad, I can't," she said, then added her usual irresistible, "Please?"

My baby girl obviously needed me and I wouldn't let her down if I could help it. Rita and I drove home, picked up the keys, and drove in to Nashville. When we got to Cumberland, I went inside looking for Bree and her class. Not wanting to disturb the lessons underway, I quietly cracked a door open. "Is Bree here?" I whispered to nearby students. She was pointed out to me. As I opened the door more so I could see her, she jumped off the counter where she was sitting, pointed to me and exclaimed, "There's my Dad!" with all the exuberance of an excited child. She bounded over to me and hugged me. I gave her the keys and we said our "I love you"s. She was so grateful.

I took Rita home, loaded up the car with my gear and headed for the gig. By about 7 p.m. I had everything set up and was talking over the show with the bandleader. It was my first night meeting him and playing with his group. Suddenly, my beeper went off. It was my home number. I quickly phoned home.

"Hi, what's up?" I asked when Rita answered.

She was sobbing. Bree had been in an accident, my wife managed to choke out, and she might not make it.

I was in shock, a vise of emotion pushing in on my head and shoulders. I ran over to the band leader and told him that my daughter had been in an accident, that he'd have to find a replacement for me. "I have to go, I'll be back for my gear later," I breathlessly muttered as I sprinted out the door. My legs felt disconnected, rubbery.

I tore out for St. Thomas Hospital, screaming down the roads at a hundred miles an hour, running stop lights and passing cars as quickly as I could. I was engulfed in fear and desperate to be with Bree—praying, hoping, afraid. I knew I had to be with my baby girl whether she was alive or not.

Through my tears and prayers, I called the hospital as soon as I was on the freeway. Was Bree alive? They wouldn't tell me anything. I began to fear this was it; I couldn't stand the thought.

Furious, I bellowed at them, "I'm driving a hundred miles an hour and I need to know now!" I demanded that the doctor be put on the line. My stomach ached. Finally, the doctor told me the truth.

Bree was dead. My heart shattered.

I phoned my twenty-nine-year-old son to tell him he didn't have to hurry to get to the hospital. I didn't want to lose anyone else or endanger anybody. I still drove as fast as I thought was safe. I ran into the hospital, screaming for my daughter. The nurse and doctor each took me by an arm and walked me about fifty feet past the room where Bree was. I couldn't figure out what they were up to. For some unimaginable reason, they were delaying me being with my daughter. Now livid, I demanded they take me to her room that instant.

When I walked in my shock was complete. The glare of the fluorescent lights was cold and disconnected. The room was pleasantly redolent of Bree. The dusky mix of her perfume and Drum rolling tobacco, the way she always smelled. Her lifeless, still-warm body had been laid out on a bed, shrouded to her shoulders in a white sheet. I could see her beautiful, gentle face. Her eyes were closed. And although her upper lip was split to her nose, she was smiling. A peaceful smile. That beautiful smile. Bree was always smiling.

I touched her ear, as I did so often. I stroked her dainty and fragile, yet powerfully healing hands. Her brother said he wanted to see her eyes. I remember thinking, I hope it doesn't leave a haunting memory. As he raised her eyelids I saw the most beautiful blue eyes, filled with great peace. Later, I found out that the corneas from those beautiful eyes helped give sight to two women who desperately needed them. Someday I hope to meet them.

As family and friends arrived, we all sank into a hell of horror and grief. Bree's car had been hit head-on by a truck; she had been hurt so badly that there simply was no saving her. My wife refused to believe it. She just knew Bree was still alive and insisted through her bounteous tears that the doctors check for any sign of life again. It was hopeless. My God, the grief.

Not even an hour after I'd arrived at the hospital, I was approached by a staffer about donating Bree's organs. I agreed. It turned out to be one of the most insensitive, heart-wrenching processes I have ever gone through. They had me on the phone for about forty-five minutes, describing to me every possible detail of what they were going to do. It was so morbid, so painful. I kept telling them they had our permission to take and use everything as long as we could still view her at the funeral, please just give me something to sign and stop this torture. But over and over again we went through the same horrifying discussion. I have tried to make my experience known to the people in charge of that organization and would like to do whatever it takes to make that process more humane for anyone in that position.

When I departed the hospital, I drove to the accident site. I wanted to see what I could find out. I came upon a man loading some stuff onto a trailer and it turned out to be the owner of the gardening company whose truck hit Bree. I asked him for the phone numbers of the driver and passengers so I could speak to them, and he gave them to me.

I found out that Bree had been driving at about 5:30 p.m. or so on this very busy street. The traffic always moved very fast at that location. Apparently, Bree was distracted and didn't see that traffic had suddenly stopped up ahead of her; out of her vision, over the upcoming hill, cars in her lane—just out of view moments before— had stopped to make turns.

When Bree reacted to the halted cars, it was too late. She slammed on her brakes, skidded several feet to the left and clipped the left rear of the car in front of her. She probably swerved left to avoid the severe drop-off on the right side of the road. That first collision put her into the oncoming traffic lane. At the same time, there was a truck—a one-ton pickup pulling a twenty-five-foot gardening trailer—about to clear the top of the hill in front of her. They collided head-on. The driver of the truck only had time to stiffen out his arms before the impact. He and his two passengers were not hurt badly. Bree, who was not wearing her seat belt, was killed instantly. Upon impact she flew forward, hitting her face and separating her skull from her neck. Her torso smashed into the steering wheel, which badly injured her internally. Her right leg was broken at the thigh, and there were many contusions. Mercifully, the coroners said she didn't feel any pain after her initial impact because of her broken neck.

That night, that awful night, when I arrived back home after leaving my daughter's lifeless body, there was a message waiting for me. A friend had called to console me about Eddie. It was April 17th. I hadn't realized.

11
Synchronicities

THE DAY AFTER BREE was killed we got a call from Jane, a close friend of both Bree and our family. She had been at St. Thomas Hospital with us the night before. When she finally got home from the hospital, she told us, she climbed into the shower to freshen up after the long, horrible ordeal. Standing under the hot, pulsing water in the dark, she had a vision in which Bree came to her and said "Michael, the archangel, helped me get here. I didn't know how to get here myself."

Later that day we received a call from another acquaintance. She really didn't know us all that well, and she wasn't sure if she should tell us what had happened to her. It all seemed so crazy. But after talking with Rita for awhile, she decided she couldn't hold back. Apparently this woman had had a few psychic experiences from time to time in her life, often preceded by severe migraine headaches. She'd had an excruciating migraine the day before, she confided to Rita. Something terrible was going to happen to someone they knew, she'd told her husband—she could feel it.

When our acquaintance finally heard about Bree, she felt an incredible pain at the base of her skull. She had a series of visions, or experiences, that left her with a knowledge of things she'd never known before. One was of an opening between the skull and the neck, something like a bullet hole separating the bones. Another was of a beautiful girl with long, blonde, curly hair—like Bree. She was dancing, moving her hands at her waist, and saying, "Heaven is bitchin'!" The flower lavender was pressed into the woman's memory, which in herbology is used specifically to heal the soul. The girl then said, "Tell Angie"—we have a close family friend named Angie—"it's breezy, not cheesy," and "Tell them to give it up, I'm fine." Bree's not earthbound, the woman said the girl in her vision told her; she travels back and forth. She doesn't need the archangel Michael now, she knows the way herself. She is spending her time helping, helping the children to cross over. As bizarre as it all was, what our friend Jane and this woman whom we barely knew told us brought us some comfort.

The next several days were the most anguished of my life. I had a pain in my solar plexus so deep and so large that I didn't know if I'd actually survive it. That ache inside me was all consuming. I cried so long and hard it seemed like there just couldn't be any more tears.

With Bree's death, my life was altered in a way that's difficult to explain. My love for her was—and is—so deep, so profound, and my grief so extreme. I can still remember the night Bree was conceived. It was one of those moments that was so special, it has stayed with me all these years. After seven years, my wife decided she wanted another child. Although we'd had a son, I'd always wanted more kids, but Rita had remained adamantly against a bigger family. She told me over and over again that she never wanted more kids. But secretly, I always believed she would have a change of heart when the time was right.

And I was correct. When Bree was born, we had her at home in our bedroom, just as we did with our next two children. When her delicate little head came out, she smiled this huge smile. I loved her from the very moment we'd created her.

I'd always worried about losing Bree, much more than with our other kids. A couple of weeks before she died, she told her fifteen-year-old sister Courtney that she just couldn't picture herself any older than she was. "Whatever!" Courtney playfully admonished her. "You're gonna be one of those old maids who lives alone with a hundred cats and eats frosting straight from the can!"

I'd always tried to get Bree to use her seat belt. In fact, just a few weeks before she died, I'd lowered the belt so it would be more comfortable on her. She had been involved in another accident about two years earlier—before she'd licked her alcoholism—in which she was thrown from her car as it flipped and cartwheeled into a field. The driver behind her said she was thrown more than twenty feet into the air and landed on her head. She fractured her C2 vertebra and was in a neck brace for months; the doctors were amazed that she survived. We used to have to wash her hair in the kitchen sink as she lay on the counter. Once she recovered, it took us about four hours to get all the mats and tangles out of her beautiful, long, blonde hair.

Bree's loss was staggering for us. She was a very special young lady and an awesome presence, who had a lasting, and oftentimes profound, effect on people. Rita and I had an incredible relationship with our daughter and I couldn't stand the thought of life without her. I could never, ever love anybody more. The love for a child is the most unbridled, unconditional, complete, and awe-inspiring love there is; there is nothing deeper or more pure. Our sense of loss was—and still is—overwhelming.

I knew we would all heal with time, and that the process would be long and extraordinarily difficult. Part of the healing for me included contacting the men in the truck that killed Bree. I knew they must have felt terrible, in some way responsible for the snuffing out of this bright, young life. I wanted them to know that they were welcome at the funeral. I wanted to let them know that I forgave them for their part in my daughter's death. When I did finally meet them, their grief was palpable. The guilt that weighed on them was heartwrenching, and in my view, unwarranted. I knew that Bree would not want them to carry any such guilt or pain. On her behalf I had to forgive them, and thank them for their courage to meet with me.

We held services for Bree on April 22 at Harpeth Hills Funeral Home and Memory Gardens in Nashville. In honor of Bree's free and fun-chasing spirit, we asked that attendees dress wildly or like hippies—Bree always told us she was a hippie born too late. We wanted her funeral to be a true celebration of her life. Although passersby may have thought that aliens had landed, it was truly heartwarming to see such a diverse crowd come to commemorate my daughter's life. So many spoke of the incredible connection there seemed to be among the attendees, all folks who loved Bree. Many found it the most moving and touching service they'd ever attended, certainly not the normal kind of grim affair. There was joy, love, tears, and celebration—heartache and jubilation in equal abundance, just as Bree would have had it. She would have danced her whirling, twirling, smiling, singing, inspired-by-life ballet. She had the most fluid way of dancing, a real joy to watch.

A week or so before Bree's death I'd ordered some promotional CDs of my latest recording project. Bree loved music and was always her father's biggest fan. I requested that I have the discs by April 22. I had no idea that would be the date I'd be burying by daughter. I had no idea, not an inkling, that she'd be gone. When I got the call that the CDs were ready, I had forgotten about the order. I remember thinking how ironic it was that I'd picked that date for delivery, that I'd stressed how important it was that I have them by then, although at the time I thought I was just making sure they would be ready in a timely fashion. I decided I wanted to give copies of the CD to all of Bree's friends, to share some of what my daughter loved with them. The order was hand delivered in time to distribute the music to all of Bree's friends at the funeral.

On July 27, 1999, on what would have been Bree's twenty-second birthday, we had a small party with some of our close friends at Bree's favorite park. It was so heartwarming to hear people continue to share the impact Bree had had on them. At the party we cried and laughed a lot. There were so many stories we all had to share with each other, some funny, some stupid, some personal. They all helped bring us closer to knowing Bree in all her special and unique ways. I love her so much and think of her many times a day, and I appreciate the way she still makes such an important impact on me every day. I thank her for allowing me to make the journey of her too-brief life here on earth with her.

It took me many months to even begin to cope with Bree's death. Often I'd burst into tears while driving by myself, motoring down the same roads Bree did, missing her and the delight I always got from seeing her, holding her, and telling her how much I loved her. I missed that so much, it sometimes seemed impossible to adjust to life without her. I found myself totally letting go on those drives, with no one there to be uncomfortable with my grief. Then I'd think of how much she would prefer it if I wasn't sad but instead was empowered by her memory. It felt good to know how much she cared about me. And I suspect she still does. So I continue to do the best I can, to bring the very best I can to life.

It wasn't too long after Bree's death that I started to notice some striking coincidences. Both Bree and Ed died on April 17. They were both just twenty-one. Both were killed in car accidents at nearly the same time. They both died of severe traumas to the head. The address where Bree was killed was 2417; two people dear to me were killed on 4/17. They both had small hands and feet, shoe fetishes, and both were big tippers. And they both came to me in my dreams. When Ed used to visit me when I was a boy, he taught me how to play music. Now my daughter teaches me how to live.

I often wonder about destiny and free will. There have been times when I've regretted moving from Los Angeles to the Nashville area in 1994. The relocation was done partially in an effort to save Bree's life; the more negative influences of LA had begun taking a nasty toll on her. I wanted all of our children to have a safer environment in which to grow up. But when I look at all the circumstances that brought us to that fateful moment of Bree's death, at that place, at that time, it is hard for me not to take solace in the realization that it couldn't have happened any other way. The synchronicities, the connections too numerous to be mere coincidences, have been undeniable. Through Bree's death, I've been given an opportunity to gain insight and peace—the messages are far too clear to me that there is more going on in life—more bubbling just under the surface—than we realize.

Although Bree, to me, was and always will be my child, she had the wisdom and insight of an old soul. It was the same thing with

Eddie. He's often been described as mature for his age, and certainly as a musician he was an old soul. Every person I've ever talked to about my uncle has said how much he affected them. It doesn't seem to matter how long or how briefly they knew Eddie. If it was a year, a day, or just an hour, Eddie made sure you never forgot him. I guess that's why he was always signing things, "Don't forget me." I just never realized the same was going to be true for Bree. And Bree, nor Ed, will never let us forget.

On October 19, 2000, a year and a half after my daughter's death, while I was on tour in Great Britain, I felt compelled to call home. I had glanced at my watch and realized that it was approximately the same time at which Bree's accident had occurred, between 5:30 and 6:00 p.m. central time. It was also about the same time Eddie's accident happened, between 11:30 and midnight London time. When I reached my wife, she was crying. On her way home that evening she'd come to a stop sign. Though the oncoming traffic was a couple of hundred yards away—she certainly could have safely made her turn—something told her to wait.

After the cars had passed, she pulled out behind them. After she drove a mile or so, the cars in front of her stopped suddenly in the middle of the road. She waited. And waited. But the traffic did not move. Soon she saw the man who was driving the car in front of her get out of his car, walk up the road and then return to his vehicle. "What's happening?" Rita had asked. The car leading their convoy of traffic had hit a young girl, he told her. The girl was dead. Rita burst into tears. If she had pulled out in front of the line of cars a few minutes ago, she would have been that lead car. She would have killed that girl.

All the horror of that night we lost Bree instantly overtook Rita. She was overwhelmed by sorrow and confusion. She thought of the pain this young girl's parents were about to go through. Why had she hesitated before pulling into that line of traffic? Why had she been at that place, at that time, so close to that accident?

When she arrived at our house, she carried some groceries into the kitchen and put the bags on the counter. When she turned around, standing inside the house, just inside the front door ,was a young girl. She was dirty and covered with debris—bits of leaves and twigs and smears of dirt. Rita was stunned. Who was this girl? Did she need help? Rita was about to ask what she was doing there, when the girl disappeared.

My wife was shocked and mystified. What had just happened? First the accident, then this. Was she dreaming? She called Angie, our close family friend, and told her of the disconcerting events. With Angie's help, Rita tried to find some meaning in the day's strange events.

Angie suggested that since we had recently lost our daughter, maybe Rita could be of some comfort to the parents of this young girl who had been killed. My wife decided to request an address from the police so that she might send a letter to the parents of the deceased girl. Rita wrote the letter but didn't immediately send it. It wasn't the right time. She mailed it about three weeks later.

Not long after I returned home from England, we received a call. It was the father of the deceased girl. The letter Rita wrote was perfect, he said. It brought his wife and him great comfort. We both wanted to talk and had a wonderful conversation about our daughters. Together, this grieving father and I laughed and cried many times during the course of our nearly two-hour conversation.

Suddenly he confided, "I'll never forget the date your daughter died because we have another daughter whose birthday is April 17th." He called a few months later and we spoke again for another two hours. He thought it odd that his address was 2119; Bree was twenty-one, his daughter nineteen. By then I knew that our daughters had many similarities and that his daughter had been adopted. "We loved her like she was our own," he told me.

And then he said, wait, he'd just remembered something. His deceased daughter's birth name was... Cochran

Another time, on a trip to California, we were driving down Interstate 40 west through Oklahoma, near where Eddie had spent some of his childhood. This was a few months after Bree's death. Bree and Rita were both interested in Native American culture, and they had always wanted to collect some owl feathers. My wife decided that we were going to find those owl feathers on this trip.

We were talking in the car when I thought I saw a dead bird on the side of the road. I wasn't sure, but it looked like an owl. I turned off at the next exit and headed back to where I thought I'd seen the bird. Sure enough, there it was, lying dead on the side of the freeway. We put the owl in a trash bag, pulled off at the next exit, and stopped on a side street of what looked to be a very small town.

My wife and daughter Courtney harvested the feathers, prayed for the bird, and conducted a sort of burial ceremony for this beautiful owl with the glorious five-foot wing spread. We'd been there for a while when my Courtney asked, "Do you know what time it is?" I looked at my watch. It was 5:30 p.m. central time, around the time of Bree's death. I looked up and noticed the sign on the building near which we were parked. It said "Hembree." Rita and Courtney had already noticed—the sign had Bree's name in it.

Then I noticed the street sign; we were parked on Donlee. That reminded me of our friend Don, who worked in the burn ward at Vanderbilt Hospital. He had helped prepare Bree's body for the funeral; he had been invaluable in repairing Bree's lip, which was badly mutilated in the accident. With his help we were able to keep the natural smile that was on Bree's face after her accident. We wanted her to look as natural as possible for her viewing in the casket at the funeral. My wife and daughter-in-law arranged Bree's hair just the way she used to like it, and they disguised some of the bruising with hand-drawn flowers on her cheek. She looked so beautiful, I can still see her now.

As we pulled onto the main street, we passed a Taylor gas station. Taylor is our youngest daughter's name. So many coincidences! When we returned home, we got together with some of our friends including Don, Jane, and Angie. We told Don about the street named after him, "Donlee." He laughed and said, "Do you know what my middle name is? Lee!"

12
Endnotes and Remembrances

ED WAS LAID TO REST on Monday, April 25, 1960, at Forest Lawn Memorial Park in Cypress, California. It was a short and simple graveside service, officiated by the Reverend C. Sumner Reynolds of Maywood Methodist Church. Mrs. Concepcion Valens, Ritchie Valens's mother, who'd been a tremendous support to Granny, joined the several hundred mourners. My father and Uncle Bill laid on the grave a wreath of red and white carnations in the shape of a guitar.

Johnny Rook traveled to Los Angeles to attend the funeral of his friend, but he just couldn't bring himself to go. He stayed at Granny and Grandpa's new house in Buena Park, about which Ed had spoken when he played in Hot Springs, South Dakota. Johnny had had visions of it being elaborately beautiful; when he arrived, it didn't even have a lawn. He was there when Ed's body arrived from England. Dad and Red went to the airport to meet the casket. When they came home, Dad looked at Granny with a pained frown and choked, "Mom, it doesn't even look like him." That's all Johnny needed to hear. It destroyed him. He couldn't bear the thought of seeing his beautiful friend dead, disfigured, and lowered into the dirt. So Johnny stayed behind while the others went to the funeral. Granny put Johnny in Ed's room the first of his four nights there. Johnny was so devastated by Eddie's death, that for four decades he was unable to listen to any of his friend's records.

Of course, Ed's death was a tremendous blow to our family, Granny in particular. I remember her collapsing on top of the casket at the funeral, a moment of indescribable sorrow captured for posterity by a nearby newspaper cameraman. Dad was right behind her, picking her back up onto her feet. After the Wiltshire Constabulary returned Eddie's guitar, Granny turned her youngest son's bedroom at her home in Buena Park—a house purchased by Gloria and Red, not Eddie, as myth has had it for too long—into a virtual shrine, keeping it just as it was while he was alive, allowing few to enter it. Sometimes she slept there. A few times I did, too, like the night Dad brought us kids over there very late, and we went home the next morning to find Mom beaten up. It was a little spooky sleeping in Eddie's room across from the display case where they kept that beautiful Gretsch and all of his guns and knives. Granny chose to deal with her grief through denial; it was as though she made herself believe that Eddie was simply away on a long tour.

After Eddie's death, Grandpa Frank started coming to our house more often. He'd bring a trunk full of pop bottles so we could turn them in for the refund. I used to think, "Boy, Granny and Grandpa must be rich to afford all those sodas." Every two weeks he would pick me up and take me with him to groom and polish Eddie's gravestone. It was a solemn time; Grandpa was very quiet. He used to take me for a haircut at the local barber shop and pay an extra dollar so that I could get the head massage. What a treat, apparently for him as much as me as it made him happy to see how much I enjoyed that. Though he seemed happy to visit with us, he still seemed so downtrodden. I never knew why that was. My sisters would sit on his lap and he would give them a quarter. Then he'd have to go home. I remember everyone's concern when, at one family gathering, the garage-door spring broke, trapping Grandpa under the heavy door. He was yelling for help. The men rushed out to lift the door from him. Everyone was concerned about his heart.

Then one day Grandpa stopped coming over. It was as though he was withering away emotionally. We had moved farther away and didn't see him hardly at all. Then word came that he died. My cousin "Little Ed" Julson, Glo and Red's son, discovered him in the bedroom, where so much of his life was spent. It seemed so inevitable. It was sad to lose Grandpa, but we had already lost him when Ed died. Everything in our family shifted when Eddie died. Granny's house was like a tomb.

My immediate family seemed to drift farther away from the rest of the Cochran clan. Dad and I stayed close to Granny, but things were strained in some way. There were hidden undertones of tension that I just didn't understand. It wasn't until the early 1990s that some things started to become clear for me. It was then that I learned of a very private family crisis that had happened thirty years before. This revelation shed light on the rift between my immediate family and the rest of the Cochrans, that, while already palpable by the early '60s, had somehow, painfully deepened from that period forward. I say these things now not to open old wounds or to hurt anybody. I love all of the Cochrans. I know how difficult it is to deal with life's tragedies and pain. I've learned that fear, anger, and hatred only serve to consume us from the inside out, and that ultimately we are best served by love, forgiveness, and compassion. Crisis in any family has to be dealt with in a positive way, in a manner that can heal and rebuild healthy, loving relationships. Our family's history of alcoholism and their ever-present fear of what others will think caused one hell of a crippling emotional barrier to any kind of healthy family functioning. In retrospect, the family was still reeling from the recent loss of Eddie and simply wasn't capable of dealing effectively with another emotional crisis. Now, the strangeness surrounding my family—the oppressive perfectionism, the secrecy, the undercurrents of tension, have begun to make a profoundly sad sense.

My father was also crushed by the loss of Eddie. Eddie was his rock, Johnny Rook remembers; there was a great bond there. Johnny doesn't think anyone loved Eddie more than Dad, they were so close. They never had to talk about it, Johnny said, you just knew it. Dad had always been very protective of his baby brother, his musical alter-ego and drinking buddy. Sometimes when Ed and his friend Ron Wilson would be playing music and my father was around, Dad would watch them intently, scrutinizing them, Ron told me. Ron can remember Dad's eyes while he was sitting in a chair, with a cup of coffee or whatever. He'd be concentrating on them as if he were studying something, analyzing, digesting. And Dad was always sticking up for Ed. I remember hearing about one time when some guy was going to whip on Ed. Ed was just about to get into it, when Dad stepped in, yelling at Ed, "No! You'll hurt your hands!" So Dad fought the guy. In another scrap on Ed's behalf, Dad ended up with a big scar on his right hand—an inch wide from his ring finger knuckle almost up to his wrist—where his fist had caught some guy's teeth.

But there was no saving Ed this time. There was nothing Dad could do. So he poured his emotion into a poem that was inscribed on Eddie's grave:

Heavenly music filled the air
That very tragic day.
Something seemed to be missing tho'
So I heard the creator say:
"We need a master guitarist and singer.
I know of but one alone.
His name is Eddie Cochran
I think I'll call him home.

"I know the folks on earth won't mind,
For they will understand
That the Lord loves perfection,
Now we'll have a perfect band."

So as we go through life; now we know:
That perfection is our goal,
And we strive for this
So when we are called,
We'll feel free to go.

Shortly after Eddie's death, Dad was in bed and suddenly bolted upright. He wildly swung a fist, as if trying to hit someone. Mom asked what he was doing. Dad told her someone had been standing there just moments before, then simply disappeared. Dad was spooked. They both came to believe that it Eddie, coming to pay a visit.

Dad always told me to make sure I called Granny. All the Cochrans loved Granny. Her iron fist, her petite frame, her unwavering devotion to the memory of Eddie, her deep Southern drawl. With Granny, most single syllable words became two syllables. She'd say, "Na-ow, B...o...bb...y..." I still miss her. It saddens me that we were not as close in her later years. There was an element of jealousy and fear that Dad spoke about. He said that on some level he thought Granny was afraid I would outshine Eddie.

Imagine! In my world nobody could outshine Eddie, he was as bright a star as there could ever be. That time Granny and I ended up sobbing together when I played "Little Lou" for her when I was fourteen was only the second time that Granny really heard me play, for just a few minutes, even though I'd been one with my guitar for nearly two years, and we always lived only minutes away. The third time was when I was with Steppenwolf at Royce Hall at UCLA several years later. I had reached my goal, I had made it as a professional guitarist; Granny still seemed indifferent to my talent. Duane Eddy once mused that Granny thought she was being loyal to her son by never acknowledging anyone else. In her mind it helped to keep her precious Eddie's image and legacy intact. I wanted nothing more than for Granny to put her arms around me and let me know how much she loved me and how proud she was of me.

When Eddie's buddies and I used to play music together when I was young, they would often say that I, even at my tender age, was already better than Eddie at some things. It always felt good to know that I was on track with my goals. But in my heart I knew that being better than Eddie at something, at anything, wasn't the point. Eddie shared a gift with me. He allowed me to stand on his shoulders, so to speak. In today's world there is so much talk of who is better than whom, so much emphasis put on the flash factor. In truth, what really matters is whether an artist can touch your soul. And Eddie touched my soul.

Duane Eddy put it well when he said, "Music is not a sport, it's not a competition. That's football. I can name you a dozen guitar players right off the top of my head that play better than I do, that have more skill of the instrument. But not one of them can make a hit record. It is not how skillful or how fast you are, or how many licks you can play. It's what you do with them, how you communicate with the instrument. If you can do that or use it as a tool to accompany you, and get your thought across as a singer, then you are way ahead of the game. That's what it's about. It's about playing for people and having them love it."

More often than not, accomplished musicians have more trouble keeping their amazing technique from getting in the way of making music. One of the hardest—but most important—lessons for any player is to let your chops get out of the way, so the music can flow through you. Otherwise you might as well listen to somebody typewrite. It may be amazing how fast they can do it, but does it touch your soul? I don't know who came up with it, but one of my favorite sayings is "God gave us music so we could pray without words." We need to honor where the music comes from. As Hank Cochran told me, "Anytime somebody gets the idea that I'm writing these songs, they are mistaken. I'm just holding the pen."

After months in a British hospital, Sharon made an appearance at a concert with Billy Fury. Even with Eddie's body protecting her— he'd pulled her into his lap during the crash—she'd suffered massive back and pelvic injuries. It was a miracle she was alive, though without Eddie she hardly felt that way. Since the accident, she'd been inundated with phone calls and visits from friends and family: Ricky Nelson and Jack Good sent flowers, Phil Everly rushed to the hospital soon after the accident, and Fury sent her toy animals.

Eddie's British fans saw to it that "Three Steps to Heaven," recorded at his final session, made it to the top of the charts after its release in May. They'd also deluged Sharon with get-well wishes and gifts, toiletries, St. Christopher medals, and spiritual and inspirational things. She was especially touched by a scrapbook sent to her by a young girl. It was full of cuttings and pictures of Eddie, obviously the fan's most prized possession.

Fury introduced her as she hobbled out onto the stage, and the crowd, roaring with compassionate applause, rose to their feet. They were sharing her pain. Sharon began to cry. She didn't want to deal with any of it. It was Gene's show—the Anglo-American package tour had been transformed into a memorial to Eddie—but Sharon just wanted to go home.

She needed to see Gene, though, to give him a hug, to say hello and let him know that, no matter their differences, he was in her heart. They were, after all, now joined by their cataclysmic sorrow. She quietly limped her way to his dressing room. She was about to walk through the door when she heard Gene speak. He was all alone. "Well, do you think I should wear the black leathers, Ed? Or do you think I should wear this blue shirt?"

Gene was chatting with Eddie, as if his best friend was right there in the dressing room with him, just as he'd always been. Sharon's heart ached as she silently shut the door and crept away.

Ed's death had a profound effect on Gene, marking the beginnings of a downward spiral of alcoholism that would take Vincent's life just a decade later. Gene had spent three days in the hospital in Bath after the crash, then flown home to recuperate from his broken collarbone and additional damage to his already-injured left leg. Although he'd intended to fly home with Eddie's body—"Eddie and I started out together, and we're coming home together," he'd told his mama on the phone—he ultimately did not, and he could not bring himself to attend Ed's funeral either. His antidote for grief was to throw himself back into work, so he'd returned to London just over a week after leaving to resume the tour. He'd become a virtual resident of England through the late '60s.

"I want to sing for you now Eddie's favorite song," a cheerless Vincent announced, rubbing at his left shoulder at the Gaumont in Lewisham, his first gig since the accident. He launched into a high, haltingly doleful rendition of "Somewhere Over the Rainbow." Tears of teenage sorrow streaked the pretty English faces of the girls in the audience, their lowing moans a mournful accompaniment. But moods soon brightened as Gene belted out a crowd-pleasing "Be-Bop-A-Lula," backed by the Beat Boys with Georgie Fame on piano.

Two nights later, on May 3, 1960, it became apparent that despite his injuries, both physical and emotional, Gene was still in peak form. Larry Parnes had almost cancelled the show at the six-thousand-seat Liverpool Stadium, believing the kids in the crowd would cause troubled because of Eddie's absence. His co-promoter talked him into saving the date, padding the bill with popular local groups, including Gerry and the Pacemakers. The four thin lads—John, Paul, George, and Stu—who'd caught Ed and Gene just a few short weeks ago at the Empire Liverpool, were again in the audience, scrutinizing Gene's every frantic move and analyzing the ruthless, reckless music that still so provoked the crowd.

After the singer's frenetic performance in the boxing ring that served as a stage, the venue just simply came apart. Gangs of youths tore seats up from the floor and hurled them across the stadium. Parnes scurried about the stage, desperate to maintain order, stomping on climbing fans' fingers to get them to fall back into the crowd. It was Liverpool's own beloved singer, the stuttering Rory Storm—whose drummer Ringo Starr would join John, Paul, and George in 1962 to complete the Beatles—who calmed the raging masses. At the height of the melee, Storm vaulted onto the stage and began to lecture with his signature speech impediment, "S-s-s-stop it, you k-k-kids!" They listened, and stopped.

Gene was never the same after Eddie's death. He kept as a treasured possession a photograph of Ed, taken the day before he died, which showed several inexplicable white cross designs scattered above Ed's head and in his hair. He was convinced they were holy crosses.

Alcohol, erratic behavior, poor business decisions, and shoddy management had put Gene on a crash course with disaster by 1968. He'd had to leave the U.K.—where he was still something of a star— because he owed a lot of people a lot of money, including the tax man and his British ex-wife. Back in Los Angeles, he became acquainted with Jim Pewter, a Hollywood disc jockey who did a rock 'n' roll show for the Armed Forces Radio Network, heard in more than thirty countries. A simple interview turned into a close friendship and business relationship, with Gene cutting Pewter's "Story of the Rockers" for an eventual single.

Jim received a call one night in the wee hours. It was Gene. He sounded on edge. He'd had an argument with his current—and fourth—wife, and he wanted Jim to come to his home. He said he had a gun. And he said he was going to use it.

Jim jumped into his car to make the hour's drive from Hollywood out to Gene's new home in Simi Valley. By the time he reached the suburb, a dense fog had settled among the hills. As Jim pulled up he could see that the front door to Gene's modest two-story house was wide open. He could hear Gene's dog barking. He sprinted inside, calling Gene's name, but got no answer. His heart throbbing, he checked each room downstairs. No Gene. He moved upstairs. When he got to the master bedroom, he found Gene unconscious on the bed. A pistol lay across his chest. Empty beer cans were strewn across the bed linens.

After disposing of the gun, rousing Gene, getting some coffee into him, and sitting up with him for hours reminiscing about his days in England, Jim felt comfortable enough with Gene's emotional state to head back to his own home. Leaving Gene's house, Jim looked up at the street sign shrouded in fog at the end of the block. A chill shinnied up his spine. Gene had purchased a house on Cochran Street. It dawned on Jim as he drove away: It was Eddie who'd sent him to Gene.

A dozen years later, nine years after Gene's death, Jim arranged to interview Sharon Sheeley. He'd always been a fan of both

Sharon's and Ed's music, but he had never had the opportunity to meet either of them. He often featured Ed's songs on his various rock 'n' roll radio shows. Their chat went well, and Jim and Sharon soon became close friends. The interview aired on Jim's Armed Forces Radio Network program in January 1981, and after its broadcast Jim phoned Sharon to tell her that he'd made a copy for her personal collection. She invited him to drop by her home in Studio City so they could listen to it together.

After listening, she told Jim something a bit strange. She said that Eddie would give Jim a sign that he was with them and appreciated what Jim was doing to keep his memory alive. Immediately the lights above them in her den started to flicker. Then they went out completely. They came back on ten seconds later. Sharon smiled knowingly.

"Eddie will give you another sign within twenty-four hours," she told Jim as he walked out her door. Jim didn't know what to believe.

When he got to his car, he put the key in the ignition. He turned it—and it kept turning, and turning, and turning, round and round in a circle. He'd never had a problem like this with his vehicle. Puzzled, he returned to Sharon's door and told her what had happened. She laughed, then told him to try again. After a few moments he attempted to start his car. This time the ignition worked, and the car functioned normally.

Driving home to Ojai, about eighty miles north of Studio City, Jim reflected on his memories of Gene. They'd often talked about Eddie, and since Eddie and Jim were both from Minnesota, Jim had always felt a certain kinship with him. Jim arrived home late that evening, and, after spending some time with his family, went to bed. The next morning he noticed his back left tire was flat. He removed the wheel and took it to a service station. They immersed the tire in water, looking for the source of the leak. But there were no bubbles, no holes. The service station staff couldn't explain it. When Jim got home he phoned Sharon to tell her about the implausible flat.

"Oh well," she said, "that's Eddie. Now you have a cherished memory."

Sharon's life after Eddie probably contributed more than anything else to the persistent sense of unbelievability in the couple's deep commitment to each other. Eddie's death, in some ways, destroyed Sharon's life. For a few brief but intense years, he was her life; when he was gone, on a certain level, she had nothing left. The all-consuming sense of loss was unceasing and undeniable. Her pain was much more than what most people will ever experience. Sharon began a steady and crippling nosedive into substance abuse. Anyone who was close to her, and some who weren't, can remember "those calls" at 4 a.m. For years she would bury her grief in the blinding, numbing haze of too much drink or too many pain pills. Anyone who knew Ed was keenly aware that he would never have been with "that girl." Those drunken moments became the norm for many years; you never knew how she would be from one moment to the next, brilliant and joyful or that other Sharon, the dark and sad soul.

Yet anyone who allowed those pained times to define Sharon Sheeley missed a rare and wonderful woman. Behind that sad exterior was a woman of rare bravery and uncommon intellect. Sharon was not only overcoming the loss of the most incredible love of her life; she was also coping with the aftermath of an incredibly painful childhood. Sharon would never heal from the physical or emotional injuries sustained in the accident—at one point she was given no hope of ever walking again. In some ways Sharon was more fragile than most of us. In other ways she was stronger than all of us. No matter how hard she tried she could never shove Eddie's death far enough behind her. Every close relationship she ever had was never without Eddie. She knew my uncle in an intimate and personal way that no one else can claim. And she would relive and long for those memories for the rest of her life.

Sharon was finally able to recognize and conquer her addiction to alcohol, and it made a tremendous difference in her life and the lives of the people around her. Sharon had a fabulous sense of humor, and we had some great times recollecting some of her worst moments, laughing and making light of them. Although she could be tough, she was one of the most vulnerable and fragile women

I've ever known. I am so proud to have been one of Sharon's close friends, and I hope to have the courage to face life with as much dignity as I experienced from her.

Was Eddie going to marry Sharon? I don't doubt that he asked. Would it have lasted? Who knows? I doubt it—look at the odds in this business. Eddie was a playboy and still a kid. Would they have grown apart? Probably—how many marriages do you know where that's happened? All I know is that I love Sharon, and I don't care whether they would have married. When she passed to the other side shortly after Mother's Day, 2002, I'm positive she was met by Eddie. She was an important part of Eddie's life, and they brought each other something rare—a sense of being loved.

Though he never met Sharon until after Eddie had passed, Johnny Rook also felt there was some sort of depth to his friend's relationship with Sharon. Eddie had never mentioned her to him; most of all he'd learned of Sharon was from what he'd read or from what Granny and Glo told him. "She was nobody to him," my aunt would say. Johnny didn't think much of Sharon's marrying radio and TV personality Jimmy O'Neill—the same Jimmy O'Neill that helped promote my early shows at the Buena Park Civic Auditorium—just a short time after Eddie's death.

But years later, when Johnny ran radio station KFI in Los Angeles, Sharon visited the station with actor Dak Rambo, hauling with her a marvelous portrait of Eddie for Johnny. It was a long framed picture, four or five feet long by three feet high. It became one of Johnny's prized possessions, ending up on his office wall every place he went from KFI on.

Sharon and Johnny wound up knowing a lot of the same people, like Jackie DeShannon and the Everlys. But to Johnny, Sharon seemed to be a woman who wanted to be known as "The Eddie Cochran Love." He didn't know if his friend's feelings for Sharon were that profound. But he did think that there was something there, because, after all, Ed wouldn't have had her over there with him, traveling around with him for that period of time, if there wasn't something special between them.

It was because of Ed that Johnny wound up knowing the Beatles. While he was working in radio in Pittsburgh, one of the bigwigs at Liberty phoned to ask, "Do you want to hear this stuff from England, the Beatles?" Johnny said sure. Soon he got a call from Beatles manager Brian Epstein, who was under the impression that Johnny was "some big, giant, important radio guy." He started sending Beatles material to Johnny; Johnny's station became the first in the country with almost every Beatle record. They would pipe the moptops' music up to WABC in New York, giving those stations almost a month's jump on the rest of the nation's airwaves for new Beatles music. When the Beatles finally arrived in America, they were well aware of Johnny, as Epstein had told them all about the influential deejay who was a friend of Eddie Cochran's. Avid Cochran fans, the lads from Liverpool invited Johnny down to the Bahamas. George Harrison went on and on about Ed, telling Johnny that in England he'd traveled with nary a pound to his name to every Eddie Cochran concert he could find. Eddie had tremendous bearing on his career, particularly Ed's guitar work. "The man's magic," Harrison mused to Johnny, "way ahead of his time." John Lennon said the same thing. Johnny can remember Harrison leaning over to John Lennon, strumming an air guitar riff and saying, "Remember this? I stole that from him."

Johnny bumped into Lennon later in Los Angeles at a concert at the Troubador by Neil Diamond, whose career Johnny helped launch while he was at Chicago's station WLS. Lennon—drunk as a skunk, according to Johnny—was seated next to the deejay at the show. Johnny, whose appearance had changed in the three or four years since he'd last seen Lennon, looked at the Beatle and asked, "Do you remember me?"

"Not really," was Lennon's reply.

"In the Bahamas?" Johnny prompted.

Lennon gave Johnny a squint, then exclaimed, "Ohhhh! Cochran!"

"That's right," Johnny said, and the two spent the rest of the night reminiscing about Ed.

Other artists would profess to Johnny their love of my uncle. Cliff Richard spent an entire afternoon with Johnny one day, telling him how impressed he was with Ed and how he grew up with and was motivated in the business by Eddie's example. Mick Jagger was amazed that Johnny knew Ed. Before the Rolling Stones even had a hit in the U.S., they stayed in the Carlton House hotel in downtown Pittsburgh, the same hotel where Eddie stayed when he visited that city. In the course of their conversation, Johnny mentioned that fact to Jagger, who replied in awe, "Eddie Cochran? You knew Eddie Cochran?" Jagger was a huge fan and spoke of how much Eddie's music had inspired him. Keith Richards went on to give Johnny a full rundown of British musicians who were influenced by Eddie. It was Eddie, Johnny soon learned from his British pals, who taught the British how to rock 'n' roll, indirectly bringing on the British invasion only a few years later.

From 1965 to 1969 Sharon Sheeley lived in London, becoming a close friend of Jeff Beck and Jimi Hendrix. The two guitarists would sit for hours playing Eddie's records, she recalled, and they would say, "If we didn't know they were cut in the '50s, and if we didn't know how many tracks he had to work with, we'd swear to God there'd have to be five guitar players on that record." They were in awe.

British fans would continue to clamor for Eddie's music years after his death. "Eddie has lived on," mused British magazine Pop Weekly in August 1963. "

> Like Buddy Holly, his releases find a huge following and, often, a place in the charts. Like "My Way," released in May 1963, which crested at Number 23 on the U.K. charts. Eddie has plenty of hitherto unreleased discs waiting to be released. That they weren't rushed out before was due to Liberty Records honestly feeling that much of his fan following had died with him. They were wrong in supposing that. So wrong that they now realize the fault... and are planning to keep Cochran releases flowing.
>
> In three years, Cochran fans have kept his memory alive by writing to magazines and record companies. Pop Weekly gets many such notes...anxious notes, sincere notes. The main result has been

that even the younger fans realize now just how wrong was his chart potential in the days when he was carefreeing his way round the one-nighters both here and in America. Eddie's biggest hits included "Summertime Blues," "C'mon Everybody," and that rocking sensation "Somethin' Else." Eddie had star quality stamped all over his frame. Among his mates in Britain were Cliff, Billy Fury, and Joe Brown. They all testify to his brilliance as a performer.

Eddie was rated as a singer. Fair enough. But he also played several musical instruments…and played them well. On some of his discs, he turned to the instrumental side, contributing excellent bits and pieces on drums, piano, bass, or guitar. He looked like [he was] becoming a useful film performer, too. Remember him, older fans, in that Jayne Mansfield sensation The Girl Can't Help It? In Untamed Youth, he had an exacting acting role, which he covered in such a way as to suggest that he'd one day be in the Frank Sinatra all-rounder class.

Eddie was a rockster. Rock 'n' roll was for him because "it comes from the heart. The craze just about got away when I signed my first recording contract. I just knew it was the field for me to work in." He worked in it with such success that he didn't clash with anybody at all…but created his own particular corner of the field.

Soon there'll be an E.P. released of four tracks from Eddie's album Cherished Memories. That, plus the success of his single "My Way," should ensure that Liberty will keep the releases a-rollin.'

And the releases have continued, in nearly every country, in every conceivable format. A steady stream of tributes, memorials, and honoraria has never ceased since Eddie's death, particularly in the U.K. In 1991, the first annual Eddie Cochran Weekend was hosted in Albert Lea, Minnesota, by the Eddie Cochran Historical Organization, founded by Bruce Blake, a Minnesota resident and Cochran fan who has worked tirelessly to support Eddie's legacy. Bruce had been in touch with Jerry Capehart, and he gave me his number.

I phoned Jerry. I hadn't seen or spoken with him since I was fourteen, since that day in Hollywood when my father and I ran into him on the street. I really had no idea what Jerry was like; I just remembered the ambiguity of that sidewalk meeting, the discrepancy between how my father emotionally embraced Jerry and the deep loathing of Jerry that the family had always expressed. Jerry was happily surprised to hear from me. For me, it was like finding a long lost relative, like locating somebody you already knew well on some level. Jerry was as excited to talk to me as I was to talk to him, and we hit it off instantly.

Years of listening to Jerry's voice on Eddie's dubs and outtakes and hearing about him from others became mixed together with my curiosity about how he and Eddie worked and created together. I wanted to get together with Jerry, who lived in Missouri, to get to know him. I thought the memorial weekend in Albert Lea—which would feature an Eddie Cochran exhibit and dedication of his gold records at the local museum, a dedication of an Eddie Cochran monument, and concerts by the Crickets and the Kelly Four— would be the perfect opportunity to get together. He was reluctant to come, given the family's attitude toward him, but I persuaded him, telling him he could room with me. It was fabulous to see him after so many years.

It was also great to see the members of the Kelly Four, with whom I was to play during the weekend. Though Dave Shriver and I had kept in touch, I really hadn't seen or talked with the other guys since I was eighteen or nineteen when we had gotten together to jam. By then I had it pretty together musically, was a professional player. And, as a confident—maybe even cocky—young man I was expecting to just blow their socks off. But I was absolutely awful. It was like my fingers didn't work, nothing worked. At eighteen I was accomplished enough to be playing with just about anybody—and was. But that day I was nervous—this was Eddie's band. Later I discovered that the Kelly Four's recollection was that I was really good; my recollection is that I sucked so bad, I was just embarrassed by my performance.

The same thing would happen again in 1979. It was strange, because with my years of experience, playing had become the most natural thing in the world for me. I seldom if ever felt nervous or afraid. I would just do what I do, the best that I could do. Then in

'79 I attended a NAMM convention, a trade show for musical instrument manufacturers. I was an endorsee for Ibanez and was performing at their booth, demoing all the new effects that would soon hit the stores. I was playing, and this guy walked up. He looked familiar. It was Paul Yandell, Chet Atkins's guitarist. Paul said he liked what he was hearing and that he was going to go get Chet. Instantly, I felt like that knock-kneed, butterfingered kid on the talent-show stage all over again—those damned nerves were back. Chet, Eddie's idol, was and still is one of my all-time favorite guitar players. The purity of tone when he simply touched a string was sheer perfection. He always seemed to know how and where to strike a note to give it the perfect resonance, the perfect tone, for the song he was playing. His arrangements were breathtaking. He was such an innovator.

A few minutes later, off to my left, I could see them coming, Paul and Chet. My heart was pounding out of my chest, and my ears clogged like I'd just descended ten thousand feet all at once. My knee started jumping up and down uncontrollably. I was sitting on a stool and felt suddenly wobbly. I was falling apart. By this time in my life I had played for literally millions of people at most every major venue in America and Canada. Working with Kindred, Steppenwolf, the Flying Burrito Brothers, Leon Russell, Bob Weir of the Grateful Dead, Bobby and the Midnights—I had played all over the world, Europe, Japan. I had been playing what felt like all my life, sometimes seven nights a week. I'd played countless sessions. I was fearless. But this was Chet—bigger than life itself. Suddenly I was twelve and a half again performing my first gig, shaking and sweating, stuttering, struggling to just keep hold of my pick. God, I was a mess.

As they approached, I started to play "Hello My Baby," one of Chet's arrangements that I had played a hundred times before. I couldn't believe what I heard come out of my guitar. It sounded like I had potatoes for fingers and a tin can for a pick. I was hitting all the wrong notes. It was one of the most embarrassing moments of my life. Thankfully, as we talked about what the effects could accomplish and I got back into my demonstration I began to calm down. But it was one of the scariest moments of my guitar-playing life.

Later, when I heard the news about Chet's passing, it hit me like a ton of bricks. I had to pull off the road into a parking lot to get it together; I was crying so hard I couldn't see. The world lost a revelation that day.

With the Kelly Four during the memorial weekend in 1991, I was determined to make up for my last shoddy performance with them. But things got off to a rocky start. When we got together to practice in the hotel room, there was no amp. I'd arranged for Fender to donate an amp to the museum, a Fender Bassman like Eddie's. So I said, "Well, let's just call the museum and have them bring the Bassman over, we could use that." But they wouldn't let us borrow it. I talked to the curator of the museum and said, "I'm the one that got that donated to you, and you're telling me I can't borrow it? I'm playing a show for you for free with Eddie's band." It didn't matter to the museum. So I called up Peavey, they phoned their local store and set it all up, and within two hours we had our amps. Peavey has kicked butt for me for years, Thank you Hartley!

We began to rehearse and reminisce. It was a poignant reunion for all of us. Jerry Capehart, Dave Shriver, Gene Riggio, Jimmy Stivers, and me, all together for the first time ever. The camaraderie between us all was instant, the feelings of déjà vu undeniable. It was truly magical, with everyone winding up in tears—the band, Jerry, me. There are certain things I do that are very much like Eddie. I don't know if it's conscious or not, I've done his music all my life, I've listened to his stuff all my life, and some stuff I just do like him. It was very emotional for everyone. And to my surprise, everyone was happy to see everyone. All of a sudden this supposed animal, Jerry, whom I'd heard the worst about for decades seemed to be best friends with Ed's band.

The show was fantastic, evoking so many familiar feels and licks for all of us. There were smiling faces onstage as well as in the crowd that night. Although the guys hadn't played together in thirty years, they did so with enthusiasm and spirit. Gene Riggio was particularly put to the test because I am pretty intense onstage. We didn't leave much time between numbers, and at one point Geno was huffing and puffing so hard I had to pause and talk to the audience so he could catch his breath. But we all had such a good time together that we made plans to get together at my home studio in southern California.

Assembled in the recording studio, I began to see some of the old tensions start to surface. Jerry had a very condescending way of dealing with the guys, even though they were no longer eighteen-to twenty-year-old kids on their first tour. These were grown men with lots of life experience, and they were not about to be treated in that way. It all came to a head one day when there was an angry confrontation between Jerry and the guys. Eventually everything was worked out and things went much more smoothly.

Most of the musicians hadn't done much playing after the 1960s, and, as I'd found in Albert Lea, their chops were understandably rusty. But we were all having fun in the studio, reminiscing and fooling around. It was a thrill for me just to be playing with Ed's pals. But the Kelly Four had some big ideas. The group had ambitions, nearly four decades after their heyday, to revive their careers and become a touring band once more. And they wanted me to join them. I was having fun, but I just didn't see things developing into a serious recording and touring relationship without considerable work. I suggested that the guys needed to get together regularly and rehearse just to get their chops into shape, and then we could take another look at the possibilities. Gene was talking about giving up his job of more than twenty years and retirement to do this band. They had dreams of touring first class and taking their families along, sort of like a current world-class successful band.

I thought those were pipe dreams. I just couldn't be involved in the group's plans. I didn't want to do anything that might tarnish Eddie's reputation, his legacy, his memory, in any way. And the only thing the Kelly Four had left, really, was the reputation they'd built for themselves from playing with Eddie. If they went out unrehearsed, unprepared, less than perfect—which is what Eddie'd always demanded of them—they'd only embarrass themselves and destroy the vibrant legacy they and Ed had left. I didn't think that was right. It didn't honor Ed's memory, or their own. So the band and I parted ways. Hopefully we will still do some things together with the intention of simply having a great time.

Jerry and I stayed in communication. Both being seasoned songwriters and producers—by that time, beyond my playing, I'd produced award-winning albums for British guitarist Adrian Legg, conducted guitar clinics around the world, and assisted in the design and development of guitars, amplifiers, and effects—our conversation naturally drifted once more to recording. Jerry was eager to get into the studio with me, he had some great country tunes he was itching to cut. I'd been avoiding the Eddie Cochran connection all my life. But the time now felt right to explore it a bit more. Plus, I knew how much it would mean to Jerry. Eddie was plucked from all of us at such an early age, Jerry no doubt never had any real sense of closure to Eddie's career. So when he met me again as a man, he said it was like seeing what Eddie might have become had he gotten a chance to mature and evolve a bit more. For me, working with Jerry would be a glimpse into some of the intricacies of what went into making Ed's records, plus a chance to learn more of the history of both Eddie and my family from an outside perspective. So I put all of my other projects on hold, and I devoted all my time to working with Jerry in my studio on what would be my first solo album.

It was illuminating to see for myself how Ed's partner really worked—the brilliant parts, as well as the thoroughly exasperating. Jerry had this little boy quality, a vulnerable side of him that I couldn't resist. He was incredibly smart, well educated, well read, and very articulate. There was something about him I really, really liked. He considered himself a religious scholar, and we used to have some rather colorful discussions on the topic.

But Jerry really did have a problem with admitting he was wrong about something or that he'd made a mistake. It was rare for him to back down, whether he believed he was right or could actually be proven wrong. I think that came from his earlier years, his mom and dad never acknowledging how good he was at what he was doing and that he had made music into a viable job. Although he talked about what a loving family he had, there was something about that family that absolutely wounded him as badly as I'd been debilitated by mine.

Jerry used to talk about emotional rejection and what an obvious problem it was in Eddie's life, my life, my father's life, and his life. I hadn't really thought about it that hard until he put it in those terms. And then I realized how profound a problem it really was in my life. I knew Granny had rejected me, had lied about me, and had said horrible things about me all my life. Anyone who knew me knew those things weren't true. I was just trading on Eddie's name, she'd say again and again, and riding on Eddie's coattails, even though I'd specifically engineered my entire life to be the complete opposite of that.

With Jerry's insight, I began to recognize what I'd been forced to do since the moment I'd picked up a guitar. It had simply become second nature to me to wall off my love and admiration for and my kinship with Eddie—to shirk from it, run from it, camouflage it, hide it. But rather than have my relationship to Eddie Cochran be something I should push away and discard, with Jerry's help I was able to see that it's something I should've been able to embrace all of my life. Of course, I did need to establish my own credentials and credibility, particularly in my own mind. But after I'd done that, why shouldn't I have been able to honor all that Eddie did, all that Eddie was? Why shouldn't I have been able to proudly say, "I am related to Eddie Cochran"? And why couldn't the family share in the joy of seeing someone they love do something wonderful, just as they had with Eddie?

Jerry put it very beautifully to Granny at the weekend in Albert Lea. He was kneeling by her wheelchair, I was a few feet from her, and he said, "Alice, do you realize how fortunate you are to have two talented people that came from your own flesh and blood? Eddie was a tremendous, tremendous talent. And so is Bobby. It's unbelievable the relationship you have with Bobby, how awful it's been, when it's really something you should be so proud of." Of course, her response was along the lines of "Yeah, yeah, yeah, leave me alone, go away." But I really appreciated the way he put it to her.

And it was gratifying for me to learn more about Eddie's musical development from someone who'd been there with him from almost the very beginning. Jerry told me that, contrary to what my family and Sharon Sheeley believed, he actually put Eddie's name on some things, that Eddie wasn't as interested in being a songwriter so much as being a guitarist and singer. Jerry tried to foster Ed's writing. I could easily imagine the "We're in this together, boy" nature of Jerry's relationship with Ed, because that's what I felt from Jerry myself. He and Eddie obviously had a unique relationship, as Ed was young and impressionable when they got together. To some degree, I think Jerry took on the role of mentor and father figure to Ed, as he did, in a way, with me. I must add, though, that Jerry's motives were perhaps not always pure: Hank Cochran tells that Jerry put his name on songs that Hank and Eddie wrote by themselves. "Jerry didn't contribute a lick to 'em," Hank asserts.

Working with Jerry was an opportunity for me to explore some of Ed's technique, as well. Everybody admired that Eddie could do the Atkins and Merle Travis kind of stuff and that he utilized it so well in his rock 'n' roll material. From Jerry, I learned that some of Eddie's solos were double-tracked. I remember Dad telling me, "Oh, Eddie did all of that all at once." I'd be listening to it and I'd say, "God, you can't do that all at once. That's impossible." I thought, well, maybe I just don't know the technique because I know with Atkins there were things that sounded impossible until you saw how he did it. It was wonderful for me to find out when Jerry and I got together that Eddie did, in fact, double-track certain things, and Jerry remembered a lot of details. It answered some questions for me. I remember one time I was introducing British guitarist Albert Lee to Jerry, and Albert was so excited to talk to him, he wanted to know how Jerry and Ed had gotten the sounds on the various records. As guitar players, we had all these questions, not being able to talk to the artist or learn about his technique in a book or on a video. And here was one of the guys who was actually responsible for the sound.

Our time together in the studio was not without disagreement. I know that Eddie detuned the guitar a whole step for "Sittin' in the

Balcony." I had never noticed that until Jerry and I were recording one day, and I was listening to one of those tracks for some reason. Detuning accomplishes two things. It helps you to sing in a different key with a certain chord structure. And, in the days when they didn't have light guitar strings, if you tuned your guitar down a whole step, all of a sudden you could bend the strings where you couldn't before. I noticed from pictures that Eddie used a capo a lot. A capo was always utilized by amateur musicians who didn't know how to play in different chord structures, it was always considered a cheater's tool. I rarely use a capo, except for when it has to be used. But when it has to be used, it's the only sensible way to do things. Jerry and I had a spirited argument about Ed and capos. He insisted, "He didn't use one of those cheater's tools!" I said, "It's not about being a cheater and not knowing what you're doing, it's about achieving your goals." We had this hot debate about it, and he never, never would change his position on it.

I found Jerry to be very stubborn. The main difference probably between Jerry and me and between Eddie and Jerry is that Eddie was very young when they got together, and although he matured into manhood, he was very young when he died. I, on the other hand, have been a professional in this career twenty, thirty years longer than Eddie got to be. What Jerry was dealing with in me was a grown man with a wealth of experience behind my concepts and judgment, as opposed to when he was dealing with Eddie in those early days. Eddie was very advanced for his age, but it wasn't like it would have been had Jerry and Eddie been able to have a career for ten more years or so.

Sadly, Jerry passed away in 1998, after a bout with brain cancer. I'd noticed that sometimes he'd scuff his foot on the ground when he walked. He wouldn't fall down or get shaken up by it, so it didn't seem to be a big deal. But other problems with balance and coordination sent him to the doctor, where tests revealed the cancer. I was shocked and saddened to tears on that Saturday he shared his news. Since I was just starting work producing an album for which I was already two weeks late, I reluctantly told Jerry, who'd moved to the Nashville area, where I lived, that I couldn't come over that day. "I've got to go into the hospital Wednesday for a biopsy," Jerry said. "It would be better to just get together on Thursday after I've come out of the biopsy and we know what the situation is.

"I'm going to pull through this," he added, in his typical ex-fighter pilot way. "I've got a lot more life in me." Jerry went in for the biopsy, fell into a coma, and never came out of it. I miss him dearly, just as so many still miss Ed.

Though he's been gone for decades now, Eddie still touches the lives of people all over the world. Some tell of visits from Eddie, though many, like Johnnie Berry, prefer to keep such intensely personal and deeply spiritual experiences to themselves. Others connect with Ed through his music, which secured his place in the Rock and roll Hall of Fame in the United States in 1987.

It's hard to say for sure what my uncle might have achieved had he survived. I believe that Eddie was going to have to overcome his drinking problem to reach the potential that everybody saw in him, to not destroy that potential. To not fall into the trap that the Cochran family fell into, total destruction by alcoholism. Destruction by this sense of rejection, that nobody was ever good enough or that nothing you ever did was good enough, which compelled you to work harder to be good enough to be worth having the success that was thrust on you. Eddie was a wonderful person and incredible talent, and he was also human. He suffered through the same things that I suffered through, that my Dad suffered through, and that Grandpa suffered through. The sins of the father will be visited on the children, the Bible says, and our family was no different.

Liberty Records would go on to become an industry leader in the '60s; Ed, had he been able to tame his demons, would have no doubt contributed much to that success. Like his friend Buddy Holly, Ed had made early steps toward functioning as a producer, and he might have gone on to helm his own record label. He'd spoken of plans to make an album on which he would play every instrument. And there was always the session work the big star with the diminutive ego so enjoyed. So much promise unfulfilled.

What we do know, however, is that Ed was a true musical pioneer, illuminating the way for generations of auteur producers, guitar gods, and stylish rock, pop, and even country stars after him. His "Twenty Flight Rock" has been performed by the Rolling Stones, Cliff Richard, Ronnie Montrose, Brian Setzer, Danny Gatton, and Robert Gordon. In addition to the Who's classic rendition, "Summertime Blues" has been covered by the Beach Boys, Blue Cheer, T. Rex, Ritchie Valens, Dick Dale, Alan Jackson, Joan Jett, the Flaming Lips, Olivia Newton-John, Buck Owens, the Ventures, and Motorhead. Humble Pie, Dave Edmunds, Iggy Pop, the Sex Pistols, U2, UFO, and even Elvis Presley have all done "C'mon Everybody." "Nervous Breakdown" has been covered by punk bands Generation X and fronted by Billy Idol, as well as the Grammy-winning Brian Setzer. "Somethin' Else" has been given the anthem treatment by Led Zeppelin, the New York Dolls, the Sex Pistols, and UFO. And a relative unknown named Sting sang "Three Steps to Heaven" in the 1979 road movie *Radio On*, playing a character called Just Like Eddie.

Embraced by rockers of every stripe—from the harmonious Beatles to the metallers of Motorhead to the Sex Pistols punks—Cochran represents the unifying, youth-empowering and universal might of raw rock 'n' roll. Just over four decades after his death, Cochran's music is still being consumed…and the demand shows no sign of slowing. His songs, both original and cover versions, can be heard every day on radios around the globe, and his limited but beloved catalog is repackaged and reissued year after year.

And he still turns up onstage—in musicals, like 1999's acclaimed *Four Steps to Heaven* in London, and in films and on television, from major motion pictures like *The Buddy Holly Story* and *La Bamba* to the BBC-TV documentary *The Eddie Cochran Story* and the CBS television mini-series *Shake, Rattle & Roll: An American Love Story*.

Without benefit of long life or long-term success, Eddie has subtly but surely become a significant part of pop culture, a rock 'n' roll icon of style, know-how, and attitude. His death is still commemorated annually in England with tribute concerts and solemn gatherings at the accident site, attended by fans from the farthest reaches of the globe, admirers who are compelled to pay their respects to the man whose music they love, whose life they honor.

Over the last several years I have had the great pleasure of attending and performing at the annual Eddie Cochran Festival in Chippenham, England. It always happens on the last weekend of September, just before Eddie's birthday on October 3rd. People were interested in having me tour more in England and Europe, but to do so I needed a band. Brian Hodgson, bass player for a band called Hogan's Heroes who frequently backs Sonny Curtis of the Crickets, helped me assemble an all-star group and find booking agents for my European dates. For the past several years the Bobby Cochran Band has consisted of Brian Hodgson, drummer Howard Tibble, keyboardist Gary Baldwin, on occasion, bassist Jim Rodford, keyboardist Rod Argent, and drummer Peter Baron.

Through Brian, I've had the opportunity to get to know esteemed British guitarist Albert Lee, who's worked with Eric Clapton, Jerry Lee Lewis, Emmylou Harris and the Everly Brothers, as well as Hogan's Heroes. Actually, I had known Albert at a distance for years. I've always loved his playing. I had shared a stage with Albert in the mid '70s during an all-star Telecaster extravaganza for *Bam* magazine. We had met then and stayed acquainted over the years, but weren't really close. Later, I introduced him to Jerry Capehart. It turned out that Albert was a big fan of Eddie and his recordings. Albert had the great fortune to get to see Eddie perform in 1960 at the Granada Woolwich Cinema, with Gene Vincent. Eddie actually borrowed Albert's Selmer amp while it was at Larry Parnes's office. Albert had lots of questions for Jerry, particularly about some of the recording techniques they used.

I was delighted to discover Albert's interest in Eddie's work; however I never dreamed that our paths would become so closely entwined. Over the last few years this association has opened many doors for me and I have gotten to know a completely new audience. In fact Albert will be doing some soloing on one of our most recent tunes with the Bobby Cochran Band, "She's So Hot, She's on Fire." It is a perfect tune for him to break out his arsenal of hot licks.

It is funny how the various connections we make in life seem so random. Yet when we look deeper we often find unthought of connections, synchronicities. I was told that Albert Lee was related to Gypsy Rose Lee, the same person who gave Eddie that unsettling yet so fateful prediction. Eddie and I were both born in Albert Lea. And though Albert and I had never talked about Eddie, when I was with Jerry Capehart and bumped into Albert one day, I just knew that I had to introduce them to each other. We three—as well as most all of the souls who people my life—are bound by our mutual love of Eddie Cochran.

With his flawless, tan complexion and sun-kissed, slicked-back hair, in his metallic vests and leather trousers, and armed with his flashy, orange hollowbody Gretsch guitar that he'd pump like a steam turbine, Eddie was a truly commanding presence. In the fledgling field of rock 'n' roll, he was unlike any other performer the world had ever seen. A romantic outlaw: dangerously intense but elegantly graceful at the same time. Teens on both sides of the Atlantic were smitten.

But for Eddie, it was the music that mattered. Though he was as proficient as a guitar player in a variety of genres—from jazz to country—it was through rock 'n' roll that he expressed himself most forcefully. Eddie didn't sing at his audience, he sang for them. With songs like "Summertime Blues," "Somethin' Else," "C'mon Everybody," and "Nervous Breakdown" Eddie gave voice to the trials and triumphs of teenage life, speaking to issues just as relevant today as they were in the 1950s: the struggle for independence and individuality, questioning of authority, generational misunderstanding, and the hopes, dreams, and desires of youth.

Yet Eddie was so much more than a mere rock 'n' roll star. As evidenced by the tremendous body of work he left as a session player, instrumentalist, and producer, he was an artist whose natural curiosity, intelligence, and passion for music informed almost everything he did. He would just as soon pick and strum on a rookie artist's debut recording session as appear coast-to-coast on television's *American Bandstand*.

I hope the world rediscovers what Eddie knew so well—the powerful and important part that music plays in our lives. In the name of profit, the record industry has too often abandoned and forgotten to nurture music and its creation. So much of what we are inundated with on the airwaves sounds a lot like music, but it is missing that vital ingredient—a connection to the heart and soul. If we honor the music that truly touches us, we will all be better for it. As Eddie knew, there are many great artists out there waiting and struggling to be discovered. That rare gift of communication is waiting to be shared. We must look past the barrage of cool-factor belly buttons and tight bodies, empty and uninspired dance routines, and manufactured pop idols with which we are supposed to be so impressed. We must look for artists who pursue something deeper, who make music because they love it. We must seek out artists who make that invisible connection to our greater self, our spirit. Artists who touch our very souls. Forty plus years after it was made, Eddie's music still touches me—and countless others around the world—in just that way.

As I wrote for the annual memorial service at Chippenham, England, on the fortieth anniversary of Ed's death, "when you're young it seems people and things will endure forever. But life teaches us a different lesson. Most of us are fortunate if we touch the lives of just a few people while we're here. Eddie had a rare gift that allowed him to reach millions. Eddie's love of music has reached out and continued to touch the hearts and souls of people all over the world. Certainly our memory of Eddie and the music he gave us has stretched far past his brief twenty-one years of life. Eddie has truly endured, and he has served as a beacon for all of us who strive for the best in ourselves and others. And we are richer for it. We love you, Eddie."

Memories are sweeter than roses,
'Cause roses will fade away.
But the memories that you've left behind you,
I'll cherish the rest of my days.

SOURCES
Interviews and Correspondence

Allison, J. I.
Belcher, Tony
Bennett, Brian
Brown, Joe
Capehart, Jerry
Carmen, Jeanne
Carter, Hal
Charles, Bobby
Clark, Alan
Cochran, Hank
Collins, Joey
Commander, Carole
(née Ward)
Curtis, Sonny
D'Andrea, Tony and Rose
Deal, Bud
Deasy, Mike
Denton, Bob
Eager, Vince
Eddy, Duane
Ennis, Ron
Facenda, Tommy
Faust, Jackie
Flock, Warren
Foreman, Chuck
Gomez, Juvey
Good, Jack
Harmony, Dotty

Harrell, Dickie
Harris, Jet
Horn, Jim
Hover, Freeman
Knight, Baker
Lambert, Gary
Lee, Albert
Levine, Larry
Locking, Brian
Mauldin, Joe B.
McCullough, Richard
Pewter, Jim
Preston, Don
Pugh, Graham
Raines, Johnnie Berry
Reynolds, Jody
Riggio, Gene
Rook, Johnny
Ross, Stan
Sheeley, Sharon and Shannon
Shriver, Dave
Stivers, Jimmy
Sullivan, Big Jim
West, Carl and Betty
Wilde, Marty and Joyce
Wilson, Ron
York, Art and Mary

SOURCES   *Photos*

Alan Clark Archives

Carole (née Ward) Commander

Tony Barrett

Johnny Rook

Ron Wilson

Richard Mc Cullough

Bobby Cochran Archive

Johnnie Raines

Sharon Sheeley

SOURCES   *Books*

Chapple, Steve, and Reebee Garofalo. *Rock 'n Roll Is Here to Pay.* Chicago: Nelson-Hall, 1977.

Clayson, Alan. *Ringo Starr: Straightman or Joker?* London: Sanctuary Publishing Limited, 1996.

Colman, Stuart. *They Kept On Rockin'.* New York: Sterling Publications, 1982.

Flippo, Chet. *Yesterday: The Unauthorized Biography of Paul McCartney.* New York: Doubleday & Company, 1988.

Marsh, Dave, and Kevin Stein. *The Book of Rock Lists.* New York: Dell Publishing, 1984.

Mundy, Julie, and Darrel Higham. *Don't Forget Me: The Eddie Cochran Story.* Edinburgh: Mainstream Publishing Company, 2000.

Stallings, Penny. *Rock 'n Roll Confidential.* New York: Random House, 1984.

Stuart, Johnny. *Rockers!* London: Plexus Publishing Limited, 1987.

VanHecke, Susan. *Race with the Devil: Gene Vincent's Life in the Fast Lane.* New York: St. Martin's Press, 2000.

Vince, Alan. *I Remember Gene Vincent.* Merseyside, U.K.: Vintage Rock 'n' Roll Appreciation Society, 1977.

White, Timothy. *Rock Lives.* New York: Henry Holt & Company, 1990.

SOURCES   *Periodicals*

Bush, William J. "Eddie Cochran." *Guitar Player*, December 1983.

Eder, Bruce. "Eddie Cochran: Somethin' Else." *Goldmine*, September 8, 1989

Eder, Bruce. "The Musician's Musician." *Goldmine*, September 8, 1989.

"Gene Vincent" from *Fusion*, 1969 in *Kicks*, No. 2.

Goodwin, Keith. *New Musical Express*, April 15, 1960.

Jamieson, Pete. "Yes I Was There at the Gene Vincent-Eddie Cochran Show April 1st 1960." *Not Fade Away*, no. 14, 1979

Kehoe, Jim. "On the Road with Eddie Cochran: An Interview with Dave Shriver." *Blue Suede News*, Spring 1989.

Kelemen, Steve. "First Love: Eddie Cochran's Junior High School Girlfriend Johnnie Berry Raines." *Nervous Breakdown*, issue 4, 1995.

VanHecke, Sue. "Somethin' Else: Bobby Cochran." *Original Cool*, October/November 1999.

SOURCES   *Picuture Books, Collections, Memorabilia, Internet*

The Big Show. 1957 Australian tour program.

Clark, Alan. *Eddie Cochran: Never to Be Forgotten*. West Covina, CA: National Rock 'n' roll Archives, 1991.

Eddie Cochran: *The Legend Continues*. West Covina, CA: National Rock 'n' roll Archives, 1994.

Gene Vincent: *The Screaming End*. West Covina, CA: National Rock 'n' Roll Archives, 1988.

Firminger, John. *Three Steps to Heaven: Eddie Cochran's Last Tour*. Self-published, 1998.

Henderson, Derek. www.derek.henderson.btinternet.co.uk.

Larry Parnes Presents Eddie Cochran and Gene Vincent. 1960 U.K. tour program.

Pugh, Graham. *The Truth About Eddie Cochran: The Oklahoma City Connection*. Self-published, 2002.

Rockabilly Hall of Fame. www.rockabillyhall.com.

SOURCES   *Radio*

"Eddie Cochran's Final Tour," BBC Radio 2, 1996.

"Jim Pewter Show," Armed Forces Radio Network, January, 1981.

"Race with the Devil," BBC Radio 2, March, 1998.

SOURCES   *Television*

Arena: The Eddie Cochran Story, BBC TV, 1982.

SOURCES   *Liner Notes*

Escott, Colin. *Somethin' Else: The Fine Lookin' Hits of Eddie Cochran.* Razor & Tie, 1998.

Finnis, Rob. *1938–1960: The Eddie Cochran Story*. EMI, 1988.

Saddler, Ian. *The Town Hall Party TV Shows Starring Eddie Cochran and Gene Vincent*. Rockstar, 1999.

EDDIE COCHRAN   *Discography*

LABEL	RELEASE NUMBER	TITLE	YEAR

U.S. Singles

COCHRAN BROTHERS

Label	Release Number	Title	Year
Ekko	1003 (78 rpm)	Mr. Fiddle/Two Blue Singing Stars	1955
Ekko	1003	Mr. Fiddle/Two Blue Singing Stars	1955
Ekko	1005 (78 rpm)	Guilty Conscience/Your Tomorrows Never Come	1955
Ekko	1005	Guilty Conscience/Your Tomorrows Never Come	1955
Ekko	3001 (78 rpm)	Tired and Sleepy/Fool's Paradise	1956
Ekko	3001	Tired and Sleepy/Fool's Paradise	1956

JERRY CAPEHART AND THE COCHRAN BROTHERS

Label	Release Number	Title	Year
Cash	1021	Walkin' Stick Boogie/Rollin'	1956

EDDIE COCHRAN

Label	Release Number	Title	Year
Crest	1026 (78 rpm)	Skinny Jim/Half Loved	1956
Crest	1026	Skinny Jim/Half Loved	1956
Crest	1026 (red vinyl)	Skinny Jim/Half Loved	1956
Liberty	55056 (78 rpm)	Sittin' in the Balcony/Dark Lonely Street	1957
Liberty	55056 (promo)	Sittin' in the Balcony/Dark Lonely Street	1957
Liberty	55056	Sittin' in the Balcony/Dark Lonely Street	1957
Liberty	55070 (78 rpm)	Mean When I'm Mad/One Kiss	1957
Liberty	55070 (promo)	Mean When I'm Mad/One Kiss	1957
Liberty	55070(picture sleeve)	Mean When I'm Mad/One Kiss	1957
Liberty	55087 (78 rpm)	Drive-in Show/Am I Blue	1957
Liberty	55087 (promo)	Drive-in Show/Am I Blue	1957
Liberty	55087	Drive-in Show/Am I Blue	1957
Liberty	55112 (78 rpm)	Twenty Flight Rock/Cradle Baby	1957
Liberty	55112 (promo)	Twenty Flight Rock/Cradle Baby	1957

LABEL	RELEASE NUMBER	TITLE	YEAR
Liberty	55112	Twenty Flight Rock/Cradle Baby	1957
Liberty	55123 (78 rpm)	Jeannie, Jeannie, Jeannie/Pocketful of Hearts	1958
Liberty	55123 (promo)	Jeannie, Jeannie, Jeannie/Pocketful of Hearts	1958
Liberty	55123	Jeannie, Jeannie, Jeannie/Pocketful of Hearts	1958
Liberty	55138 (78 rpm)	Pretty Girl/Teresa	1958
Liberty	55138 (promo)	Pretty Girl/Teresa	1958
Liberty	55138	Pretty Girl/Teresa	1958
Liberty	55144 (78 rpm)	Summertime Blues/Love Again	1958
Liberty	55144 (promo)	Summertime Blues/Love Again	1958
Liberty	55144	Summertime Blues/Love Again	1958
Liberty	55166 (78 rpm)	C'mon Everybody/Don't Ever Let Me Go	1958
Liberty	55166 (promo)	C'mon Everybody/Don't Ever Let Me Go	1958
Liberty	55166	C'mon Everybody/Don't Ever Let Me Go	1958
Liberty	55177 (promo)	Teenage Heaven/I Remember	1959
Liberty	55177	Teenage Heaven/I Remember	1959
Liberty	55203 (promo)	Somethin' Else/Boll Weevil Song	1959
Liberty	55203	Somethin' Else/Boll Weevil Song	1959
Liberty	55217 (promo)	Hallelujah! I Love Her So/Little Angel	1959
Liberty	55217	Hallelujah! I Love Her So/Little Angel	1959
Liberty	55242 (promo)	Three Steps to Heaven/Cut Across Shorty	1960
Liberty	55242	Three Steps to Heaven/Cut Across Shorty (green label)	1960
Liberty	55242 (promo)	Three Steps to Heaven/Cut Across Shorty (black label)	1961
Liberty	55278 (promo)	Sweetie Pie/Lonely	1960
Liberty	55278 (promo)	Sweetie Pie/Lonely	1960
Liberty	55389 (promo)	Weekend/Lonely	1961
Liberty	55389	Weekend/Lonely	1961
Liberty	54502	Sittin' in the Balcony/Hallelujah! I Love Her So	1962
Liberty	54503	Summertime Blues/Teenage Heaven	1962
Liberty	54504	C'mon Everybody/Twenty Flight Rock	1962
United Artists	014	Summertime Blues/Cut Across Shorty	1972
United Artists	015	C'mon Everybody/Twenty Flight Rock	1972
United Artists	016	Sittin' in the Balcony/Somethin' Else	1972

U.S. EPs

Liberty	LEP-1-3061	Singin' to My Baby (Vol. 1)	1957
Liberty	LEP-2-3061	Singin' to My Baby (Vol. 2)	1957
Liberty	LEP-3-3061	Singin' to My Baby (Vol. 3)	1957

LABEL	RELEASE NUMBER	TITLE	YEAR

U.S. LPs

Liberty	LRP 3061	Singin' to My Baby	1957
Liberty	LRP 3172	Eddie Cochran: 12 of His Biggest Hits (retitled Memorial Album)	1960
Liberty	LRP 3220	Never to Be Forgotten	1962
Sunset	SUM-1123, SUS-5123	Summertime Blues	1966
United Artists	UAS 9959	Legendary Masters Series, No. 4	1972
United Artists	LA.428-E	The Very Best of Eddie Cochran	1975
Liberty	LN-10137	Singin' to My Baby	1981
Liberty	LN-10204	Eddie Cochran: Great Hits	1983
EMI	SQ-17245	Eddie Cochran: On the Air	1987

U.S. CDs

Curb	77371	Eddie Cochran: Greatest Hits	1990
See for Miles	271	Eddie Cochran: The EP Collection	1991
Capitol/EMI	80240	Singin' to My Baby/Never to Be Forgotten	1993, 1996, 1999
Disky	TO8605952	Eddie Cochran: The Original	1995
Music Club	MCCD318	Rare 'n' Rockin'	1998
Razor & Tie	RE 2162-2	Somethin' Else: The Fine Lookin' Hits of Eddie Cochran	1998
EMI	TOCP-53091	Memorial Album	1999
EMI Plus	5761430	Eddie Cochran: The Story	2000
EMI	7981232	Legends of Rock 'n' Roll: Eddie Cochran	2000
Capitol/EMI	5336312	12 of His Biggest Hits/Never to Be Forgotten	2001
EMI Plus	5761430	Eddie Cochran: The Story (with bonus CD-ROM)	2002

U.K. SINGLES

London	HL-U 8386	Twenty Flight Rock/Dark Lonely Street	1957
London	HL-U 8433	Sittin' in the Balcony/Completely Sweet	1957
London	HL-U 8702	Summertime Blues/Love Again	1958
London	HL-U 8792	C'mon Everybody/Don't Ever Let Me Go	1959
London	HL-U 8880	Teenage Heaven/I Remember	1959
London	HL-U 8944	Somethin' Else/Boll Weevil Song	1959
London	HL-W 9022	Hallelujah! I Love Her So/Little Angel	1960
London	HL-G 9115	Three Steps to Heaven/Cut Across Shorty	1960
London	HL-G 9196	Sweetie Pie/Lonely	1960
London	HL-G 9362	Weekend/Cherished Memories	1961
London	HL-G 9460	Jeannie, Jeannie, Jeannie/Pocketful of Hearts	1961
London	HL-G 9464	Pretty Girl/Teresa	1961
London	HL-G 9467	Stockin's and Shoes/Undying Love	1961

LABEL	RELEASE NUMBER	TITLE	YEAR
Liberty	LIB 10049	Never/Think of Me	1962
Liberty	LIB 10088	My Way/Rock 'n' Roll Blues	1963
Liberty	LIB 10108	Drive-in Show/I Almost Lost My Mind	1963
Liberty	LIB 10151	Skinny Jim/Nervous Breakdown	1964
Liberty	LIB 10233	Comon Everybody/Summertime Blues	1966
Liberty	LIB 10249	Three Stars/Somethin' Else	1966
Liberty	LIB 10276	Three Steps to Heaven/Eddie's Blues	1967
Liberty	LBF 15071	Summertime Blues/Let's Get Together	1968
Liberty	LBF 15109	Somethin' Else/Milk Cow Blues	1968
Liberty	LBF 15366	C'mon Everybody/Mean When I'm Mad	1970
United Artists	UP 35361	Somethin' Else/Three Steps to Heaven	1972
United Artists	UP 35408	Summertime Blues/Cotton Picker	1972
United Artists	UP 35796	Summertime Blues/C'mon Everybody	1975
United Artists	UP 36121	C'mon Everybody/Milk Cow Blues	1976
United Artists	UP 603	C'mon Everybody/Don't Ever Let Me Go (picture sleeve)	1979
United Artists	FREE 12	Think of Me/Pretty Girl (included with first pressing of The Singles Album, UAK 30244)	1979
Rockstar	RSR-SP 3001	What'd I Say/Milk Cow Blues	1979
Rockstar	RSR-SP 3002	Skinny Jim/Half Loved	1979
United Artists	UP 618	Twenty Flight RockTeenage Cutie (picture sleeve)	1980
United Artists	UP 36520	Three Steps to Heaven/Cut Across Shorty	1980
United Artists	UP 36521	Somethin' Else/Boll Weevil Song	1980
EMI	G45 19	Summertime Blues/Twenty Flight Rock	1984
Liberty	EDDIE 501	C'mon Everybody/Don't Ever Let Me Go (picture sleeve)	1988
Liberty	EDDIE 502	Somethin' Else/Boll Weevil Song (picture sleeve)	1988

U.K. EPs

London	RE-U 1214	C'mon Everybody	1959
London	RE-U 1239	Somethin' Else	1960
London	RE-U 1262	Eddie's Hits	1960
London	RE-G 1301	The Cherished Memories of Eddie Cochran	1961
Liberty	LEP 2052	Never to Be Forgotten	1962
Liberty	LEP 2090	Cherished Memories Volume 1	1963
Liberty	LEP 2111	C'mon Everybody	1963
Liberty	LEP 2122	Somethin' Else	1963
Liberty	LEP 2123	Cherished Memories Volume 2	1963
Liberty	LEP 2124	Eddie's Hits	1963
Liberty	LEP 2165	C'mon Again	1964
Liberty	LEP 2180	Stockin's and Shoes	1964
Rockstar	RSR-EP 2003	Let's Coast Awhile	1979
Rockstar	RSR-EP 2004	Walkin' Stick Boogie	1979

LABEL	RELEASE NUMBER	TITLE	YEAR
Rockstar	RSR-EP 2005	Tired and Sleepy	1979
Rockstar	RSR-EP 2006	Country Style	1979
Rockstar	RSR-EP 2007	20th Anniversary Special	1980
United Artists	Free 16	20th Anniversary Album Sampler (DJ issue to promote box set ECSP 20)	1980
Rockstar	RSR-EP 2009	Pink Peg Slacks	1981
Rockstar	RSR-EP 2010	More Sides of Eddie Cochran	1981
Rockstar	RSR-EP 2012	Rare Items	1986
Liberty	12 EDDIE 501	C'mon Everybody	1988
Liberty	12 EDDIE 502	Somethin' Else	1988

U.K. LPs

LABEL	RELEASE NUMBER	TITLE	YEAR
London	HA-U 2093	Singin' to My Baby	1958
London	HA-G 2267	Memorial Album	1960
Liberty	LBY 1109, LBL 83072, LBS 83072	Cherished Memories	1962, 1967, 1968
Liberty	LBY 1127, LBL 83009, LBS 83009	Memorial Album	1963, 1967, 1968
Liberty	LBY 1158, LBL 83152	Singin' to My Baby	1963, 1968, 1968
Liberty	LBY 1205, LBL 83104, LBS 83104	My Way	1964, 1968, 1968
Liberty	LBS 83337	Tenth Anniversary Album: The Very Best of Eddie Cochran	1970
Sunset	SLS 50155	C'mon Everybody	1970
United Artists	UAS 29163	The Legendary Eddie Cochran	1971
Sunset	SLS50289	Cherished Memories	1972
United Artists	UAD60017/18	Legendary Masters Series	1972
United Artists	UAS29380	On the Air	1972
United Artists	UAG29760	15th Anniversary Album: The Very Best of Eddie Cochran	1975
Liberty-Fame	FA3019	"	1982
Rockstar	RSR-LP1001	The Many Sides of Eddie Cochran	1979
United Artists	UAK30244	The Eddie Cochran Singles Album	1979
United Artists	ECSP20	20th Anniversary Album (box set)	1980
Rockstar	RSR-LP1004	Rock 'n' Roll Heroes	1981
Rockstar	RSR-LP1005	Words and Music	1982
Rockstar	RSR-LP1006	The Young Eddie Cochran	1982
Liberty	LBR1827011	Cherished Memories	1983
Liberty	EG2607571	The Best of Eddie Cochran	1985
Liberty	EN2605323	25th Anniversary Album	1985
Rockstar	RSR-LP1008	Portrait of a Legend	1985

LABEL	RELEASE NUMBER	TITLE	YEAR
Rockstar	RSR-LP1009	Hollywood Sessions	1986
Music For Pleasure/ EMI	MFP415748I	Rock 'n' Roll Greats: Eddie Cochran	1986
Conifer	CFRC505	The Many Styles of Eddie Cochran	1986
Ace	CHA237	The Early Years	1988
Liberty	ECRI	C'mon Everybody: 20 Rock 'n' Roll Classics	1988

U.K. CDs

LABEL	RELEASE NUMBER	TITLE	YEAR
EMI	CDECB1	The Eddie Cochran Box Set	1988, 1999
Rockstar	RSRCD14	Don't Forget Me	1988
Ace	CDCH237	The Early Years	1992
Remember	RMB75054	Summertime Blues	1994
EMI	TO860952	The Original	1995
EMI	CDMFP6268	Best of Eddie Cochran	1996
EMI	5217152	Legends of the 20th Century	1999
Rockstar	RSRCD001	Rock 'n' Roll Legend	2000
Rockstar	RSRCD003	L.A. Sessions	2000
Rockstar	RSRCD008	Mighty Mean	2000
Rockstar	RSRCD09	Cruisin' the Drive-in	2000
Rockstar	RSRCD010	One Minute to One	2000
Rockstar	RSRCD014	Don't Forget Me	2000

Sources: *Goldmine*, September 8, 1989; *The Eddie Cochran Box Set* discography by Derek Glenister; www.ubl.com; www.towerrecords.com; www.uk.towerrecords.com.

Additions and corrections welcome at:
www.bobbycochran.com
www.eddiecochran.com

Bobby is currently working with:

Burrito Deluxe, a continuation of his Flying Burrito Bros. heritage, featuring:
Garth Hudson: Keys (The Band, Bob Dylan, Norah Jones, member of the Rock and Roll
  Hall of Fame, CSBS Lifetime achievement award)
Sneaky Pete Kleinow: Steel Guitar (Flying Burrito Bros., John Lennon, Rolling Stones,
  Fleetwood Mac)
Rick Lonow: Drums / Vocals (Flying Burrito Bros., Johnny Cash, the Bellamy Brothers,
  Vince Gill)
Dave Roe: Bass / Vocals (Johnny Cash, Flying Burrito Bros., Jerry Reed)
Carlton Moody: Guitar / Vocals (George Hamilton IV, The Moody Blues, double Grammy
  nominee, three time International Country Music Award winner)

The Bobby Cochran Band , featuring The UK All-Stars:
Brian Hodgson: Bass, Vocals (Albert Lee and Hogan's Heroes, Matchbox, Billy Fury,
  Marty Wilde, George Harrison)
Gary Baldwin: Keys / Vocals (Georgie Fame, Fats Domino, Kiki Dee)
Howard Tibble: Drums / Vocals (Shakin' Stevens, Cliff Richard, Paul McCartney,
  Little Richard)

Bobby Cochran's "Rock Around The Clock Show"

EDDIE COCHRAN IN THE CHARTS

Title:	Label/No.:	Peak Date:	Peak Position:	Weeks on Chart:
U.S.				
Sittin' in the Balcony	Liberty 55056	March 1957	18	13
Drive-in Show	Liberty 55087	September 1957	82	6
Jeannie, Jeannie, Jeannie	Liberty 55123	March 1958	94	1
Summertime Blues	Liberty 55144	August 1958	8	16
C'mon Everybody	Liberty 55166	November 1958	35	12
Teenage Heaven	Liberty 55177	March 1959	99	7
Somethin' Else	Liberty 55203	September 1959	58	4
U.K.				
Summertime Blues	LondonHLU8702	November 1958	18	6
C'mon Everybody	LondonHLU8792	March 1959	6	13
Somethin' Else	LondonHLU8944	October 1959	22	3
Hallelujah, I Love Her So	LondonHLW9022	February 1960	22	3
Three Steps to Heaven	LondonHLG9115	May 1960	1	15
Sweetie Pie	LondonHLG9196	October 1960	38	3
Lonely	LondonHLG9196	November 1960	41	1
Weekend	London HLG9362	June 1961	15	16
Jeannie, Jeannie, Jeannie	London HLG9460	December 1961	31	4
My Way	Liberty LIB10088	May 1963	23	10
Summertime Blues	Liberty LBF15071	April 1968	34	8
C'mon Everybody	EMI EDDIE501	July 1988	14	7

EDDIE COCHRAN   *Index*